John H. Eichinger

CHICKEN EVERY SUNDAY

CHICKEN EVERY SUNDAY

My Life with Mother's Boarders

BY

ROSEMARY TAYLOR

Illustrated by Donald McKay

THE SUN DIAL PRESS · GARDEN CITY, N. Y.

1944
THE SUN DIAL PRESS

CHICKEN EVERY SUNDAY

Printed in the United States of America

For Mother

Contents

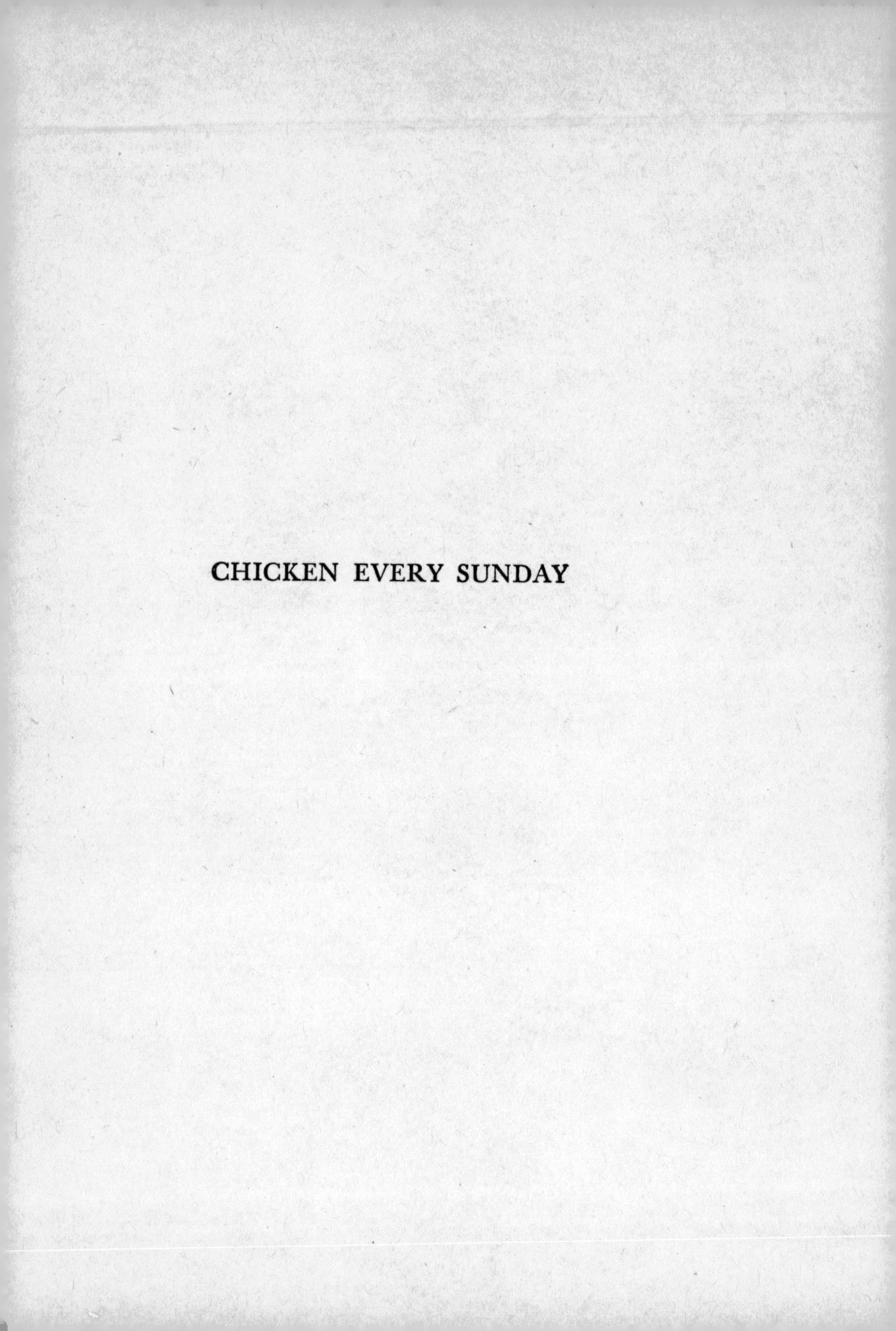

CHICKEN EVERY SUNDAY

CHAPTER 1

A Little Sin at Midnight

THE FIRST boarders I can remember are Miss Gilley and Mr. Robinson. Mr. Robinson was sleeping with Miss Gilley, and that was why Mother told me the facts of life. She hadn't intended telling me so soon, but there was Mr. Robinson tiptoeing into Miss Gilley's room at night—it *was* footsteps Mother heard and not creaks as Father said—and there was that business of the Indian jumping at Miss Gilley from the bushes, which was really the reason for Mr. Robinson's going into her room. Naturally all this was pretty puzzling to a child of seven, and I was pestering Mother with questions.

"All this" happened in Tucson where Mother and Father had come after Father bought the laundry.

With part of the money they got from their property in Phoenix they bought two lots in Tucson and built the "big house." We call it the big house, for after a while Mother built a little house in back of it.

But when they built there wasn't a house between us and the Catalinas to the north. About a mile away to the east was the university. (Father loved to tell how Tucson happened to get the University instead of the insane asylum, which was what it really wanted.) A half mile to the west was the Indian school and the

Roskruge Grade School, where I went, and which was the reason we got Miss Gilley and so many other teachers as boarders.

Uncle Harry, Father's brother, said, "I think you two are crazy to build so far out; the town will never catch up with you." (And now we're zoned for business.)

A streetcar drawn by two little horses linked us to town and went on through open country to the university. Father was the manager of the streetcar company—yes, he'd got into that shortly after coming to Tucson. This was convenient for Mother when she forgot to order the meat in time for the morning delivery. She could telephone Pusch and Zellweger to put her chops on the streetcar. Then when the car got in front of our house, the driver yelled, "Whoa!" wound his reins around the whip, and delivered the meat to Mother. Yes, sometimes the passengers complained.

Mother had had boarders in Phoenix—I remember some of them vaguely—but now Father said why did she have any more. After all, Mother had three children now—me, the oldest; Phillip; and Oliver, the baby. Besides, in spite of Mother's predictions that the laundry would go broke because Father had put his barber in charge of it, it was really doing awfully well.

"Take in boarders if you like," Father said, "but you don't have to. I think it would be nice to have our home to ourselves for a while."

So Mother was a little surprised when shortly after that Father asked her if she wouldn't take in Mr. Robinson for a month or two.

Mr. Robinson was a mining man, from a company

back east that had a lot of money, and he was looking for prospects.

"Robinson hates living in a hotel," Father said, "and you know how it is—he'll be sitting around that lobby and someone will sell him a mine."

"And why," Mother wanted to know, "do you care if someone sells him a mine?"

"Because," explained Father, "then he probably won't buy the Oro Blanco."

"Oro Blanco?" puzzled Mother.

"It means white gold. Pretty name, isn't it?"

Mother put her hand to her head. "Don't tell me you've bought a mine!"

Bought the Oro Blanco! Not at all. He just had an option on it. And if Mr. Robinson's company took it over, Father's commission might easily be $25,000. "And," gloated Father, "you can't sneeze at $25,000."

"No, you can't," Mother agreed, "not until you have it."

So Mr. Robinson moved in with us, but Mother didn't put him in the big front room. She put him in the room next to it, the middle room. She put a school-teacher, Miss Gilley, in the front room.

"Well," reasoned Mother, "if we're going to have one boarder, we might as well have two. Miss Gilley will be here all the year and will pay me $40 a month. And," said Mother firmly, "I don't sneeze at $40."

Miss Gilley taught history and girls' athletics and was a great big blond woman who didn't wear corsets. She was always telling Mother not to lace so much, and Mother said she didn't lace at all. But Miss Gilley said no one could have as small a waist as Mother and not lace, and that she'd pushed herself all up and down.

"Am I all up and down?" I heard Mother ask Father once. And Father said of course she was and wasn't she glad she had an up and down and wasn't all level like Miss Gilley.

Mr. Robinson didn't seem to mind Miss Gilley's being level, for he liked her very much. "Your food is wonderful," he told Mother, "but what I like best is the kind of people you take in." And he would smile at Miss Gilley.

"Do you think those two are sweet on each other?" Father asked Mother.

"I shouldn't be surprised," Mother said.

Mr. Robinson always brought Miss Gilley a box of candy when he came back from his trips. He brought us children a box, too. And he used to give us specimens. He'd open up his bags and give each one of us two or three pretty stones and tell us, "Now that's molybdenite. And that's porphyry. And that's malachite." Then he'd tie up the bags very carefully and put them in the hall closet and say to us, "Now you children wouldn't salt them on me, would you?"

Father had specimens, too, and he was always trying to show them to Mr. Robinson. "That's from the Oro Blanco's new crosscut, and here's something from Level No. 6." And Mr. Robinson would nod his head and say, "Yes, yes. Very nice." Then he'd look around and ask, "Where's Miss Gilley? When is she coming out?"

Miss Gilley was very peculiar in one way. She was scared to death of Indians. Even though Father told her there hadn't been any bad Indians around Tucson for years, Miss Gilley still felt the only good Indian was a dead Indian. Of course in those days there were lots of Indians about. There was old Meta who came to wash for us every Monday—except the Mondays she had a baby and then she came Tuesdays—and the Indians who used to sell us wood, and the boys and girls from the Indian school. Sometimes we had Indian girls as cooks, but when Miss Gilley was there we had Ruth, a darky from Georgia.

Miss Gilley's room had an outside entrance, and she didn't like the latch on the French doors. She said anyone could push those doors open with one good push, and even if she screamed we were so far away no one would hear her. Mr. Robinson said he'd surely hear her and would come right in to rescue her. But lots of times Mr. Robinson wasn't there, and then Miss Gilley was far away from anybody, for we slept on a big screen porch at the rear of the house—all five of us, in five beds, lined up like a dormitory. Mother thought fresh air was good for us, and if it was good for us in the daytime it was good for us at night. And besides, that way we had more rooms to rent.

So Mother put a big bolt on the French doors to keep out the Indians, and Miss Gilley felt happier. But Mother didn't put any bolt on the door into the little hall that led into Mr. Robinson's room.

However, the Indian didn't try to push in the French doors. He jumped at Miss Gilley from the bushes.

I remember it was just at dinnertime when it happened. Mother had put Oliver to bed and was helping Ruth bring on the ham and vegetables when we heard

screams and footsteps running on the porch, and in burst Miss Gilley in a dreadful state. She fell into a chair, and kept swallowing and swallowing, and trying to tell us something. You could hear her heart, it was beating so hard.

"Indian . . . he . . . he . . ." and she'd stop and wave toward the street with a long purse she was carrying.

"Was someone trying to get your purse?" Mother asked.

"Not my purse—not my *purse!*" And she let out another shriek.

"What *was* he trying to get, Miss Gilley?" asked my brother Phillip. Phillip was always the one who asked the questions.

"You children go on out," Mother ordered, and, "Ruth, put the dinner back on the stove."

Father came from his room where he'd been having a before-dinner snooze, and we children listened at the swinging door that led into the pantry. Little by little we pushed the door open until we were back in the dining room again.

Finally Miss Gilley got out what had happened, how she'd been walking home from town, not wanting to wait for the horsecar, and across the street, right in front of our house, where the bushes were thick because of the little arroyo, an Indian—a great big Indian—had leaped out at her. And she said again, "He wasn't after my purse, but I hit him with it." She started to scream again.

"Now, now," soothed Mother, "you've got to get hold of yourself."

"We must call the police!" cried Miss Gilley. "Maybe he's left footprints. Maybe they can track him down with bloodhounds."

Father said he didn't think the town had any bloodhounds. But he called Ed Peters, the chief of police, and then he went outside to look for footprints.

"Did you find any?" Miss Gilley asked when he came back in.

"No," said Father, "not a footprint. But I found the Indian. He's lying out there in the street. You said you hit him, didn't you?"

"As hard as I could."

"Hard enough. He's out cold. Smells to high heaven of booze, too. He's just a little fellow, looks about seventeen. Probably one of those boys from the Indian school."

"But it was a great big Indian," protested Miss Gilley.

"No, he's little. I dragged him into the yard."

"Into the yard?" gasped Miss Gilley and Mother at the same time.

"He was on the streetcar tracks. Did you want him run over? Do you want," asked Father severely, "to destroy the evidence?"

"I want to see the Indian," cried Phillip and dashed out with me after him. He was a little one, too, in blue overalls and a purple shirt. Phillip leaned down and smelled him. "Nasty," he said.

But Father came out and dragged us back into the house, and Miss Gilley was now saying that if only Mr. Robinson were there.

Mother said what could Mr. Robinson do more than they were doing, and for her to go to bed and have her dinner on a tray.

Miss Gilley said, oh, dear, she couldn't sleep in that room away off by herself and Mother said for her to go into Mr. Robinson's room, that the sheets were clean on the bed, and she'd be nearer us.

So Miss Gilley went into Mr. Robinson's room, and Mother asked Father if there was any danger of the Indian coming to and getting away.

"I don't think so," said Father, "but maybe I ought to bring him in here where we can watch him." So Father lugged him in and dumped him on the parlor floor. Then Ed Peters drove up and Mother took him in to talk to Miss Gilley. After a while they came out and Ed Peters said they'd have to get hold of the people who were selling liquor to Indians.

"She's crazy scared of Indians," Father told Ed Peters. "I don't believe that little fellow tried to do anything to her. I think he just stepped into the bushes to . . . well, you know what . . . and then came staggering out and fell against her."

"Sure," agreed Ed Peters, "probably held on to her to keep himself from falling."

"After all," Father went on, "if a man had that in mind, why would he pick on a woman twice his size?"

And Mother sniffed and said when men had that in mind they didn't ask how much a woman weighed.

Ruth brought in the dinner and Ed Peters took one look and one smell at the ham and said, my, wasn't that a good ham, and how he was simply crazy about ham.

Mother said for him to sit down and have some dinner with us, but Ed Peters said he'd better take the Indian over to the school and talk to the superintendent, and anyway he had to go home to his own dinner. But then he took another smell and said yes, he would have just one little bite.

So Ed Peters sat down and ate three slices of ham and some candied sweet potatoes and some baby Lima beans, and then he said he must get along to his own meal, and for Father to give him a hand.

"Mother," I asked, when they'd carried the Indian out, "if the Indian wasn't after Miss Gilley's purse, what *was* he after?"

"My dear," said Mother, "there are bad men in the world . . ." Then she stopped. "Probably," she began again, "he was after her beads, those pretty beads she wears."

Miss Gilley's beads were pretty. They were of turquoise and Mr. Robinson had brought them to her from New Mexico. Once or twice she had let me wear them.

Phillip said if he wanted the beads he wouldn't jump at her from the bushes; he'd wait until she took them off to wash her neck and then he'd get them.

"But you live here," I told him. "You know when she's in the bathroom."

"Now you children stop talking and eat your dinner," Mother ordered, "and put all this out of your mind entirely."

But I couldn't help thinking about it and somehow Mother's bead story didn't satisfy me.

One day just before lunch Mr. Robinson came back from Mexico. Of course we told him about the Indian, and he said if he'd been there he'd have torn the Indian limb from limb.

Mr. Robinson had a whole lot more specimens with him and some queer Mexican candy made of peanuts and brown sugar. Mother told us not to eat it before lunch. But we played with the specimens and Father brought out some of the Oro Blanco specimens which he said were from Level No. 7, and he said some people went chasing all over the country trying to find something when all the time it was in their own backyard.

That afternoon after school Mr. Robinson came up in a buggy and took Miss Gilley for a ride. They were gone so long they were late for dinner. Mother said it was all right with her if they wanted to eat burned-up roast.

Mr. Robinson said the roast wasn't burned; it was wonderful. Then he turned to Father and said, "I ran that Oro Blanco ore this afternoon and it's wonderful. Everything is wonderful." And he looked at Miss Gilley and laughed.

And that was the night I woke up and heard Mother and Father arguing about the footsteps.

"It's creaks," I heard Father say, "you know this house creaks."

"No," insisted Mother, "it's footsteps. I know a footstep from a creak."

"Well," demanded Father, "do we wait for her to scream, or do we go running in now and make damned fools of ourselves waking her out of a sound sleep?"

"She won't scream," said Mother. "I'm positive she's not going to scream."

Said Father, "You women! Nice charitable minds you have!"

"There . . . listen! Those are footsteps."

"Creaks," repeated Father. "Go to sleep."

"There . . . he's opened her door."

By this time I was wide awake. "Mother," I cried, sitting straight up in bed, "is Mr. Robinson after Miss Gilley's beads?"

Mother reached over and caught my arm. After a minute she said, "What's the matter, dear? Did you have a nightmare?"

"But I heard you and Father talking. . . ."

"You must have been dreaming. Lie down and go to sleep."

So I lay very still and took deep breaths pretending I was asleep.

Pretty soon they began to talk again, but this time they whispered.

From Mother, "The first thing tomorrow I tell them to go."

"W-h-a-t!" hissed Father, "just when he's going to buy the Oro Blanco, just when we're going to be on Easy Street."

Mother said Easy Street was Easy Street, and she'd like to have a look at that street, but there was also such a thing as easy virtue, and she wasn't going to have it in her house.

"There's such a thing as minding your own business, too. Just because a floor creaks. Women have the most suspicious minds. You have no proof, absolutely no proof. . . ."

"Keep your voice down or you'll wake that child again."

So then they talked so low I couldn't hear them.

In the morning Mother talked to me about my dream. She said yes, it was a very queer dream, and people often had queer dreams, but I mustn't mention it to anyone.

The queerest change came over our house after that. Mother got polite and called Miss Gilley "Miss Gilley" instead of "dear" or "honey," and Mr. Robinson "Mr. Robinson" and not "Mr. Man" as she usually did. And at the table she didn't say, "Pass your plate this way," or "Here's a chop with your name on it," but merely, "May I serve anyone anything?" Father looked worried and talked a lot, mostly about the Oro Blanco, and I knew something was terribly wrong.

Two or three times at night I woke up and heard the noises and heard Mother and Father arguing in whispers about them. Sometimes I thought Father was right—that they were creaks—and sometimes I sided with Mother and was sure they were footsteps. And once I heard Mother say, "I'm not going to put up with this much longer."

Then Mr. Robinson got a very bad cold. But Mother didn't make him any hot lemonade or tell him he ought to go to bed or in fact pay any attention to it.

Mr. Robinson's cold got worse and worse, and one Sunday he coughed so hard he could scarcely eat. Mother didn't mention it, but Father said, "You sound like a lunger. Are you doing anything for that cough?"

And Miss Gilley said, "I certainly am. I got up three times last night and rubbed his chest, and I . . ."

Then all of a sudden she stopped talking, and there was the strangest silence. I looked up from my drumstick to see what was the matter. Miss Gilley was fiery red and Mr. Robinson had his handkerchief over his face as if he were trying to hide it. Father was patting his mashed potatoes into a neat little mountain, and Mother looked pleased as anything.

"You say you got up three times last night and rubbed his chest," Mother repeated very carefully as if she hadn't heard Miss Gilley the first time.

Then Mr. Robinson came out from behind his handkerchief and gave a great big laugh. He slapped Miss Gilley on the back. "Well, old girl, you'll have to tell them now."

Miss Gilley and Mr. Robinson were married! They'd got married the afternoon they were late for dinner. They were going to wait until school was out, but because of the Indian Miss Gilley was afraid to sleep in the front room by herself. They didn't want to tell anyone, for in Tucson a schoolteacher had to give up her job when she got a husband, and Miss Gilley wanted to teach until the end of the year.

" 'Fraid cat—that's why I got her," laughed Mr. Robinson.

"Well, for Heaven's sake," said Mother, "as if you couldn't trust us not to tell."

And she kissed Miss Gilley, and Father shook hands with Mr. Robinson, and Miss Gilley kissed me, and Father got out the bottle of brandy Mother kept to flavor desserts, and we were all very happy. The brandy did Mr. Robinson's cold a lot of good, for he stopped coughing and sat there with his arm around Miss Gilley.

"You sure spilled the beans, old girl," he teased her.

But Mother said she hadn't at all, that what really spilled the beans was Mr. Robinson's tiptoeing around like an elephant.

Then she turned to Father. "You and your creaks!" she scoffed.

That night when I was helping Mother with the dishes—Ruth didn't come back for Sunday suppers—I asked her what I'd been wanting to ask all afternoon.

"Why," I demanded, "is it all right for Miss Gilley to rub Mr. Robinson's chest now, when it wasn't before?"

Mother swished the dishrag around furiously for a

minute, and then she said, "I didn't intend to tell you so soon, but perhaps I'd better."

And she turned her back on me and ran a lot of water and began a long story about men and women loving each other and having babies and how it was all very beautiful and wonderful, and please would I bring her that platter to wash. She said maybe I wouldn't understand it all now, but I would later on, and anyway that was how God had arranged matters, and I'd just have to accept it.

Poor Mother. I can remember how embarrassed she was, and that's about all I can remember. She must have been pretty confusing, because for years I thought you got babies by rubbing people's chests.

CHAPTER 2

Father Slept on the Floor

OF COURSE Mother had boarders long before she had us children. In fact, the first ones she had she got soon after she was married, and she sneaked them into the house when Father wasn't looking.

I've heard Father tease Mother with the story so often —usually at mealtime, with some later-day boarders as audience—that it almost seems as if I'd been there myself.

"Yes, sir," Father would say, "I left the house one morning, and when I came home there were this man and woman in our bedroom, and all she had for me to sleep on was a mattress down on the floor."

"Don't forget I was sleeping on it, too," Mother would put in, "and it was only for one night until I could get a bed."

"Then I went away on a trip," Father continued, "and she got two more people and put them in that bed, and this time what she had for me to sleep on was a 5-foot cot (Father was 6 feet) in the dining room, and my feet could just hang over."

"They did not hang over," protested Mother. "I had that orange box at the end."

"That's right," said Father. "My bed was in two pieces, and one of the pieces was an orange box. It certainly was comfortable."

Whenever Mother was put out, her Virginia accent came in thick and strong. "Well, Ah got $30 each from those boarders. That was $120. And Ah reckon you liked that all right." And she would put her chin up in the air and pretend she was hurt. But actually she wasn't. I think she liked Father to tease her.

"You bet I liked it," said Father. "I still like it when you bring in money." And he'd lean back in his chair and grin at the boarders. "I never worry about going broke. I've got a smart wife. She can support herself, and the kids, and me, too."

"I should think you'd be ashamed," Mother would scold, "wanting a woman to support you."

"I don't want you to support me, but it's good to know you can if you have to." And Father would ask, "You wouldn't turn me out, would you?"

"No, I wouldn't turn you out, but I wouldn't have you sitting around the house doing nothing. You'd certainly have to help me with the work."

And then we children and the boarders would all laugh, for Father was one of those helpless men about the house, and the idea of his doing any domestic chores struck us as extremely funny.

But Father never quite went broke, although he teetered on the edge of it most of the time. So he never had to help Mother with the boarders.

Mother and Father were married in 1897. They lived in Phoenix first in a little brick house on Second Avenue, which they'd built with the money they'd saved before they were married. It was an unpretentious, little cracker box of a place—after all you can't save much on a schoolma'am's salary of $75 a month and a wholesale-house clerk's remuneration of $100. But it had a parlor, dining room, bedroom, kitchen, and two-thirds of a bathroom. Since there were no sewer connections on Second Avenue, there was only the tub and basin inside—with the waste water flowing out on the trench where Mother had planted the roses. The other necessary one-third of the plumbing was taken care of by a little house in the rear.

Since the house had cost $1,500 to build instead of the $1,200 they'd planned, they had to skimp on furniture. They had a golden-oak dining-room set, a bed and a bureau, a kerosene stove and a table in the kitchen, and nothing at all in the parlor. They kept the parlor shades down and took any callers into the dining room.

Father was still at his job in the wholesale grocery store and one day happened to tell Mother about a liquor salesman who had come into the office, a Stephen Kane.

"Seems like a nice fellow," said Father. "He's going to locate here and work out of Phoenix."

"Where is he staying?" asked Mother.

"At the hotel, but he has a wife and wants to find a room in a private home."

As soon as Father left Mother telephoned to the wholesale house and asked if Mr. Kane were there. He was, and Mother said to him, "Mr. Kane, my husband tells me you're looking for a room. I wish you'd come out and talk to me."

When Father came home that night and started up the walk, he saw sitting on the porch a shirt-sleeved man who looked vaguely familiar.

Father didn't go in the front door but went around to the back and into the kitchen.

Thundered Father, "Who's that man on the porch?"

"Shhh," cautioned Mother. "You know him; it's Mr. Kane."

Just then there bustled into the kitchen a plump little woman whom Mother introduced as Mrs. Kane. Mrs. Kane went over to a kerosene stove, a duplicate of Mother's, that Father hadn't seen before, and began dishing something out of a pot.

"We feel so grateful to you," Mrs. Kane beamed at Father, "for telling your wife about us."

Father gurgled something in his throat, and then in came Mr. Kane and thanked him again.

The Kanes sat down at the kitchen table and began to eat, and Father and Mother went into the dining room where the argument went on in whispers.

"Taking in roomers!" hissed Father. "People will think I can't support my wife."

"Who cares what they think?" soothed Mother. "We'll have $20 a month, won't we?"

"But how have you worked it? That room had no furniture."

"Oh, I've given them our room," explained Mother.

"Our room!"

"Don't worry. I've got some furniture for us."

"No privacy," mourned Father, "strangers all over the house."

"They won't bother us. They'll stay in their own room and they'll eat in the kitchen. You won't even see them."

At this point Mrs. Kane came in and asked if she

could have a little of Mother's mustard until she got some tomorrow.

"Certainly," said Mother. "Help yourself."

"Thank you," smiled Mrs. Kane, and then, putting her head around the door again, "I do think it's too mean to make your husband sleep on the floor. We should have stayed at the hotel tonight."

"Oh, he won't mind a bit," Mother assured her, trying not to see Father's expression.

"Well, anyway, it's awfully nice of him," and she withdrew her head.

Without saying a word Father rose to his feet and stalked over to the parlor and opened the door. Mother followed him.

There was nothing in the room but a mattress on the floor where Mother had made up the bed and, holding their clothes in place of a bureau, three orange boxes piled one on top of the other.

While Father stared in speechless fury, Mother babbled, "Tomorrow, the first thing, I'll go down and buy a bedstead and a bureau. I couldn't do it before; he didn't give me the $20 until tonight. It's a good mattress. I borrowed it from Mrs. Bennett. Mr. Kane carried it over. Well, you needn't look like that. I don't know any easier way of making $20 than sleeping on the floor for one night."

Still speechless, Father went back to the table and sat down, while Mother kept on talking.

"It's wicked to keep that room to ourselves when we don't need it and they do. You know there isn't a place to stay in town. If they lived at the hotel all he made would go for their room. And it's wicked not to get that money, when it won't inconvenience us at all, when we won't even *see* them. . . ."

Mrs. Kane now appeared in the doorway with a platter in her hand.

"Won't you have some of our meat balls? I made too many and they're awfully good." She put some on Mother's plate, and despite Father's violent gesture of protest, on his plate, too.

"Thank you," said Mother, "and won't you have some of our salad?" She put it into the plate that had held the meat balls.

Mrs. Kane stood in the doorway tasting. "My, that's good. You'll have to give me the recipe for your dressing. Now I'll hurry and get my dishes out of the way before you come in."

Exploded Father, "This is the damnedest, silliest arrangement! Two women cooking on two stoves, eating at two tables, swapping food back and forth! Hell! If we're going to have them in the house, they might as well eat with us."

"I think so, too," agreed Mother.

So the next day they took the kerosene stove back, and Mother charged them $30 each for room and board. After a few days Father stopped sulking, for Mother fixed up the parlor very comfortably, and the Kanes were really awfully nice. And he could see the extra money was going to come in very handy.

In fact, because of it—and also because Steve Kane kept telling him he was being wasted in office work—Father gave up his job in the wholesale grocery store and took on the agency for Arbuckle's coffee for Arizona and New Mexico.

"I wouldn't have done it," Father told protesting and panicky Mother, "but you've got that board money and I know we won't starve. Now I've got a chance to get ahead. Look what Steve makes on his liquor sales. I can do the same with coffee."

So Father and Uncle Steve—as we children called him later—traveled about the territory and over into New Mexico getting orders for liquor and coffee, both happy that their wives had each other's company.

When Uncle Steve was away Mother deducted 50 cents for every day he was gone. But even so she made money on what the Kanes paid her. Food was very cheap in Phoenix then. A chicken cost 25 cents, eggs were never more than 15, and sometimes 10, cents a dozen. Vegetables were almost nothing, and besides Mother had a little garden of her own where she grew potatoes and beans and onions and carrots. An expensive item was ice. It was 3 cents a pound, and she got two 50-pound pieces a week. These she wrapped carefully in newspapers before putting them in the ice chest, and of course they were never chipped. For cool drinking water she depended on an earthen olla which swung on the porch. Kerosene was cheap, and, because of the Phoenix climate, she needed a fire in the dining-room stove for only about 4 months of the year, and then usually just in the morning and at night. The wood was brought in by Indians who drove along the streets in their creaking old wagons crying, *"Quiere leña?"* These wood sellers, and the occasional squaw who came to the door selling baskets, were about the only picturesque notes in Phoenix.

Phoenix, unlike Tucson, had no old Spanish background but was settled by Americans in the sixties, and, with its little brick houses and tree-lined streets, might have been any Midwestern town.

Right from the first Father did well with his coffee, selling worlds of it to the wholesale houses, the ranches, the mines, the Indian trading posts. But of course he didn't have a steady income. Some months his commissions were big; some months they were small. This worried Mother, who liked to know, as she put it, "where she was at."

Mother, having been born right after the Civil War, had gone through those poverty-stricken times of the ravaged South. She had been brought up on a war-ruined plantation, with its trunkfuls of Confederate money and not one penny to buy anything. Mother had a terror of not having something laid by, of a precarious income. Whenever there was the possibility of making money, Mother felt she had to seize it, but it had to be a pretty certain possibility.

Father also had known poverty as a child. Mother might be an F.F.V., but Father was an F.F.A.—First Family of Arizona. His father had come west in '54. His mother was the second American woman to arrive in Tucson. Father was brought up in an adobe house with a dirt floor and no windows. At the age of six years Father was adding to the family income by selling newspapers on the street and sweeping out the saloons in the morning. Father didn't want to miss any opportunities for making money either. But unlike Mother he was after "killings." "I can't waste time on this penny-ante stuff," he'd tell Mother.

It happened once that when Father was away on an

extended trip, Mother heard of another couple, the Sawyers, who were looking for a room. They were from Michigan, and Mrs. Sawyer had lost a child and was so melancholy about it that her husband had brought her out to Phoenix to see if she wouldn't pick up in the warmth and sunshine.

Mother couldn't resist this chance to make a few dollars. So she gave the Sawyers her and Father's room, and for herself rented at a dollar a week a couch which she put in the dining room. It was one of those contraptions that fold up into a bench in the daytime and then unfold into a bed at night.

She warned the Sawyers they could stay only by the week and that when Father came home they would have to go.

Since the only entrance into the bathroom was through one of the bedrooms, she brought her things out and washed at the sink.

"I don't know any easier way of earning $2 a day than washing at the sink," she told Aunt Rose, Uncle Steve's wife.

Father always let Mother know when he was coming home, and she thought she could get the Sawyers out before he appeared. But this time he walked in unexpectedly, just before dinner.

"Having someone in?" he asked, seeing the extra places at the table. And then, noticing the couch, "What in the name of God is that thing?"

"Well," said Mother, "it's this way. Mrs. Sawyer lost her baby, and Mr. Sawyer wanted to get her out in the sunshine. . . ." And Mother hurried on with explanations.

Of course Father blew up. He raved, he stormed, he shouted so loud Mother dragged him into the kitchen where the Sawyers couldn't hear him.

"You ought to be ashamed of yourself," scolded Mother. "Here that poor woman's lost her child and you're carrying on like this."

"I'm sorry she's lost her baby," cried Father. "It's tough to lose a baby. But is that any reason for me to wash in the sink and sleep in a couch with my feet hanging over?"

"Why will your feet hang over?" demanded Mother.

"Because that couch is too damn short. I should think you could tell by looking at it. That's a child's bed!" And Father strode into the dining room and flung himself down on the couch. Mother saw it was true. There was a foot less of couch than there was of Father.

"I'll fix it," promised Mother. "I'll make it longer."

"How can you make it longer?" snorted Father. "Are you a magician?"

"I've got an orange box. I'll put it at the end. I'll put a pillow on the box. It'll be perfectly comfortable. It's just for three days. Their week is up Sunday."

But when Sunday came the Sawyers didn't want to leave. "Please let us stay on another week," Mr. Sawyer begged Mother. "My wife is so much better. She's almost happy here. I know that couch isn't comfortable for your husband. I'll buy you another one. And come through our room to the bathroom. We won't mind."

"What can I do?" Mother said to Father. "We'll have to stand it one more week. And we're getting a present of a new couch."

But at the end of the week it was just the same. Mr.

Sawyer pleaded, "My wife says she must stay here, she simply *must*. She says this is the place for her. . . . Well, this is the place for her to get well. I know it's lots of work for you. I want you to get yourself a maid, and I'll pay her wages."

"I can't put them out," Mother told Father, "and it will be fine having a maid."

"Well," moaned Father, "I'm away a lot. At least I can be comfortable away from home."

But he couldn't stay mad. Mrs. Sawyer was so pathetic, such a thin little thing. He joined with the others in trying to make her eat and in trying to amuse her. And Father couldn't be indifferent to all that money coming in. Sixty dollars from the Sawyers, besides the $3 they paid to the Indian maid, and from $45 to $50 from the Kanes, depending on how many days Uncle Steve was home.

They now had quite a little nest egg in the bank, over which Mother gloated proudly.

But then one time when Father was in Tucson a queer feeling came over Mother—she was always getting queer feelings of one kind and another, and usually they were right, too—that that nest egg was no longer in the nest. So persistent was this idea that she put on her hat and went down to the bank and asked for their balance. It was something under $9!

Yes, said the cashier, her husband had drawn out the money some time ago.

Mother was almost beside herself with anger and curiosity. Why had Father taken that money? What could he be going to do with it? She got him on the long-distance telephone—an unheard-of extravagance.

Father was soothing, but vague. Yes, he'd drawn out the money. Yes, he had a deal on. What was she worrying about? Didn't she have her boarder money coming in regularly? Yes, he'd be home in a week and tell her all about it.

The next day Mother got an envelope addressed to her in Father's handwriting and in it was a handbill:

Acreage to Be Cut Up

CHOICE LOTS

Will be Auctioned Off

TUESDAY

April 3

Follow the Brass Band
to the

UNIVERSITY

Join the Crowds
under the

BIG TENT

Bargains in Home Sites

LOTS OF LOTS FOR LOTS OF PEOPLE

Free Transportation   Free Lemonade

COME ONE   COME ALL

And there wasn't another thing in the envelope.

Consumed by angry curiosity, Mother waited for Father to come home.

He arrived one night a little after dinner, looking as smug and complacent as the canary-eating cat. The Kanes and the Sawyers, sensing a domestic crisis, vanished into their rooms.

After listening to a furious lecture on the way he had treated her, taking "our" money out of the bank without consulting her, Father calmly announced that he'd bought a lot of land around the university, about 80 acres, in fact.

At that time Tucson's university consisted of one extremely ugly brick building and two stone dormitories, set down in the midst of the mesquite and cactus about two miles from the center of town.

"University!" wailed Mother. "Why would you buy land around the university, 'way out there in the country?"

"I got it cheap," explained Father, "around $4 an acre."

"Four dollars an acre!" gasped Mother, for that meant he'd spent the entire nest egg. "What will you do with that land?"

"Didn't you read the handbill I sent you?" demanded Father.

"Of course I read it, but I don't know what it means."

"Just what it says. I cut up those acres into lots. I rented a big circus tent and a brass band. I hired an auctioneer and a lot of carriages. I got the people out there and auctioned off the lots. Gave them free lemonade, too."

"Of all the crazy schemes! Spending our money on such foolishness!" As an afterthought, "Did you sell any lots?"

Father nodded casually. "A few." Then he got up and pulled down all the shades, doing it slowly and carefully. Father knew a dramatic moment when he had one.

"Yes, I sold a few," repeated Father, standing before the table. Then before Mother's popping eyes he began to empty his pockets, pulling out roll after roll of bills until the table was covered with them. Last was a canvas sack of gold and silver coins.

"Want to count it?" asked Father. "I think it amounts to $1,827."

Father had made a "killing."

The handbills, the brass band, the free carriages, had drawn Tucsonans out to the university by the hundreds. Under the stimulus of the free lemonade and the auctioneer's gavel, they'd bought lots hand over fist, bidding $5, $10, even as high as $20 for some of the choice lots. When all expenses were paid Father had over $1,800.

"Well," gloated Father, "what do you think now?"

Mother was so excited she couldn't talk. "I think you're wonderful," she got out finally.

Father gathered up the money. "I guess we'd better sleep with this." He let down the couch and stuck the wads of bills and sack of coins under the covers.

"Here I am a rich man, and I've got to sleep on this damn couch. I tell you, if those Sawyers don't go soon, I'm going to build on another room. But what would be the use? I'd go away on a trip, and you'd have that rented, too. When *do* you suppose the Sawyers will go?"

"I don't know," said Mother, "but you know we could take part of that money and put on one or two more bedrooms and . . ."

"Nix," interrupted Father, "I've got a place for that money, and it's not in more bedrooms for more boarders."

"Now don't put it into anything foolish," begged Mother. "Another bedroom would be sensible; you wouldn't have to sleep on the couch."

"Why I don't mind the couch," said Father, "not with this wad of money in with me. And a pretty girl," he added gallantly. "Let the Sawyers stay on forever."

But then a few days later Mr. Sawyer came to Mother, his face beaming, and said they'd be leaving for Michigan the next day. And Mrs. Sawyer looked radiant, too, and for the first time gobbled up her dinner like a little pig.

Afterward she took Mother into her room for a long talk.

"What do you suppose struck them?" Father asked Mother when they went to bed. "All this time they couldn't leave, just *had* to stay here, and now they're off in this awful hurry. It sure is a mystery."

"No, it isn't," said Mother. "She told me why. She's going to have a baby."

"Oh, she is. Well, that's good. That'll cheer her up. But it's still no reason for this hasty exit."

"I think she's a little bit crazy," said Mother. "She told me she had to stay here until she got pregnant, that if she went away before, she knew she wouldn't get pregnant."

"Of all the loony ideas!" snorted Father. "Couldn't she get pregnant back in Michigan? Any particular magic in this house?"

"Maybe," said Mother.

Father pondered on that. "What do you mean 'maybe'?"

"Well . . . Rose Kane is going to have one."

"Oh! Well, that's fine."

"And," added Mother casually, "we are, too."

"Great jumping grasshoppers!" cried Father. "Why don't you tell a fellow?"

CHAPTER 3

Ten Young Men

MOTHER's next surprise for Father was taking in the ten young men as roomers, although this shouldn't have surprised him. Knowing Mother and her aversion to missing any chance for gain and at the same time doing somebody else good, he should have seen it coming. But he didn't, and suddenly there it was—a rooming house, and ten young males ready to move in as roomers. All of which requires a little explanation.

After the Sawyers left, Mother and Father went back into their bedroom.

"Now, please," begged Father, "let's not have anybody but the Kanes."

But then Steve Kane's territory was changed to California, and the Kanes departed for Los Angeles.

Immediately two young men from the wholesale house asked if they could have the room. One of them had the fantastic name of Casimir Casoo and the other, Jerry Blake. However, with Father away half the time, Mother knew she could not have men in the house. Two or three other boys asked about the room—Phoenix, like any young community, was full of unattached young men, and there was very little accommodation for them. Reluctantly Mother told them all "No."

"It's a shame," she said to Father, "that this town doesn't have a place for nice boys like that."

Then one evening two young and pretty schoolteachers came to ask about room and board. Mother said she'd let them know.

"What's the matter with them?" asked Father.

"They are so young and pretty," Mother explained.

"What's that got to do with it?"

"Well, you *do* like women."

"Don't you like men?"

"Not the way you like women."

"Good night!" snorted Father. "If you don't trust me right here under your eye, how you must worry when I'm away on trips!"

"I do worry," admitted Mother.

"Well, then, don't rent the room. Don't take in anybody." But he didn't say it very emphatically. He'd got used to that $60.

So, no married people putting in appearance, Mother accepted the schoolteachers. Having workingwomen, she found, was very convenient, for she could give them lunches to take with them, and they were away all day.

In the meantime Father was making his trips about the territory selling his coffee. But Mother needn't have worried. He had his mind on finances, not females. He saw such tempting opportunities for "killings," and the money he'd made in Tucson was burning a hole in his pocket. There were those mining claims near Globe he could pick up for a song. There was the gas franchise in Bisbee. There was an ice plant in Nogales. And there was more land in Tucson.

But Mother, too, had her mind on a piece of real

estate, and it was the lot next door. (She also wanted Father's money invested in something sensible.)

"We've just *got* to buy that lot," Mother insisted.

"Why, for heaven's sake?" Father wanted to know.

"Because if we don't, Mr. Schmalz is going to buy it."

"Great jumping grasshoppers!" gasped Father.

Mr. Schmalz was the town cobbler and had eleven children, the oldest fourteen.

"We'll have just about enough," Mother continued, "to pay for the lot and a five-room house."

"House?" questioned Father.

"It's no use having an empty lot; we'll have to build a house to get something out of it."

Father thought this over and figured it was a good idea, that the house could be sold to people with fewer children than old Schmalz, and they'd have their money back and a profit besides. In the meantime he could decide whether to make his "killing" in an ice plant or a copper mine.

So they bought the lot and Mother drew the plans for the house, deciding to be her own contractor and hire the workmen herself.

"Why do I need a contractor?" she replied to Father's protest. "I watched our house being built. I'm just duplicating it with one extra room. You remember how I asked all those questions. I've got all the specifications right here in my recipe book." And she brought forth the book, and there, mixed in with how to make a one-egg cake and how to roll out noodles, were the "recipes" for cement and plaster, and the proportions of color and oil for paint, and how many nails to put in a shingle, and the right width between floor joists and between lathes, and a whole lot of other information she'd pestered out of the contractor who'd built their house.

Gloated Mother, "I knew sometime I'd be building a house myself."

So, recipe book in hand, she made her contracts with the cement men and the bricklayers, the plasterers and painters, the carpenters, plumbers and electricians. And from dawn until dark, every minute she could spare, she watched the work being done. The foundation men found they couldn't skimp on cement; the plasterers mixed the lime and sand under her very eye. When the paint was stickier than she thought it ought to be, she had it analyzed and found that molasses had been used instead of oil. Off came the paint, and the next batch she mixed herself. She made the carpenters tear up their No. 2 floor boards when No. 1 was what she had bargained for. She kept an eagle eye on the electricians and plumbers. She called up to the roofers, "Now you put the right number of nails in each of those shingles, or you'll just have to go up there and do it over." And she made Father climb up on the roof and count the nails.

How the workmen must have hated her!

"Cuidado, aquí viene la molona!" she heard one mutter as she came over. She asked Father what it meant.

Father grinned. It means "Look out, here comes the old pest!"

"They'd better look out," Mother warned, "for I'm going to keep right on being a pest."

Mother got the most enormous kick out of being capable. Here she was, a Claiborne of Virginia, with all

those ancestors, from such "nice people," waited on hand and foot as a child, really such a lady, and just look at what she could do. Build a house. Boss a lot of laborers. Outsmart them when they tried to cheat her. Knowing about cement and plaster and painting and plumbing, and how many nails to put in a shingle. Not to mention cooking, sewing, taking in boarders, and being equal to such household crises as unstopping sinks, repairing leaky faucets, replacing blown-out fuses, mending broken electric contraptions.

"You know," she told Father, "whenever I have anyone fix something I always watch, and the next time I can do it myself."

Father, on the other hand, was decidedly not a fixer.

Father's response to any domestic S.O.S. was, "I don't know how to do it. You'll have to get a man."

Father, I'm afraid, got a kick out of being helpless. He had no background of past grandeur. Nobody had waited on him as a child. He had done plenty of menial work. Now he could hire someone to do it. "I'm just a roughneck," he would say. "I had no education. I don't talk good grammar." And for a few sentences he'd be determinedly illiterate. When he wasn't thinking he scarcely split an infinitive, for schoolma'am Mother had done a good job on polishing up his English. Being an omnivorous reader he had educated himself a whole lot better than most men. But he was fond of referring to himself as "just an ignorant cuss."

He certainly was a pretty unobservant cuss about the new house, for it was in its final stages before he noticed anything peculiar about it.

One day after a tour of inspection, he came storming in. "What's all this? What under the sun? The men say there's to be no kitchen over there. How can you sell a house without a kitchen?"

"But we're not going to sell it," soothed Mother; "we're going to rent it."

"Rent it?" boomed Father.

"Rent it," echoed Mother, "and for $75 a month."

"Are you crazy?" he exploded. "Nobody rents a house without a kitchen. No family will give you more than $25 for it."

"But I'm not going to rent it to a family," said Mother.

"Then to who?" demanded Father.

"To whom, you mean," corrected Mother. "Well, I'll tell you. All those rooms are going to be bedrooms."

"All bedrooms!"

"Let me tell it. Yes, all bedrooms. Why waste a room on a parlor or a kitchen when the boys wouldn't need them anyway? Of course the plumbing attachments are there, so we can have a kitchen later if we want it. But now we'll have just bedrooms, and there can be two boys in each room. At $7.50 a month each, that's $15, and 5 times 15 is $75."

While Father stared at her speechlessly, Mother went on. "Boys don't need much furniture, just a bed and a bureau and chair. They'll be gone all day, so there won't be much wear and tear on things. I'll have a little electric plate in the bathroom for their shaving water. A stove in the hall will give enough heat, I think. As for the wood, the boys can just buy their own."

"What boys are you talking about?" snapped Father.

"Why, Cass Casoo and Jerry Blake and their friend, Walter Hanny, and they know three others who'll come. That makes six already. They say they won't have any trouble getting the other four."

"My God!" gasped Father. "You didn't want Schmalz and his eleven children, and now you want ten boys living next to us."

"But the boys will be gone all day."

"But they'll be there at night. Suppose they have drinking parties, bring in women. . . ."

"But I'm getting the kind of boys who won't do those things. Cass is a nice boy—he teaches in the Sunday school—and Jerry is nice, and they'll get their friends.

It won't be a rooming house. It'll be a sort of club, the Second Avenue Club."

Mother waxed Biblical. "You know what happened to the man who hid his talent in the ground. I have this talent for making people happy—you know how no one wants to leave me—and I mustn't bury it in the ground. We need the money, and these boys need rooms. Just because a boy has a small salary is no reason he doesn't want a clean comfortable room. Why, Cass tells me his room has bedbugs in it, and he's paying $12 a month. When we have this opportunity to do good and at the same time help ourselves, it's wicked not to take it. Besides," Mother hurried on, "instead of your investing in some crazy scheme, here's our money in something sound and sensible, something we can keep our eye on, and it's practically all profit, too."

"Are you going to take care of the rooms?" asked Father. "Make all those beds?"

"Losa will do it. I'll give her an extra $1 a week."

"What's the use of my saying anything?" groaned Father. "You'll do what you want. Rooming house! My wife running a rooming house!"

After a while he got out an envelope and pencil and started figuring. He began to look more cheerful.

"What are you figuring?" asked Mother.

"Your expenses. Let's see: Fifty-two dollars a year for Losa. About $20 a year for taxes, and I guess $20 for water. Electricity shouldn't be more than $4 or $5 a month, say $60 a year. That adds up to $150. Take that from your annual rent and you've got $750 clear. You know, you're right. It *is* going to be almost all profit."

"That's what I'm telling you."

Father put the envelope back in his pocket. "That's a pretty sound proposition. You could borrow money on a setup like that."

"Now you're not going to borrow. . . ."

"Did I say I was? I just said it was a sound proposition."

So with Father calmed down and the house almost completed, Mother went into the second phase of her rooming house, furnishing it. She bought the cheapest kind of bureaus and chairs, but good mattresses and springs. For $2.50 each she had a carpenter make her frames for the springs; in this way she got out of buying bedsteads. As for the rugs, curtains, sheets, quilts, towels, she saw no reason to buy these. Not when she had a sewing machine and plenty of energy. The curtains she made out of scrim. She bought bolts of sheeting and hemmed the sheets and pillow slips, thirty sheets and twenty pillow slips—Mother changed but one sheet at a time, the bottom one off, the top one on the bottom, and a clean one on top. She made her spreads of unbleached muslin with a gingham trim. She bought hucking for towels and washcloths. She made the quilts, getting help from her friends by inviting them in to quilting bees. She crocheted rag rugs, begging scraps from everyone she saw. In the evening, while the schoolteachers sat around the dining-room table, she had them turning down hems and cutting up scraps for rugs. Tom Sawyer getting his fence whitewashed had nothing on Mother. If Father was home, he usually read aloud to the three of them, calling them his harem and flirting with the teachers outrageously.

"I think it's a shame the way she works you," he commiserated.

"They don't mind," said Mother. "Look at the beaux they'll have, and right next door." (Mother no doubt was glad Father was going to have this competition.)

And the teachers giggled, and Father said women were the biggest bunch of matchmakers.

Of course my advent was getting closer, and, with all this sewing, tiny garments were conspicuous by their absence. Once Father observed, "You seem to be sewing for the roomers, all right, but what about the baby?"

"Heavens," said Mother, "it's months yet, and all a baby needs in the summer is diapers, anyway."

What might have occurred to them both, that Mother should not do all this work in her condition, did not occur to them. Mother was from a family of twelve, Father from one of ten. A baby was a pretty commonplace happening. One wasn't incapacitated just because one was having offspring.

So the house was finished and furnished, and the ten young men moved in. There were of course Cass Casoo and Jerry Blake and Walter Hanny from the wholesale house, and Reginald Eadie and Chris Paterson from the railroad offices. There were Herbert Trivers who worked in a shoe store and Carl Richardson who had a laundry route and Lester Jones who was a bank clerk—he had the best job of all, $18 a week—and Arthur Stayner and Pete Campbell who were salesmen in a gents' furnishing store.

The Second Avenue Club was on its way. As Mother had said, the boys liked this domitory life. Being by themselves, they felt free and easy without the restraint that a landlady living in the house would have given them. From next door Mother kept an eye on things and took up matters that needed to be taken up with Cass Casoo, the house president.

"Look here, Cass," she'd say, "if your friends are going to use my towels to polish their shoes, I'm not going to provide any towels. But here are some soft old rags you can use."

The boys were gone all day, and Losa took care of the rooms. Monday was the most strenuous day when Losa did the washing. Besides the linen from our house, there would be on the line ten sheets, ten pillow slips, ten towels, ten washrags.

"Looks like a tenement house," snorted Father, and complained that his own shirts were being skimped.

They were a nice group of boys, and Mother played the role of elder sister to them, having them over by twos and threes to a meal, bossing them when they needed bossing, listening to their love troubles, telling them to get haircuts, taking care of them when they were sick. Every once in a while Father and Mother would have to sleep on the dining-room couch again because Cass, or Pete, or Chris would be in the bedroom.

"That boy almost has pneumonia," Mother would tell Father. "I've got to have him over here where I can look after him."

When there was a vacancy, members of the club chose the next inmate. This made for congeniality. Of course Mother was lucky in that Phoenix had a dearth of cheap, comfortable rooms, and there was always a waiting list.

So now Mother had quite an income—$60 from the teachers, $75 from the Second Avenue Club.

Father by this time was entirely reconciled to both boarders and roomers. "I've got a damn smart wife," he'd tell people. "She can support herself and me, too. I'm thinking of retiring."

At the same time Father was doing very well with his coffee. But, whereas he used to tell Mother just what he was making, reporting proudly on his sales after each trip, now he became vague and reticent, merely saying, "Oh, I did all right," in answer to her inquiries.

"If you're doing so well, why is our bank account so low?" Mother would ask.

"Oh, I've opened up an account in Tucson," Father explained.

It was the beginning of the division of their finances into "his" money and "her" money.

"Why do you worry what I'm making, when you're bringing in enough for us to live on?" Father asked.

"I actually think you like me to work," pouted Mother.

"I do," Father agreed with her, "because you like it so well. When you stop liking it, you can stop doing it."

"How can I stop when I know you're going into these crazy schemes?"

"They're not crazy," Father protested; "they're golden opportunities. It would be wicked," he went on, using Mother's own argument, "when I see them to let them pass by."

And opportunities did abound in those booming days of the young West, when you could sell almost anything you bought at a profit, if you held on to it for a while.

When cities and towns and communities were clamoring for railroads and streetcar lines, for ice plants and gas plants and powerhouses, for schools and post offices, for hospitals and hotels. A man who could anticipate—or wangle a tip from someone in the know—where these were going could buy shrewdly and profitably. All that was needed was a little cash and a gambler's courage. And if Father guessed wrong, wasn't Mother still there bringing in the beans?

So there it was, the circle complete—Father feeling he could plunge because Mother was making money and Mother feeling she must make money because Father was plunging.

Nor could Mother hold Father in check by saying he shouldn't take such chances when she was going to have a baby.

"What difference will the baby make?" demanded Father. "Will the teachers leave because you're having a baby, or the boys next door? Now if you were working in a store or going out as a dressmaker, I can see a baby would be difficult. But you're in a business where it won't matter. You're a damn smart woman!"

This constant reiteration by Father of how damn smart she was irked Mother. She wanted to be smart, able to make money, but she didn't want Father to take it so as a matter of course. She was learning, dear Mother, that you can't eat your cake and have it, too. You could be a clinging vine in the Southern tradition and lean on the menfolks, or you could be a sturdy oak, in which case the menfolks just let you be a sturdy oak.

And so I arrived and, as Father had predicted, made

no difference to Mother's business and, weighing but 3 pounds, almost no difference at my coming.

"Heavens," said Mother, "why, this is nothing."

"Easiest birth I ever saw," marveled the doctor.

According to Mother, I was an awfully good baby. I got fat and pretty right away, and slept and ate when I should have done so, and scarcely ever cried. And smart! Why, I was talking at nine months! "You really were the smartest little baby," Mother always boasted.

Even though my arrival didn't affect it, it must be admitted that there were occasional problems at the Second Avenue Club.

There was, for instance, the matter of Norville Roth. Mother found out about him when he asked her to build the fire for his hot water.

Mother had that little electric plate in the bathroom to heat shaving water, but for bath water there was a boiler on the back porch which was heated by a wood stove. The boys paid for their own wood and usually attended to their own fires. But it took about an hour for the water to heat, and occasionally a lad who was taking a young lady out to dinner would telephone about five o'clock and ask Mother to start the fire under the boiler so the water would be hot by the time he came home. And Mother would go over and build the fire.

A supply of wood was supposed to be kept on the back porch, but sometimes this was neglected, and then Mother would have to go out and carry in wood.

"Don't carry in wood for those lazy loafers," Father ordered. "If it isn't on the porch, let them bathe in cold water."

Mother would be very firm over the telephone. "If

there's no wood there, there's not going to be any fire," she'd tell them. But she usually weakened and did it "just this once."

Then one day a perfectly strange voice called up and told her somewhat peremptorily to have the water hot by six o'clock.

"Who is this speaking?" asked Mother.

"Norville Roth, a friend of Cass Casoo's."

"Why don't you bathe where you live?" asked Mother. "Why do you want to take a bath in my house?"

"I am living in your house," said Norville Roth.

"You're visiting Cass?"

"Not visiting him, living with him."

"But where are you sleeping?"

"With Cass."

"In that bed? It's too narrow."

"Yes, it is. You'll have to put in a larger one."

"I don't know anything about you. You're not paying me any rent."

"I'm paying it to Cass."

"How much?" demanded Mother.

"Five dollars a month. So will you please have the water hot."

"I'll do it just this once. But hereafter if you want hot water, get Cass to light your fires."

Mother was furious over this subletting. "Now Cass is getting his room for $2.50," she told Father. "Pretty soon they'll all want to do that, and there'll be twenty boys in the house instead of ten, and all that extra wear and tear on the furniture without my getting a cent more for it."

"Next time," Father advised, "stipulate there's to be

no subletting. But I wouldn't worry. Cass'll get tired of sleeping two men in a bed."

"I'll certainly not give them a double bed."

The next day Norville telephoned again. "You'd better hurry and get that double bed in," he ordered, "and Casoo wants a bath tonight; so light the fire."

Mother telephoned Cass.

"Cass, are you taking a bath tonight?"

"Why, no, I'm not."

"I didn't think you were," said Mother, "because you had a bath two days ago. Well, your roomer just phoned, and he wants hot water ready, so you'd better come up and light the fire."

"Now, please . . ."

"I only light fires for people who pay me rent. And I'm not putting in any double bed, and I'm not furnishing another pillow, and I'm not supplying any more towels."

It was shortly afterward that Norville left.

"Women trouble" came up only once. One day when Mother was over in the house with Losa on a tour of inspection, the closet door in Cass and Jerry's room stood open—or she opened it—and there hung a woman's sealskin cape, a very beautiful little cape.

Mother was filled with outraged anger. A woman's cape in her rooming house!

When questioned that evening, both Cass and Jerry denied any knowledge of the cape. They had never seen the cape before. Didn't even know it was in the closet. Didn't know any woman who owned such a cape. Mother questioned the other boys in the house and got the same story from all of them.

"Now see here," announced Mother, "that cape didn't walk in here by itself, and the woman who wore it didn't walk in by herself. One of you boys brought her. Who was it?"

"Maybe it was Norville," suggested Cass helpfully. "Norville knew a lot of women."

"If it's Norville, tell him to get that cape out of here. And don't you ever let me find any more women's clothes in this house."

But Norville had left town, and for weeks and weeks the cape hung in the closet until finally Mother took it over to her house.

"But you can't take some woman's cape," Father told her.

"I'm not going to leave it over there for the moths."

"I'll go and talk to them. I'll find out who owns it."

But even Father's man-to-man talk elicited no further information.

"Maybe it really was Norville," Mother said. "I hope so. I hate to think Cass or Jerry would do a thing like that."

"What under the sun will you do with the cape?" asked Father.

"Do with it? Why, wear it, of course. I need a coat, and it's the right style for me for just now." ("Just now" referring to the fact that Mother was again pregnant.)

"You're not going to wear some prostitute's coat," cried Father. "Suppose she sees you!"

"Let her see me. Let her ask for it. I'll give it to her if she can prove it's hers. Finders' keepers," said Mother, whose philosophy was nothing if not realistic. And she wore the little cape for years. I remember it. It was very pretty, with a collar that turned up and a cape part that swirled down to her hips. When it was worn out, she cut it up and trimmed our coats with it. She still has bits of it wrapped up in moth balls.

If the owner saw it, she never peeped. But Father fumed every time Mother put it on.

"Whenever I see a woman eying it, I get cold chills."

"Well," said Mother, "you'd better get over your chills, for I'm going to keep on wearing it."

After a while Father switched his tune and began hinting of a coming event that would make her change her mind.

"What's going to happen?" demanded Mother.

"I'm going to be a rich man," he promised her. "I'll soon be buying you a coat that will make that one look like 30 cents."

"What wildcat scheme are you into now? You remember you promised. . . ."

"This isn't wildcat," he assured her. "This is sensible —as sensible as your rooming house." But that's all he would tell her, until one day he came back from Tucson with what Mother called "that look" on his face.

"Well," groaned Mother, "what is it? What have you bought now?"

"A laundry," Father beamed at her. "I've bought a laundry over in Tucson."

CHAPTER 4

A Very Clean Business

FATHER couldn't see why Mother was so upset about his buying a laundry.

"But do you know anything about running a laundry?" demanded Mother.

"No, I don't, but the same foreman—and he's a humdinger—is staying on. Only now he's working for me. Instead of the former owner's getting the profits, I'll get them. And they're big—I've seen the books—they'll average $300 a month."

"Why does anyone want to give up such a nice business?"

"Because Stacey's tired of Arizona. He wants to retire. He's going back East where his children are.

"This is so sensible," Father went on. "It's the only laundry in town. People always have to have their dirty clothes washed, just the way they have to have food and shelter. See," concluded Father, pleased with the comparison, "now we're both serving the public. You feed them and room them, while I clean them up."

"But why didn't you talk it over with me first?"

"Because there wasn't time. I was afraid someone else would buy it. Stacey—he's a prince of a fellow, you'd like him—made me a wonderful proposition. A small down payment, the rest out of earnings. Why, it would be *wicked* not to grab an opportunity like that! It's a fine little plant. Thirty employees, four wagons, four good horses. And all set and running. I won't have to lift a hand. The money will just roll in."

Mother shook her head. "It doesn't make sense to me. Three hundred dollars doesn't come rolling in without lifting a hand."

"Oh, well," admitted Father, "maybe I exaggerated a little. I suppose I'll have to drop around occasionally, do a little work, but Stacey says he never goes near the place, just lets the foreman run it."

"There's something very, very fishy about all this," prophesied Mother. "It's not going to work out."

And she was right. It didn't.

Old Man Stacey turned out to be, not a prince of a fellow, but, in Father's own words, "a damned, dirty, yellow skunk." Instead of going back East he stayed on in Tucson and, immediately the papers were signed, started another laundry. He took with him the drivers, the humdinger of a foreman, several key workers, and most of the customers.

"But how can he do this?" asked Mother. "Can't you stop him?"

"I can't," groaned Father, who was now as far down in the depths as he'd been up on the heights. "There's nothing in our contract that says he can't go into the laundry business again. I never thought . . . I've just been played for a sucker. He wanted a larger building and new machinery, and he's using my money to get them. In the meantime he takes my customers, my drivers, my foreman. Played for a sucker, that's what!" And Father moaned and groaned and paced the floor.

"I haven't any business. I can't meet those payments. What am I going to do?"

"Do? I'd get out," advised Mother. "Let him have his old laundry. Take your loss, and let it be a lesson to you."

"No," Father decided, "I'm going to fight him. I'll get hold of some cash. Look, we can borrow some money on this property. . . ."

"Never!" Mother broke in, "never, never! I'll not borrow money on these houses. They're our living. I'm not going to be on the street with two babies and no home." (The second baby was young Phillip, born shortly before Father bought the laundry.)

"So you won't help me out."

"Not in throwing good money after bad, I won't. The money would be gone, like that, and then where would we be?"

"I've still got my coffee commissions."

"You can't count on those; they aren't steady."

So Father went back and forth between Phoenix and Tucson, struggling with a business he knew nothing about, fighting the dirty skunk's competition as best he could. Each time he brought back a worse report. He couldn't eat, he couldn't sleep.

"You're letting that old sidewinder ruin me," he accused Mother.

"That old sidewinder may ruin you," Mother told him, "but he's not going to ruin me. I'm going to keep these houses."

Then one day Mother heard Father coming up the path whistling. His pace was jaunty. He had the look on his face. Mother knew he had something to tell her.

But he waited until after dinner and the teachers had gone to their rooms.

"Well, Mother," he gloated, "I think you're going to sell these houses."

"Now we've been over all that."

"Look, what have we got in them—$4,000? Now suppose we could get $5,000 for them."

"We couldn't get $5,000, and I wouldn't sell anyway."

"Six thousand—would you take that?"

"No," said Mother.

"Seventy-five hundred?"

"No."

"Ten thousand?"

"What is this?"

"Well, then, $12,000? Will you sell for $12,000?"

"Will you stop being so silly?"

"I'm not silly. Will you sell for $12,000? Yes, or no."

"Yes, then. Of course I'd sell for $12,000. Now are you finished playing your little game?"

"I'm finished," grinned Father, bringing out some papers. "I thought $12,000 would get you. Sign here."

It was one of those fantastic real-estate transactions that happened so often in the boom days of the young West. The word had got out that a big Water Users' Building was to go up in Phoenix. There was a mad scramble to buy property around it. And Mother's and Father's houses were but half a block away.

Mother made one stipulation. She refused to sign unless $4,000 were given to her for a house in Tucson. "And," said Mother, "it's going to be a big house, with lots of bedrooms—for boarders!"

So Mother started packing. The schoolteachers had to

find themselves another room. The furniture in the Second Avenue Club was sold to the new owner, who agreed to let the boys stay on until he tore the house down for an office building.

The family moved to Tucson—Father and Mother, young Phillip and I. They rented a little three-room house, all they could find, downtown near the Carnegie Library.

While Father battled Old Man Stacey, Mother busied herself with plans for the new house.

It's no use going into that old laundry scrap. But, heeled with cash and righteous wrath, Father went after that old son of a you-know-what, and put the damned dirty skunk out of business. He wound up owning both laundries and running old sidewinder Stacey out of town.

Now Father consolidated the two laundries and set himself to build up the business.

Mother was amazed and delighted at the way Father was working. He really seemed to be settling down. He talked no more of "killings" but concentrated on such problems as getting the Pullman Company to put its linen off at Tucson rather than at El Paso, and in getting more and more dirty clothes away from the washerwomen. Every time he saw a row of washing on a line, it was a challenge to him. That wash ought to come to him.

Occasionally he'd say, "You know, there *is* a satisfaction in it—seeing all those bundles come in, mussed up, smelly, filthy, and then seeing them go out so nice and clean."

"I'm sure there must be," Mother agreed, and glowed that Father had at last "found himself."

There was something Spartan in Mother's nature that derived satisfaction out of money made from hard work and preferably from something rather menial. The laundry business suited her exactly—an honest, lowly business. "Such a clean business, too," as Father always said. And *very* profitable. Mother could see that, as more and more people came to Tucson with more and more dirty clothes for Father to wash, he might very well get on that street he was always talking about—Easy Street.

Mother drew a big breath of relief. She relaxed. Now she knew where she was *at*. She allowed herself a few frills with the new house. It would cost $40 to have hardwood floors instead of pine—all right, she'd have hardwood floors. She also floored over the attic just in case she ever wanted bedrooms up there.

And then with everything looking so rosy and peaceful, Father suddenly retired from the laundry and put his barber in charge. Oh, it didn't happen quite so quickly as that, but with old Stacey beaten and the business booming, Father became bored and irritated by the countless details involved in washing people's clothes. Where before no trouble had been too great to gain a customer or to keep a customer, the complaints now got him down.

"Why, they stop me on the street," he told Mother, "to show me a button off their shirts!"

"You ought to carry some buttons with you," advised practical Mother, "and hand them out to them."

"Now isn't that a bright idea!" scoffed Father. "I suppose you'd like me to carry needle and thread, too, and do a little sewing right on the spot."

"It wouldn't hurt you," said Mother.

And of course after hours, or early in the morning, people would telephone Father at the house about their troubles.

"My dress shirt's not back. . . ."

"You've sent me somebody else's nightshirt. . . ."

"Where's my tablecloth? . . . "

"I can't get into my socks. . . ."

I can remember Father coming back from these calls, crying, "Grief! Grief! All I get is grief!"

"Every business has some annoyances," Mother would try to pacify him.

But Father would shake his head and mutter, "I'm meant for better things than a lot of old dirty clothes."

I remember early one Sunday morning the telephone's ringing, and it was the Episcopalian minister saying the surplices for the choirboys weren't at the church and please would Father get them there right away. I can hear Father banging down the receiver and swearing he'd be damned if he wasn't going to get into a business where he could at least have Sunday off. And then the telephone rang again, and it was a restaurant complaining that the waiters' jackets hadn't been delivered.

"Oh, God! Oh, God! Oh, God!" swore Father.

"Now you hush such talk around the children," Mother ordered. "You ought to be ashamed, carrying on like this. Instead of being grateful you have the business and wanting to set matters right."

"I'm going to do something about this," raged Father,

struggling into his clothes. "Other men can have Sunday off. But I've got to go down and hunt up a lot of surplices and waiters' jackets."

So Mother wasn't too surprised when he came home one day and said, "I've found a man to run the laundry."

"Who is it?" demanded Mother.

"Russ Logan."

"Who is he?"

"You don't know him. He's my barber."

"Your barber! Has he ever run a laundry?"

"No, but he's a good man."

Mother had hysterics. Had Father gone stark, raving mad?

"But I know he's the right man," Father insisted. "I've got a hunch. Besides, he's buying 40 per cent."

"Where did he get the money to buy 40 per cent of that business?"

"Well," admitted Father, "it's this way. I'm paying him so much a week to be the manager"—mentioning a sum that made Mother gasp—"but I pay him only half of it in cash. The half I don't pay him goes to pay for his 40 per cent."

"Which means you're making him an outright gift. Well," sighed Mother, "if that's what you've done, that's what you've done. I know what I'm going to do. I'm going to add a big screen porch to our house. We can all sleep out there and use the little back bedroom for a dressing room. That'll give us three rooms to rent to boarders.

"I simply don't understand you," she went on. "Here you've got something that brings you in a nice income.

You could drop your coffee business, not have to make these trips, stay home with your family. But you can't stand a little grief, a little annoyance. Because someone calls up about a lost shirt, you want to hand your business over to someone else."

"But I'm not handing it over to him. I'm keeping 60 per cent. I'll still have my salary as president."

"How can the laundry afford to pay him a salary and you a salary for doing nothing?"

"He's a go-getter. He'll get a lot more customers. It's going to be all right, I tell you."

Unbelievably enough, it was.

The barber, knowing nothing about running a laundry, did the obvious thing and got an extremely competent man from back East as the plant foreman. Russ then concentrated on his real gift, which was making friends, and where he made friends he made customers. He widened his circle by joining everything there was to join—Masons, Elks, Odd Fellows, Knights of This and That. He worked indefatigably for civic and charitable organizations—Chamber of Commerce, Big Brothers, Orphans' Home, Sunshine Club—Russ was in them all.

And as for complaints, he ate them up. He had a bicycle with a large basket on the handle bars. After hours he'd pedal out miles to deliver some late bundle or to listen to some tale of woe about a torn sheet or faded apron. No matter how trivial the claim or how unjustified, Russ was ready to make it right.

"Honestly," said Father, "he's wonderful. I sure picked a winner." And Father drew his check as president and never went near the place. Now he had more time for his coffee work and for scouting out another place to make a "killing."

Mother knew he was going to get into something and braced herself for whatever it would be.

Finally it came.

"You know," said Father, "there's a company here that wants to start a brewery. . . ."

CHAPTER 5

The Big House

FATHER wasn't actually going into the brewery business, as he kept reassuring Mother. He was merely buying up options on the land around where the brewery was to be.

"I'm going to put up a lot of little houses," he told her, "and sell them to the workers. This plant will be immense. People will come from all over the Southwest to work in it. I'll make a killing."

Fortunately for Father, before he got too deeply involved, it occurred to the brewery company to have Tucson's water analyzed. It was found to be too alkaline for beermaking. The project was abandoned, and Father was left holding the options.

But was Father downhearted? No, indeed. He'd now heard of those wonderful Oro Blanco mining claims, and there was Mr. Robinson sitting around the San Xavier Hotel lobby just waiting to find something to invest in.

By this time our new house was built, and we'd moved in. I've already told you how it was Father who started Mother on the boarders again by asking her to take in Mr. Robinson.

From then on Father kept getting into more and

more schemes, and Mother kept taking in more and more boarders.

Father had had his brief period of sticking to one business. But Father was a promoter. Once a thing was under way he lost interest. Temperamentally he was unfitted for the steady plugging, the nose-to-the-grindstone stuff. As Mother once said to me, but really talking *at* Father, "Your Father gets a fire started under one pot, and as soon as that starts to boil, he takes his fire away and puts it under another pot; then when that begins simmering he's off with his fire for still another pot."

But that's the way Father was. He could no more change wanting to put his fire under many pots than he could change the shape of his nose. He couldn't bear not to seize every opportunity that came up. As Tucson grew and grew there were plenty of schemes to get into. And Father got into them. Not only with his own money, but with other people's. Father was extraordinarily persuasive; his enthusiasm was contagious. After Father talked to you about some "sure thing," you wanted to put your last cent into it. Father made money for himself and for his friends—and also lost it. But when Father made a piece of money he seldom cleaned up the obligations involved in making it. Why pay your debts when you could go on to further ventures? And whatever business Father launched, he soon put someone else in charge of it. With Russ Logan he was lucky; he was never that lucky again. In fact, some of his choices were God-awful.

Subdivisions, streetcar lines, cattle ranches, hotels, theaters, mines, a bank—oh, that disastrous bank—real estate, business blocks, oil wells, grocery stores, paving, a railroad—Father was in them all. And each one of them was going to put us on that fabulous street Father was always talking about—Easy Street. "Well, kids, we'll soon be on Easy Street." How often I've heard him say that.

But we were always hard up. Father was always coming home crying he was going broke and for Mother to "go easy" on the groceries. And the next day borrowing $10,000 to put in a gold mine!

No wonder Mother took in boarders.

"Well," she'd say to Father's occasional—very occasional—protest, "you tell me you're going broke. Someone's got to have money to raise and educate these children." And she kept the house full. Except in summer I never knew a time when we didn't have people with us.

The house Mother built in Tucson was well suited for boarders. Outside, although it was of no particular style unless it was a combination of California bungalow and early mission, it was attractive—the kind of a house you'd like to live in. It was of white stucco with a huge porch on two sides, and, just as soon as she could get them growing, Mother had roses and ivy and flowering vines climbing all over this porch.

Inside it was big and roomy. The large entrance hall, the parlor, and the dining room all opened into one another and made for spaciousness. However, sliding doors could shut off the dining room, and in winter we used them. The parlor and dining room had beamed ceilings and bay windows. Beneath the dining-room bay was a long curved window seat.

The big front bedroom, the "living room" as we always called it, besides opening on the main entrance hall, had an outside entrance to the front porch through its French doors. The three back bedrooms opened on the long inner hall, so that each one, although leading into another room, could be shut off and entrance gained only from the hall. Since the bathroom was at the end of the hall, one could get to it without going through any other room.

Sometimes Mother had three bedrooms rented. What remained for the family then was the screen porch at the side, and the last little bedroom as a sort of passageway and dressing room.

In the summer the boarders left—being for the most part teachers or tourists—and we would spread out all over the house. Mother would say, "Now next fall I'm not going to have so many people." But fall would come and she'd rent the living room, then the next room. Then there would arrive unexpectedly some people who'd boarded with us before—and how could she not take them?—or some friends or relatives of erstwhile boarders. Or Father would be particularly needing extra money at this point. There would be the third room rented, and the family telescoped into the little back room again. Well, we each had a bed, a bureau, a couple of hangers in the closet. What more did we want?

We never had all-year boarders. These would have been working people who wouldn't have wanted to pay Mother's prices. Mother's idea was that it was better to rent for a higher price at a shorter time. Besides, in the summer we usually went away ourselves for a couple of months. That is, Mother and we children did. Father stayed in Tucson to look after his business and the house—although he always let the grass die—and came up to see us for a week or two.

Mother's brother, Uncle Tom, worked in the Southern Pacific's office in San Francisco and always sent us passes for our trip to California and return. To get passes, Uncle Tom had to say that we were dependent on him, and this irked Father.

"But you're *not* dependent upon Tom," he'd complain.

"We're dependent on him for these tickets, aren't we?"

"It's cheating the railroad," Father would argue, but not very emphatically.

After a while Father was made a director of the Arizona Eastern Railroad, a small subsidiary of the Southern Pacific, and then we didn't have to ask Uncle Tom for passes, for Father could get them for all of us for all over the United States. Those were certainly the days when it came to getting passes. Father also got a $20 gold piece every time he went to a directors' meeting, which was about three times a year, and these he gave to Mother.

We did stay in our house all winter, though, and it wasn't always comfortable because at first it had no furnace—just fireplaces in the parlor, dining room, and living room, and flues for stoves in the bedrooms. Cold? You bet it was cold. I don't care if we are the Sunshine City with roses blooming in December, in wintertime it's freezing nights and mornings. Our house was drafty, because, when it was being built, it rained so much the wood warped and shrank. But as Mother said, "I've never seen the wild flowers so beautiful as they were that year." So the wind whistled about our feet, and we stuck rugs around the door cracks, stuffed the windows with paper, and huddled over the fires. We never thought of weather stripping.

While the boarders sat by the fire in the parlor, we children usually undressed in the dining room. I can see Mother now warming our pajamas by hanging them over the fire screen. When they were baking hot she plumped us into them, and we'd rush off to bed before the heat was all gone. Colonel, our black cocker spaniel, waited by the fire with us and then ran as fast as we did and hopped up on a bed. Sometimes in the night he'd whimper, and then we'd take him under the covers. On very cold nights Mother heated flatirons on the kitchen stove, wrapped them up in newspapers, and put them in our beds. Oh, but they felt grand!

Mornings we dressed in the kitchen where the big wood stove made things as warm as toast. The boarders, too, had fires to dress by, for the maid's first chore was to build fires in the little stoves and in the grate in the living room. Mother kept a box of chips and kindling especially for this purpose because they made a quick blaze.

For several years we had but one bathroom. One bathroom for a family of five, two to six boarders, a cook, and, when we children could sneak him in there for an occasional scrub, our dog, too. But we seemed to get along all right. A bathroom then was a luxury, to be used sparingly. (After all, we were not far removed from those two-fisted times when the plumbing was all outdoors.) It was long before the advertisements of delectable ladies sitting modestly in soapsuds the while giving themselves facials and manicures at a bathtub tray. A bathroom in those days was a place to do what one had to do in it and leave, not a place to rest, cold-cream one's face, or read a book.

When the door handle rattled, one sang out apologetically: "Just a min-nit," and hurried up. And if there ever came an emergency when one *had* to get in, but couldn't, well, my goodness, wasn't there all outdoors . . . and bushes and bushes and bushes?

Mother started early with her garden, digging up the *caliche*—hardpan—hauling in good, rich, river-bottom dirt, planting the lawn, the palms, the pepper and umbrella trees, the peach and apricot and fig trees, the lilac bushes, the row on row of roses, which were to make our home such a show place.

In the process an amazing number of creeping, crawling things came to light—tarantulas, scorpions, centipedes, little horned toads. And of course lizards all over the place. They even got in the house.

In the brush, quail were still around and jack rabbits, and at night we could hear an occasional coyote.

The rabbits sometimes ate our seedlings, but the worst damage was done by Mr. Mendoza's chickens. Mr. Mendoza was a Mexican and lived a couple of blocks to the south of us on Stone Avenue. His chickens were not penned up and naturally made a beeline to the delicious grubs and worms in Mother's new soil.

"Mr. Mendoza," Mother told him, "your chickens are scratching up my plants. You'll have to pen them up."

Mr. Mendoza promised that he would but, *mañana*-like, never got around to it.

"Mr. Mendoza," Mother warned, "your chickens are still digging up my garden. Now I've made a pen in my back yard, and if you don't pen your chickens up at your home, I'm going to pen them up at mine."

Mr. Mendoza swore he'd make the pen that very night.

But the next morning, bright and early, there were the chickens. Mother went into the kitchen and crumbled up some bread crusts.

"Here, chickie. Here, chickie," she called, letting the crumbs trail through her fingers and so enticing the chickens into the makeshift pen.

"But you can't keep the man's chickens," protested Father. "That's stealing."

"Those chickens were stealing from me, destroying my garden."

And she kept the chickens, building a regular pen, feeding them on scraps from the table. Later on, when the flock increased, she had extra eggs that she sold to the neighbors—including Mr. Mendoza.

The chicken pen Mother put on our adjoining lot next to the little shed where we kept our wood. Eventually when the town built up to us Mother meant to sell this lot. When that time came she could take down the pen and shed. But because they were on the other lot now, there was plenty of room behind our house. Mother began to brood about this and say what a shame it was, all that good space going to waste.

"What do you mean good space going to waste?" demanded Father.

"Well," said Mother, "the Second Avenue Club was such a success, we might build a little house back there and call it the 'Seventh Avenue Club.' " (Our house was on the corner of Third Street and Seventh Avenue.)

"Now look here," cried Father, "I had all those boys next door to me. I'm not going to have another batch in my back yard."

"It couldn't be as big as the other club," Mother went on, "probably only three rooms. But if I could get six boys, and I think I could get $10 a month from them, that would be $60, and 12 times 60 is 720. . . ."

"No! No! No!" roared Father. "I absolutely forbid it. I guess I've got some rights around here, and I don't want you taking in a lot of hoodlums."

"I never did take in hoodlums, but if you don't want me to build the house I won't do it. It was just an idea of mine."

"Well, let it stay just an idea."

And so it did until a couple of years later when Father became a third owner in an automobile. Then he thought he had to have a garage.

"You certainly should," Mother agreed quickly.

Father as usual left the details of the building to Mother and didn't notice a thing until the edifice was well on its way.

He came in one day with fire in his eye. "Now what are you doing? That's a house out there, not a garage."

"Half of it's a garage," Mother corrected. "The other half will be two rooms and a bath."

"But why . . ."

"It isn't costing much more," Mother soothed, "and I've already got two schoolteachers to take those rooms."

"Schoolteachers, are they?" Father perked up. "Are they good looking?"

"*Quite* nice looking," Mother assured him.

What she didn't tell him was that they were middle-aged!

CHAPTER 6

Good Food and Some Fun

SO THE years came and went, and so did the boarders, hundreds and hundreds of them. I can't remember them all—the schoolteachers, pretty girls who stayed with us for a year or two and inevitably got married; the mining men, coming and going on mysterious trips, sending telegrams, making long-distance calls; the college professors, male and female; the scientists who worked at the Desert Laboratory; the later-day tourists who came out for sinus and arthritis or to be near a sick relative or merely to bask in our sunshine.

I remember the Woolleys and the Merrills—the Woolleys so religious and the Merrills not so. I remember the Admiral and how he paid his rent to Father instead of to Mother, and what Father did with the money. I remember Miss Sally Lynch and the fun it was to watch her do her face. And there were Rita Vlasak, who was crazy about men, and old Miss Russell, who quarreled with Father about Theodore Roosevelt. There were Dr. Law, who was studying the effect of sun on bone diseases, and Mr. Dobson, the Chili con Carne King of St. Louis, and Mrs. Dobson, who was run down and had to be fattened up—and how Mother loved that. There were the lawyer and his wife from Duluth, and the Sewards from Cleveland—he came out on crutches and left playing golf. And Mrs. Lawson and Jeffrey.

And Floyd, who knocked out Jeffrey's teeth—and what a blessing that was. There were the Hughstons, who quarreled with Father about Franklin D. Roosevelt. There were the Lathams, who bought the mine in Mexico, and the Harmons from Vancouver, and the pretty schoolteacher from Kentucky whom my younger brother married, and many, many more.

It is a list of boarders and a list of friends—people we kissed good-by at the train, with whom we kept up a correspondence, whom we visited during the summers, who came back to stay with us again and again, and who sent us their friends and relatives.

Why? Did Mother love the people she took, or did she take only those she could love? I think it was the latter. When it came to people there was and is something psychic about Mother. As she thumps a melon—thump, thump, thump—and always gets a good one, so metaphorically she "thumped" the people who wanted to come and stay with us. She'd say, "Yes, indeed, I can take you," or she'd be vague and apologetic, "Well, I don't know. I have a room, but my brother and his wife may come out from St. Louis. . . ."

Of course Mother was lucky in that Tucson in those days presented a landlady's market. There were more people than rooms. Mother could pick and choose, and she chose those she felt would be happy with us and with the people already in the house. She made very few mistakes.

Why were all these people so happy with us? I think one of our boarders summed it up when he said upon coming to us, "You know, I was told that in your house I'd have good food and some fun."

"Good food and some fun." What better reasons to be happy? What a solution for the world's woes! Do well-fed, amused people start wars?

Certainly our food was good—more of that later. And certainly we had fun. We were harum-scarum, happy-go-lucky ourselves, and we made the boarders part of the family.

And when I say part of the family, I really mean it. Our boarders lived all over the house, and we had no reverent feeling about their rooms. If we had a party, they were of course included. If we needed their rooms to dance in, down came their beds, up came their rugs. We had them painting place cards, icing cakes, beating mayonnaise, rolling up rugs, carrying borrowed furniture. We were famous for our hot tamales, and many a boarder got a stiff arm grinding chili. In one way or another we got a lot of work out of our boarders.

When the cook left, the boarders pitched in with the dishes. They helped us nurse Colonel through distemper, picked cactus thorns out of his ears. They drove cars for us during elections—we were always hot and bothered about some local issue. They drove stakes in Father's subdivisions and often found themselves buying some of the lots. They felt free to invite their friends to drop in for meals or to have a party themselves. Obediently they went off to the movies with the family while I held sorority initiations. Home life they had paid for, and home life they got.

Mother charged a lot and was a good manager. And because she had a generous margin of profit, she wasn't too worried about the extras—the munching from the icebox, the electric iron used for hours at a time, the guests brought home for meals.

"Things even up," she'd say. "Mr. Bayless uses all that hot water, but he doesn't eat any meat."

Now that I look back upon it I see that in regard to boarders, Mother—and the rest of us following her lead —was really unique. That pathetic, forlorn note so much a part of most boardinghouses was lacking in ours. We *liked* having boarders. It was a family enterprise with us. Our wares were food, shelter, and love. We sold them happily and proudly. Possibly it was a combination of Virginia hospitality combined with the "Light, Stranger, and eat" of the young West. It did not occur to us to be apologetic, to feel that we were coming down in the world because we were sharing our home.

Mother never got over being surprised and pleased at how much money she could make in spite of her being such a lady. And Father was pleased because she was pleased—and also because she was bringing in the beans no matter what kind of a jam he got into.

Since I've been grown up I've boarded in private homes myself, and how different I've found it—the wife keeping up a determinedly brave front and a watchful eye on the amount of hot water used, the husband, crushed and humiliated, sulking in a corner, the children indifferent and resentful. And that awful feeling I've had of being an outsider, of being an unwanted but necessary nuisance. Keeping boarders is a business, and, as in any business, one can't be down in the mouth about it.

Of course it must be remembered that, lucrative as

the boarders were, much as we depended on them for our cash income, they were a side line. Father, after all, had his business—or businesses—and lots of money was passing through his hands, although very little stuck to them.

If Father had really lost everything, I wonder if we might not have been pathetic, too. I don't know. I can't visualize Father helping around the house, making a bed, shelling peas. Just why making beds or shelling peas is humiliating, I don't see, but I appreciate the fact that most masculinity is unequal to it.

If I could give any rule to would-be keepers of boarders, I'd say, "If you have a husband around the house, have him cheerful. If he can't put on a cheerful front, let him pretend to have a job and go sit in the park or the public library each day. *Don't* have him puttering about the house looking forlorn."

Although Father never helped with any domestic chores, he did hold up his end as a host. From the first greeting, "So these are our new boarders," to the time he drove them to the train, Father seemed glad to have them there. Lady boarders he flirted with discreetly—once or twice not so discreetly—men boarders he introduced at the club, took to council meetings with him, invited on his trips around the territory and into Mexico.

Father was a wonderful storyteller and had a fund of stories about old Tucson. After all, when Father was a little boy, they were still fighting Indians. As a young man, Father had worked in hell-roaring Tombstone. Father knew the Earps and the Clantons, Curly Bill and Six-toed Pete.

Father's present was as interesting as his past. Father was always in some kind of trouble, and it made a good story: the time the laundry boiler blew up and all the dirty clothes had to be sent to Phoenix; Father the receiver for a mine taken over for taxes, and the owner driving off Father and the sheriff with a shotgun; Father clerk of the court and hearing tales of opium smuggling, of Chinamen crossing the border; Father president of a cattle company in Mexico and bandits stealing our cows; Father telegraphing Secretary of State Bryan, going down to Mexico himself, coming back with bullet holes through the car.

Mother also had her stories of the old South, but Mother for the most part was carving and saying, "Pass your plate again." Unless people took a second helping, Mother felt like a prima donna being hissed.

We children were the claque both for Father's stories and for Mother's food. How we loved the stories! We were the straight man to Father's comedy, laughing in the right places, asking the right questions, waiting eagerly for the point and the roars from the boarders. The same with Mother's food. Gloatingly we watched her angel parfait coming in, waited breathlessly for the boarders to take the first bite, waited for the appreciative smack of the lips. We waited, too, for Mother's inevitable remark, "I'm afraid it isn't quite so good as I usually make it."

We had an untidy house. Mother was, and is, a terrible housekeeper. None of us put anything away until absolutely necessary, and then it was thrust hurriedly into a window seat or a closet or on top of a shelf. To this day in Mother's house you open a closet door warily, or objects fall down on your head.

We never threw anything away, for Mother was a saver-upper, fearing to discard things lest she could use them later—and usually she could. But what junk we hoarded—broken picture frames, handleless cups, tennis shoes with the soles worn out, discarded schoolbooks, old magazines, old and broken furniture. There was half a dictionary—one of those big ones—that for years I tried to throw out. What became of the other half, how Mother let that escape, I don't know, but she clung to this half. Each of us children had sat on it at the table, and Mother had a sentimental feeling for it.

We had the most harum-scarum equipment—napkins made out of old tablecloths Mother had retrieved from the laundry, dime-store silver, cracked plates. We had gorgeous silver in the bank, Haviland china gathering dust in the cupboards, beautiful linens packed in trunks.

To a new boarder unfolding half a napkin or picking up a tin fork, Father's remark was always the same, "We've got nice stuff," he'd say, "but it's too good for us."

And Mother would retort, "I'm saving the silver for Rosemary"—I've been married for years now and haven't got it yet—"and you know what your laundry would do to my good napkins."

Of course this casualness of housekeeping made for easy living. Mother worked on the theory of the superiority of the animate over the inanimate. The house was to live in, furniture to use. If in the process there was damage to either, then too bad for the house and furniture. So we put our feet on the davenport, teetered on the back legs of chairs, left the dime-store silver rusting in water while we went off to the movies. Mother didn't say much more than, "Oh, children," when we took the sheets and blankets into the yard to make wigwams with them.

But there was nothing harum-scarum in the kitchen. The housework might be neglected but never the cooking. No matter how good the cook was (once we had one who had formerly worked for the King of Sweden and had come to Tucson to visit a tubercular brother), Mother was out there in the kitchen telling her how to do it, superintending, if not doing, the actual cooking.

No dish came on the table without her tasting it, giving it some touch that made it different, exciting. A tomato salad might be two slices of tomato on a leaf of lettuce to some. But to Mother it was a tomato cut in eighths and swirled into a rosette, garnished with a ball of cottage cheese, strips of bell pepper, a piece of celery heart, and for dressing, the most super-scrumptious mayonnaise, the kind that's made slowly and lovingly, the oil poured in drop by drop. A baked apple had to be baked with a spoonful of brown sugar and marmalade in its center. String beans were cut sliver thin, cooked in chicken soup or liquor from the ham. Corn was buttered, salted, the grains slit, before it ever came on the table. And Mother's stuffed baked potatoes —my mouth waters at the thought. The outer skins scrubbed to whiteness; the potato scooped out after baking and the *insides* of the skins buttered, salted, peppered; then the potato, enriched with cream, butter, seasonings, stuffed into the skins again. More butter on the top, salt and pepper. Into the oven once more and out again, a last garnish of two sprigs of parsley and a dash of paprika. Oh, heavenly baked potato, to be devoured to the last bit, the buttered, crackly skins the best of all.

Mother was, and is, an utterly divine cook. It isn't that I'm her daughter. It isn't just a nostalgic backward look at my childhood. But, just as there are artists who paint, sing, sculpt, so there are also artists who cook. There are Carusos, Pavlovas, and Michelangelos. There is also Mother over the cookstove. And like any artist she needed a public. She had it in the boarders. The curtain went up three times a day, and she took her applause in the chorus of appreciation and also in the visible poundage that went on the eaters.

Father certainly was an example of what good cooking could do. One hundred and forty pounds when she married him, Father went up and up and up to 220. Father used to complain though that steaks were not so good as when they were first married. Whenever he said this, a queer little smile would go over Mother's face. Of course when Mother had just Father, she always gave him the filet. Now the children got it, or a boarder.

Mother cooked by instinct, and it was very hard to get a recipe from her, for her system was to take a little of this and a little of that. I used to feel sorry for our servants when they tried to follow her directions. She knew so exactly what she wanted but was no good at communicating it. Nor could she leave a task to anyone. She hovered about and made people nervous. It usually ended with the maids doing the housework and Mother doing the cooking.

She'd say, "Now tonight we'll have some good old Virginia spoon bread."

"What's the recipe?" the cook would ask.

"Oh, you don't need a recipe for spoon bread. Just take some corn meal. . . ."

Pressed for more definite measurements Mother would say, "Oh, quite a lot of corn meal."

Pressed still further, she'd give out, "Well, that blue bowl almost full." And then to us children, "Heavens, if you have to tell them everything, you might as well do it yourself."

"Moisten the lady fingers with some milk," she'd give directions for making one of our favorite desserts. But how could she give an exact amount for the milk? If the lady fingers were dry you used more milk; if soft, less milk. You *knew* when they were moist enough.

The same with the time element. You cooked one steak 7 minutes, another 10. A pudding, a meat loaf, a cake stayed in the oven until it was ready to come out. Good Lord, you couldn't give an exact time; you cooked things until they were done.

With nothing was Mother more accurate in this uncanny time sense of hers than when soft-boiling an egg. Mother put the egg into a pan of boiling water, took the pan off the fire, and after a little while—never looking at the clock—took out the egg. It was always perfect. Not too runny, not too hard, just right.

"But it's so easy," Mother would say. "A small egg you take out a little sooner, or one with a thin shell. And you feel it; if it's especially cold, you leave it in longer."

Mother's menus were varied and had a quality of unexpectedness. One reason was her system of giving foods a "rest" as she called it. If we had a roast one day, we didn't have cold meat the next. Instead the roast, wrapped up in waxed paper, "rested" in the icebox, and fried oysters or spareribs or creamed eggs on toast would appear. Two or three days later we'd have the cold meat. And if there were any bits of that left it was given another "rest" before coming on in croquettes or stuffed bell peppers. You always got Mother's leftovers, but you never knew when, or in what form they'd appear.

She had a great variety of recipes. As someone said to her, "I've been here a month and never had the same dessert twice."

"That's only thirty desserts," said Mother. "I certainly know that many desserts."

As a matter of fact, the same dessert had been served more than once. Like a woman with one costume, changing her accessories, Mother knew how to disguise her dishes with different sauces and fixings.

There was a frozen custard she made, simple and inexpensive. She varied it by serving it one time with maple sirup and chopped nuts, and the next time she might have crushed strawberries or raspberries over it. Or she might use crushed peppermint candy sticks, or a chocolate sauce, or a butterscotch sauce, or sliced fresh figs. It was the same custard but not the same trimmings.

Mother never threw anything away. Vegetable water —never very much because Mother cooked in as little water as possible—was poured into a jar and kept in the icebox until it was ready to be used in soup. Ham liquor was saved to boil vegetables in. Little dabs of peas, cauliflower, string beans, or carrots were used in salads. Bits of applesauce, jelly, and honey went into bread puddings.

All leftover pieces of bread and toast were made into crumbs. A cup of bread crumbs would be used to replace that much flour in waffle or pancake batter. Toast crumbs went into the melted butter which was poured over cauliflower. Cauliflower isn't cauliflower to me without that peculiarly nutty flavor which those buttered toast crumbs give it. And of course Mother used bread crumbs in meat stuffings. Her stuffed shoulder of lamb was so good, and the lamb went a lot further when you ate dressing with it.

A little hot-cake batter could be used later for fritters. A couple of ears of corn could have the grains scraped off and be combined with onions and bell peppers to make a succotash. Leftover squash or asparagus could go into soufflés. If there was also a little lamb left it could be creamed and put in the middle of the soufflé ring. A smidgen of chicken could have a can of tuna mixed with it and still be creamed chicken on toast.

Leftover mashed potatoes became potato cakes or potato soup or were whipped into turnips, making them fluffier and taking away the watery consistency which turnips so often have.

Another way Mother saved was to have on the table a lot of "befores," as she called them, dishes of celery, raw carrot strips, onions, radishes, and the like. When we sat down Mother started passing these around with the result that both family and boarders had the edge of their appetites dulled by inexpensive raw vegetables before the main dishes came on. Whether this was deliberate on Mother's part or just happenstance, I don't know, but there always seemed to be a lot of leftovers for other meals.

Mother did the carving. Father's explanation for this was that as a child he'd never had anything to eat but beans—which wasn't quite true—and that he didn't know the first thing about carving.

"You could learn," Mother told him. "I didn't do any carving as a child either."

"But you at least could watch something being carved. You had those wonderful Virginia hams, those marvelous Virginia chickens, while I"—and Father would put a tremolo into his voice—"while all I had to watch was my mother dishing up those Arizona frijoles."

I never could tell whether Father was really serious or just making fun of Mother. Anyway, she did the carving. She was so short she had to stand up to do it. The procedure was always the same. She would pick up the carving knife, run her thumb down its edge, say, "Mm, mm, I could ride on this," leave the table and go into the back hall where a big brick chimney ran up to the roof. Immediately would come the sound of a knife being honed vigorously against bricks. We had a carving steel, but Mother preferred the chimney.

To Mother food was the remedy for any crisis—local or national. If friends were ill, Mother found out what they could eat and sent it over. At a death, Mother didn't send flowers to the bereaved, but a baked ham, a frozen salad, cakes, and cookies. "There'll be lots of people coming and going," she would say, "and she won't feel like cooking." During the First World War from one to six soldiers were always turning up for meals. During the depression she had a stew kettle going all day long.

Unfortunately, as Tucson became more and more of a health resort, Mother began to get people who had arthritis or sinus, were on diets of one kind or another, and had to have stale bread and stewed prunes and things like that.

"How can I charge what I do," Mother would ask, "and give you raw carrots?"

So to salve her conscience she'd provide the raw carrots, but also the rich, forbidden dishes she would have cooked ordinarily. "Just a little won't hurt you," she'd say temptingly.

I remember Mr. Clampitt who finally asked if he couldn't have his Spartan fare served in his own room on a tray. "I just can't stand it," he said, "seeing those good things and not eating them."

"You know," I heard Mother tell Father, "I feel guilty charging him what I do, and giving him just those few vegetables."

"Why don't you cut it down then, don't charge him so much?"

"But if he weren't here, I'd have someone who could eat my food."

And she tried to make it up by feeding Mrs. Clampitt double, urging food upon the poor woman until she gained so much she couldn't get into her clothes. I remember this distinctly, because when she left she gave Mother half a dozen dresses bought at Saks.

"Fine racket," sniffed Father. "Feed her so she can't wear her clothes; then get the clothes for yourself."

CHAPTER 7

God's Day and the Boarders

WE WEREN'T a very religious family. Mother went to church every once in a while, occasionally with Father, although he'd usually beg off with, "You pray for me, honey, that'll be enough." Starting in November we children went faithfully to Sunday school—we wanted to be in on the Christmas tree. For the most part we got boarders of like fervor.

The churchiest people we ever had were the Woolleys. He was a retired banker from Kansas and had been a deacon or something, and she had done a lot of missionary work. At the time we had the Woolleys we had Dr. and Mrs. Merrill. Dr. Merrill was a Ph.D. doctor and so was Mrs. Merrill, and they both worked on plant nutrition at the Desert Laboratory. Dr. Merrill was always saying he didn't believe in God. We also had little Mr. Plummer who taught Latin at the high school, and I don't know what he thought about God, for Mr. Plummer was a nice little nobody who seldom opened his mouth about anything.

Until the Woolleys came, Sunday was just Sunday to us; but the Woolleys tried to turn it into "God's Day" and wanted us to stay home and read the Bible and sing hymns and not go to baseball games and movies or on picnics or even for drives into the country. The Woolleys said when you profaned God's Day you got punished for it. According to them God had nearly smothered Oliver in that cupboard the Sunday we drove out to inspect that house; and, the next Sunday when we went on a picnic, nearly drowned Mr. Plummer in the river; and, the Sunday after that, while we were at a baseball game, sent the skunk to hide under our house.

But Mother had different ideas about Sunday. As a little girl in Virginia Mother had been brought up very strictly and knew all about God's Day—the gloom descending as the sun went down Saturday night; the little pickaninnies vanishing into their quarters; no games, no laughing, no loud talk, just prayers and church, and prayers again; a solemn hush over everything. If a child forgot and let forth a shout or picked up a toy, there was the quick admonition, "Children, remember: This is God's Day." And this had to be endured until sundown Sunday night when, as the sun sank beneath the hills, one could once more play and sing and shout and rejoice, because at last God's Day was over.

Mother decided that her own family was not going to have this kind of a Sunday. And we didn't. I can remember Sunday as quite the nicest day in the week. One could wake up lazily with the knowledge that there was no school to go to. Of course there was no school on Saturday either, but Father went to work on Saturday. On Sunday he could stay in bed, too.

Pajama-clad, one of us children would scamper out to get the morning paper. Somehow or other all three of us would manage to get into bed with Father. (Mother was already up seeing about the breakfast.) Father would burrow deeper into the pillows, protesting that we ought to let a fellow sleep on Sunday. But we'd pound at him and wrestle with him until finally he'd yawn, rub his eyes, and sit up and read us about Little Nemo and the Katzenjammers and Foxy Grampa.

Breakfast was any time anyone wanted to come for it, although if the boarders were too late Mother would send it in to them on a tray. On Sunday morning Father took his weekly hot bath—on other days he had cold ones—and would come to the table all pink and glowing and saying, "Well, boys and girls, I'm the cleanest man in this house."

If we children didn't go to Sunday school—and Mother was not very firm about our going—we usually went downtown with Father to get the mail from the post-office box and then over to his real-estate office with him. Once in the office we made a beeline for the back where the bags of Arbuckle's coffee were stored (Father was still their agent). In each bag was a stick of peppermint candy, which we filched. We had taken out so many peppermint sticks that it was quite a hunt to find a bag with the stick still in it.

Of course the most exciting place to be on Sunday morning was our own kitchen. Sunday dinner was an enormous meal with us, and what a bustle and to-do there was about its preparation—the old kitchen range going full tilt and Mother saying to whoever was about, "There's lots of hot water; it's a good time to have a bath." There was usually a cake dish to be licked or bits of nuts to be eaten up, and one could watch chickens being stuffed. Almost always we had chicken on Sundays. When we didn't have chicken we had turkey. (Mother didn't have turkeys just at Thanksgiving,

Christmas, and New Year's, but every few weeks or so She said a turkey was economical for a large family because one could get so many meals from it.)

The boarders—the ones who weren't going to church—would drift in and be given tasks of one kind or another—cracking walnuts, peeling grapes for the salad, slicing string beans. Mother, who was faster than any three people, usually got through what she was doing and snatched the task away with, "Oh, you're breaking those nuts to bits," or "I said *slivers,* not big hunks." No one ever sliced string beans thin enough to suit Mother. She used a very sharp little pocketknife and achieved a bias cut about one-sixty-fourth of an inch thin. I've never seen it equaled. Usually, too, she had saved a bit of chicken broth or ham liquor to cook them in and also put with them a slice or two of onion and a strip of bacon—to "whet them up," as she called it.

Our maid was seldom in the kitchen Sunday morning, for Mother took upon herself the Sunday dinner. The maid busied herself with making beds, straightening up the house, and setting the table.

As Mother worked she would say, "Now I must keep an eye on that clock, for I want to go to church." But often she wouldn't look soon enough and then it was, "There, now, I've missed church!" When she did go, there was awful chaos as she changed into her "best" clothes with many half-dressed sorties to the kitchen to turn or baste or stir something that was cooking. In the meantime we children scurried about the house looking for her gloves or her prayer book and finding some money for her to put in the collection. Mother always had change stowed in odd places about the house. At last she'd be off with many final directions to the cook about dinner and the warning to Father—if he was there —that the next time he'd certainly have to come with her.

Of course the Woolleys never failed to go to church and would come back and tell us about the sermon and make remarks concerning people who didn't have even one hour a week to give to God. It was the Woolleys who started our saying grace at meals.

"I don't see why I have to let my soup get cold while the old codger mumbles away," complained Dr. Merrill.

"Your soup doesn't cool off too much," soothed Mother, "and those few words of blessing will do you good."

As I said, our Sunday dinners were enormous, and we ate enough to make us groggy. But we never took naps. Sunday afternoons were far too nice to spend in sleeping.

When it was "our" Sunday we had to go out and see the town. That's how Father always put it. "Well, boys and girls, it's our Sunday. Let's go out and see the town." That might mean going to the movies or a baseball game or just driving around.

When it wasn't "our" Sunday, it was the Pryce's Sunday, for the firm of Lee, Drachman and Pryce, of which Father was the Drachman, was the proud possessor of an automobile, a Reo, a magnificent piece of mechanism which was cranked at the side and whose tonneau—entrance at the rear—could hold a lot of children and boarders provided the boarders took the children on their laps. The car was used for business purposes during the week, and we and the Pryces took turns having it for pleasure on Sundays and holidays.

Mr. Lee, a widower without children, had passed up his Sunday after an unfortunate experience at the very beginning when his mind became a total blank as to how to stop the damn thing.

Mr. Lee had learned to start the car all right, and he thought he knew how to stop it. On his first solo he went around the block several times while Father and Mr. Pryce stood on the sidewalk and applauded him. About the fifth time around Mr. Lee shouted something to them.

"What did he say?" Father asked Mr. Price.

"Couldn't hear him with all that noise. Something about stopping."

"Yes," agreed Father, "it's time he stopped. He's got an appointment."

So on Mr. Lee's sixth time around Father called to him, "Better stop now. Bates will be here."

"I can't stop," yelled Mr. Lee and was gone in a cloud of dust.

So Mr. Pryce and Father started running to meet him coming the other way.

"Push in your clutch," yelled Father.

"Shift your gear," bellowed Mr. Pryce.

"Where is the clutch?" wailed Mr. Lee, and was gone again.

They say it was a wonderful sight in the town—Father and Mr. Pryce panting after Mr. Lee, roaring directions to him, and Mr. Lee in spite of himself outdistancing them and having to wait until he came around again to get some more advice.

Finally Father managed to jump on the car and get it stopped.

When the limp and shaken Mr. Lee was helped out he swore he'd never touch the blank, blank contraption again. The firm might be "Lee, Drachman and Pryce," but as for that blank, blank car, that was strictly and entirely "Drachman and Pryce."

So "our" Sunday came every other week. We always took as many boarders with us as the car would hold. Sometimes they'd say, "But aren't we intruding? Wouldn't you like to be alone sometime?"

"Alone?" asked Father. "What fun would that be?"

And he was right. We liked an audience, we liked to show people things. We missed it when boarders weren't smacking their lips over Mother's food or listening spellbound to Father's stories, or when we couldn't take them on a Cook's tour of Tucson.

Naturally we invited the Woolleys to go with us on our Sunday excursions. They always refused with many dark hints of God's punishment to fall on those who profaned His day.

"How will God punish us, Mrs. Woolley?" asked Phillip one Sunday. Phillip always wanted specific details.

"That I cannot say," stated Mrs. Woolley, "but punish he will."

"I don't want God to do anything to me," Phillip appealed to Mother as we struck off into the country.

"He's not going to do anything to you."

"Maybe we ought to stay home on God's Day."

"Every day is God's Day," Mother told him, "not just Sunday."

"You will get those hell-bent-for-heaven people in your house!" said Dr. Merrill.

This afternoon we drove out quite a way to look at some property Father thought he might buy.

"As if you didn't have enough land already," Mother protested.

"But the town's coming this way," argued Father.

That was his favorite slogan. And there was scarcely any way the town wasn't coming. New houses were going up everywhere. We liked going through them, walking precariously on unfinished floorings, taking in the room plan, criticizing this, admiring that. We children liked the long "shavings" that we tucked under our hats for curls. Mother was always picking up a molding board to use in edging her garden beds.

"Put that down," ordered Father; "it doesn't belong to you."

But Mother said probably boards were taken from our house when it was being built, and she was just evening things up.

We were investigating a practically completed house on the edge of town when suddenly we missed four-year-old Oliver.

"He's fallen down the cellar," Mother cried.

But he wasn't in the cellar or in the attic or in any of the rooms. So then he must have wandered off into the mesquite. Mother put Phillip and me into the car, made us promise not to leave it, then she and Father and the Merrills started off in four different directions. We could hear their voices getting fainter and fainter as they called, "Oliver! Oliver!"

It seemed hours before they came back. It was probably about half an hour. They hadn't found him, and Mother was crying.

"Get in," Father ordered. "We've got to find Ed Peters and get a posse out here before it's dark."

Mother started to get in the car. Then suddenly she stopped as if she were seeing something.

"He's in the house," she cried in a loud voice and ran straight toward it.

We all ran after her. Mother went straight to the kitchen, straight to a cupboard under the sink, and opened the door. There lay Oliver, purple-faced and half-smothered.

"I was playing hide-and-seek," he managed to say when he could talk, "but nobody came to find me."

Alone for a minute in the kitchen he had crawled into the cupboard under the sink and pulled in the door. The outside latch had snapped, and of course he couldn't open it from the inside. He heard us calling him, but in hide-and-seek you don't give away your hiding place but wait to be found. By the time he began to make noises and bang on the door, we were outside and couldn't hear him.

What made Mother know Oliver was in that cupboard? Was it mental telepathy—a panic-stricken child getting his message through to his mother? Was it some queer psychic power on Mother's part? I don't know. "But I *saw* him," said Mother, "I *saw* him in that cupboard."

The Woolleys said God had meant to punish us for profaning the Sabbath but had been merciful and relented.

"Will He get me next time?" asked Phillip.

"One cannot say," answered Mrs. Woolley. "He strikes where and whom He will."

Mother sent Phillip off to bed, and I heard her say to Father in the kitchen, "I'm not going to have her frightening the children like this."

The next Sunday we nearly lost Mr. Plummer. We had made no plans for the day—whether this was in deference to the Woolleys I don't know—but suddenly the cook said she was sick and was going home, and the Pryces telephoned that their children had the chicken pox and did we want the car.

"We'll have a picnic," Mother proposed, "and eat our dinner out in the country."

"Not on God's Day," said the Woolleys.

"Surely God won't care whether you eat indoors or outdoors."

Put in Dr. Merrill, "I should think He would prefer the fresh air."

Still the Woolleys would have none of it. So we left food for them at home, and off we went to the foothills where we selected a picnic place on the bank of a dry river bed.

In the middle of the sandy stream was a big tree, making a nice shady place.

"Why don't we go there?" asked Mr. Plummer.

"Not this time of year," warned Father. "There's been lots of rain up in the mountains; we might get drowned."

"Drowned?" queried Mr. Plummer, looking at the dry sand.

"You don't know about Arizona 'flash' floods, do you?"

"Yes, I've heard of them, but surely we could see and hear it coming and get out of the way."

"Maybe," Father nodded, "but they come down fast and furious. I've seen one catch a flock of wild turkeys. Do you think you're faster than a turkey?"

So we ate on the high ground and afterward spread out blankets, and the grownups snoozed while we children and Colonel went chasing through the brush scaring up quail and rabbits.

Suddenly Father sat up. "Hear that? It's coming!" He began gathering up our possessions. "I don't think it'll come this high, but just in case." He started counting noses, "Rosemary! Phillip! Oliver! Plummer," he yelled, "where's Plummer?"

"There he is, Father," said Phillip, pointing.

Under that tree in the middle of the stream bed lay Mr. Plummer, sound asleep. And coming down toward him was a wall of curling brown water.

"Plummer!" roared Father, running toward him.

Mr. Plummer was a little man, and Father picked him up bodily and ran back to us. He beat the water by seconds.

The flood roared by, and Mr. Plummer, sitting on the bank where Father had dumped him, stared popeyed at the angry, rushing water. "Does . . . does it come like that?" he squeaked.

"Yes," snapped Father, "it comes like that. You damn fool, sleeping under that tree! It's a wonder you weren't drowned!"

Of course the Woolleys were terribly pleased.

Gloated Mrs. Woolley, "Twice the sword of God has almost struck. Will you risk its wrath a third time?"

I really think none of us wanted to go out next Sunday, but there were the Pryce children still sick with chicken pox, the car available, and a good baseball game on.

"I don't want to go, Mother," said Phillip.

"Of course you do; you love baseball."

"But God is mad at us."

Warned Dr. Merrill, "You're going to have a neurotic child on your hands if you don't put a stop to this."

We went to the baseball game, and it was a very good game and nothing happened to us.

"See," said Mother to Phillip, "God wants us to enjoy ourselves."

But when we got home, there on the porch sat the Woolleys, church literature on their laps, looking as pleased as punch.

Mr. Woolley beamed, "While you were away at a baseball game, a strange animal has been running in and out under the house."

"What kind of an animal?" asked Father.

"It's black," said Mr. Woolley, "with a bushy tail."

"With a streak of white down the back," added Mrs. Woolley.

"A skunk!" said Dr. Merrill.

"A skunk!" echoed Father. "Is he under the house now?"

"Yes," nodded Mr. Woolley.

"Get the dog," yelled Father. "Get him inside quick and lock him up. If Colonel ever gets after that skunk, God help us!"

From Mrs. Woolley, "I wouldn't take the name of the Lord like that."

"I mean," cried Father, "if that skunk lets go . . . if he ever squirts . . . I mean, we'd have to move out!"

I caught Colonel and dragged him into the house.

"Let's all go inside," Father ordered. "We don't want the skunk to hear us talking."

"Why do we care if the skunk hears us?" asked Mr. Plummer.

"Because," explained Father, "if he hears us he'll get frightened, and if he's frightened, he'll *squirt*. Come on in, and don't walk too heavily."

So we tiptoed into the parlor and sat down. It was really quite exciting—like being besieged.

"Now," said Father, "let's do a little planning. We've got to kill that skunk. . . ."

"And kill him quick," put in Dr. Merrill.

"Quick is the word," agreed Father, "before he knows what's happening to him. Now if someone crawls under the house with a gun . . ."

A wicked gleam came into Dr. Merrill's eyes. "But you're too big for that, and I'm too big. It'll have to be Mr. Woolley, or maybe Mr. Plummer."

Snapped Mr. Woolley, "I can't shoot."

Quavered Mr. Plummer, "I can't, either."

Dr. Merrill clucked his tongue. "Most unfortunate."

"No one is going to crawl under that house after the skunk," Mother put in quickly, giving Dr. Merrill a look. "The skunk has got to come out."

"And come out happy," Dr. Merrill added.

"But how?" asked Father.

"We might sing to him," suggested Dr. Merrill. "Music hath charms. A hymn, perhaps, seeing it's Sunday."

"Now you two stop," ordered Mother. "It's perfectly easy to get the skunk out. We'll put food in the yard; he'll come and eat it."

"Of course," said Father. "Then we shoot him. How good are you with a gun, Doc?"

"I can shoot, but I'm no Deadeye Dick."

"Neither am I," mourned Father, "and we've got to get him with the very first shot."

"You see," commented Mrs. Woolley, "what happens when you profane the Sabbath."

"You were here reading your Bible, but still the skunk came. Why was that?" demanded Dr. Merrill.

"We were very quiet. If the children had been here playing and the dog, I'm certain the skunk would have passed us by."

"Yes, and no," pontificated Dr. Merrill. "He might have still come, and the dog might have chased him, and there would have been . . . squirts. Or the dog might have been bitten, and if he's a hydrophobia skunk—some of them are, you know—the dog would have got hydrophobia, and maybe bitten the children, and the rest of us, too. . . ."

"Dr. Merrill!" scolded Mother.

"Yes," said Father, "let's stop this might-have-been stuff. What we've got to decide is when the skunk comes out to eat, who tries to shoot him, Doc or I."

"If I had my bow and arrow," Mrs. Merrill said, "I'd get him."

"She could, too," boasted her husband. "She was archery champion at Vassar."

But of course Mrs. Merrill didn't have her bow and arrow, so it was still up to Father or Dr. Merrill.

"I don't think anyone should *try* to shoot the skunk," Mother advised. "I think we ought to get someone who can really shoot."

"I think you're right," agreed Father. "Well, I could get Old Man Hawkins. He used to shoot Indians and would probably be glad to pick up a dollar or two."

"I've heard of him," nodded Dr. Merrill. "He always shot them in the left eye, didn't he?"

"That's the kind of a shooter we need," said Mother.

"All right, I'll go get him," said Father. "The rest of you stay inside and don't make too much noise."

"What food shall I put out?" Mother asked. "I've got some pieces of fried chicken and those lamb chops I was going to have for tomorrow."

Dr. Merrill's mouth started to pucker up in the queerest way. "Woolley," he said, "help us out. Imagine yourself a skunk. What would you like to eat, fried chicken or lamb chops?"

"I'm sure I don't know," Mr. Woolley answered coldly.

"Well, Plummer, if you were a skunk, what would you like?"

Interrupted Mother, "He'll probably like the lamb chops because they're raw. I'll give him those."

Father came back with Old Man Hawkins, who was a very dirty old man with a long white mustache and quite, as Mother would say, "odoriferous."

"Where shall I put this meat?" Mother asked.

Dr. Merrill grinned. "Depends where you want the squirt in case Mr. Hawkins misses."

"I don't miss," growled Old Man Hawkins through

his long mustache. "If you put it in the back, I can hide behind that there lilac bush and I'll be down wind."

Phillip clapped his hands. "Then we can watch from the back porch."

"No," said Old Man Hawkins, "all you stay inside. The fewer humans he smells the better. Smelling me'll be enough."

"Quite enough, I should think," murmured Dr. Merrill.

So we all sat inside and listened. It seemed like an awfully long time before we heard the bang of the gun.

Father got to his feet. "Wonder if he got him."

"Stick your nose out," advised Dr. Merrill, "and see."

Father opened the front door a crack and took a deep breath. "He got him!"

We all rushed forth to view our late enemy, now stretched out on the ground before his last meal. He was awfully pretty with his jet-black fur and silver streak.

"Aren't the skins valuable?" asked Mother.

"You're not going to peddle any skunk skin," cried Father. "Into the garbage can he goes!"

"No, give him to me," said Old Man Hawkins. "I'll skin him and keep him as a trophy."

Father found a gunny sack, and Old Man Hawkins departed with the skunk over his shoulder.

We went back into the house, and Mrs. Woolley began talking about the sword of God and how it had almost struck again.

"Mrs. Woolley," Mother interrupted sharply, "I want to have a private talk with you and your husband. Shall we go into your room?"

So Mr. and Mrs. Woolley and Mother went into the living room, and after a while Mother came out.

"There are times," she announced, "when you have to put your foot down. Of all the silly things, trying to make out that God sent that skunk!"

Whatever Mother said to the Woolleys, it did the work. For the rest of the time they were with us, they observed Sunday in their fashion and we in ours. And no more remarks were made about God's sword.

CHAPTER 8

Mother's Accounts

ALTHOUGH Mother did her figuring on scraps of paper and the backs of envelopes, and her receipted bills were always crumpled into little wads from being carried so long in her purse, she really had her financial situation pretty well in hand. All the scraps and bills eventually came to rest in the drawer in the kitchen table, and there Mother studied them at her leisure.

On her bills marked "Paid" she'd make notes of the household situation at the time. On grocery bills would be penciled such memos as:

"Four boarders. Parties."

"Six boarders. Two cooks."

"Two and a half boarders. Stirling."

A half boarder was someone who was there only half the month. Stirling was Mother's brother, who paid us a 3 months' visit. The same with other bills. On the gas and electric light bill would be "Three boarders. Mrs. Yates ironed a lot." The second item accounted for the bill's size. Or the next month the explanation might be "Mr. Bloom's insomnia." When Mr. Bloom couldn't sleep at night he got up and played solitaire and turned on the electric heater to keep warm.

When the cash-and-carry markets came in Mother saved each day's slips and added them up at the end of the month. Of course on these slips a lot was listed that wasn't food, such as floor wax, soap, matches, etc., but Mother said you needed these things to run a house, and she lumped them with the food under the title "Food and."

When Mother studied over her bills and slips she knew how many people had been in the house in any given month and how much "Food and," electricity, gas, furnace oil had been used. Therefore she had a pretty good idea of the expenses for one person and could charge accordingly.

Also on certain bills for the upkeep of the house would be revealing notes. For instance, "Mr. Meade's hair" on the bill for recovering a chair. Mr. Meade dyed his hair, and the dye had come off on a certain chair he liked to sit in.

"Mr. Meade really ought to pay for it," I heard Mother tell Father, "but it would break the old fool's heart if he knew I knew he dyed his hair. So after he goes I'll get the chair recovered."

Mother paid everything she could by check and when the canceled checks came back from the bank she pinned them on their stubs in her checkbook. It made a very good record of what she had spent and furnished receipts. And she could tell in this way just which check was uncashed, for a stub without a check meant the check was still out. She liked people to cash her checks immediately and was very cross when they didn't.

Yet she was a great one for holding up checks herself. She somehow felt that it was a saving, that once the money got in the bank it was drawn on—which it was—and most important, Father would know about it.

"You know," said Father, noticing several checks tucked away in her bureau drawer, "it's a pretty dangerous thing you're doing holding up those checks."

"They're perfectly good."

"Suppose someone drops dead. Then you can't cash the check until the estate is settled. Or if someone goes broke. You don't like checks out, so cash these."

Mother said she would, and sometimes she did, but more often she held onto them until she actually needed the money.

Mother didn't like cash around the house and was always hiding it somewhere and then when she did need it, it was an awful panic to find it. She kept it in such odd places—in her powder box, in her bedroom slipper, in the icebox, in an empty pancake-flour box in the pantry. Once when there was $80 in this pancake-flour box—boarder money paid in cash instead of by check—the cook threw the box into the garbage can thinking it empty. Father had to go down to the city dump to retrieve it.

"Why don't you keep your money in your purse like other people," he snorted.

What cash Mother had usually came from her sales of figs, flowers, milk, and eggs. She had envelopes marked, "Cow," "Figs," "Chickens," "Flowers," and would keep the money earned by these in their appropriate envelopes. These envelopes she hid in various places, too, and would forget where, and we children were always having to hunt for them.

When the cow needed some feed she took the money from the "Cow" envelope. She liked to think that the cow bought its own hay, the figs and flowers their fertilizers, the chickens paid the vet who cured them of their ailments. Occasionally the cow would be broke, in which case she might borrow from the figs and Mother would put into the "Fig" envelope an I.O.U. from the cow reading, "I.O.U. $3.40. Cow." Mother loved to study these envelopes, shuffling them back and forth, writing little notes and putting them inside.

"Honestly," said Father, watching her, "I never saw such a silly way of keeping accounts. The money is all yours. Why do you do it that way?"

"Because," Mother told him, "I like to do it that way."

Mother did not put her "boarder" money into her and Father's joint current account at the bank, but into her own current account which Father was not supposed to draw on. Mother's reason for this separation of their money was a good one. At the beginning of each month, when she got the boarders' checks, she'd have from $200 to $500 to deposit, depending upon the number of people she had in the house. She knew if such a lump sum were in their joint account it would be too much of a temptation for Father. He would surely take it for one of his schemes or as a down payment on some land. So she paid the bills from the joint account as long as that held up and then drew on her own. Whatever was left Father usually got for one thing or another—taxes, interest, insurance, or for an investment that even Mother knew was too good to pass up.

Another advantage to Mother's keeping the boarder money in a separate account was that from time to time she could sneak a little out of it into her savings account without Father's knowing it. But then Father would get himself into the kind of a financial jam where he just *had* to have some money, and out would come Mother's nest egg.

"I hate taking it," Father would apologize, "but it's only to protect what I'm building up for you and the children. After I'm gone you'll have all my property and insurance."

"After you're gone," Mother scoffed. "You know you're going to outlive me. I'm just saving up for your second wife."

And then they would start wrangling happily about whether or not Father would marry again and how long he'd wait. Mother gave him 6 months. "And she'll probably be a little fly-up-the-creek," Mother said. "You've had one sensible wife; so you'll want a change next time."

When Father asked Mother for money he called it "shaking the money tree."

"Well, Mums," he'd say, "how about shaking the money tree for me?"

And Mother would reply, "That money tree has been picked pretty bare lately."

Once when Mother refused to shake the money tree, Father just went and shook it himself.

Commander Hill was with us then and helped Father with the tree shaking. Commander Hill was a retired naval officer and he and Father were great buddies. Father called him the Admiral and since Father had once been a second lieutenant in the Arizona National Guard, Commander Hill called Father the General.

For a long time Father had been doing a lot of figuring on the backs of used envelopes that he kept in his pocket for this purpose, and he'd been putting out hints in Mother's direction that he sure knew where he could use a little piece of money. But Mother was turning a deaf ear.

So Father went on figuring and got to the stage where he was continually drawing little pictures.

"What's that, Father?" I asked, when I saw one.

Answered Father, "Why, that's the Arroyo, and that's the railroad track, and that's the Stone Avenue Bridge."

It didn't seem very interesting to me, but the Admiral said, "The General's planning a campaign."

The Arroyo was a great ditch—a sort of dry creek—probably 30 feet deep and 50 feet wide, which ran through the city of Tucson from east to west and for part of its course along the north side of the railroad track. It was dry most of the time, but when there was rain in the Rincons to the east it could be a roaring flood.

Father was interested in the Arroyo where it crossed Stone Avenue (the Stone Avenue subway is there now). I remember one Sunday he stopped the car on the bridge, and he and the Admiral got out and looked raptly at that big cut in the earth.

"Why do you two want to look at that hole in the ground?" Mother asked.

"It's a hole in the ground now but some day it's going to be a very valuable piece of property," explained Father. "Some day the city is going to put a big culvert in that Arroyo and fill in around it, and then there'll be a whole block right on the railroad track."

"But who wants to be on the railroad track?" demanded Mother.

"Plenty of businesses," said Father.

"There's lots of room on the other side of the track."

"There won't always be. The man who owns this will take $500 for it."

"I should think he would," scoffed Mother. "I should think he'd take 50 cents."

"The General's got a good idea there," praised the Admiral.

"Don't encourage him," begged Mother; "he'll be buying it next."

"It's an awfully good investment for the future," prophesied Father, "and dirt cheap." He looked at Mother.

Mother shook her head vigorously. "Don't look at me. I'm not buying any ditch."

But she was. For when it came time for the Admiral to pay his board he didn't give it to her. Mother waited about a week and then spoke to Father about it.

"Now don't go dunning him," ordered Father. "He'll pay it when he gets around to it."

So Mother waited another week, throwing out hints from time to time as to how it took money to run a house.

"Quit that," Father told her. "The man's good for his board. Can't you wait a little bit?"

"Of course I can wait, but I think he ought to say something to me about it. He shouldn't just ignore his obligation."

"He's probably hard up just now and embarrassed to talk to you about it. Now don't you mention it to him."

But when it was almost time for the Admiral to pay

another month's board Mother could keep silent no longer, and asked him for the money.

The Admiral looked uncomfortable. "Well, you see . . . I thought I wasn't to pay any board."

"Not pay any board!" gasped Mother.

"Didn't the General tell you?"

"Tell me what?"

"I mean . . . I paid my board money to the General."

"Paid my husband!" cried Mother.

"Yes, I paid him for five months—gave him $500."

"But, why . . . ?"

"He needed the money to buy that property."

"What property?"

"You know, that ditch, that Arroyo."

"You mean he took my money to buy that ditch!"

"Yes," nodded the Admiral. "And he said if he didn't pay me back, I could just not pay you board. I thought you knew."

Naturally Mother was furious.

"The very ideah," she accused Father, "taking mah money before Ah even get it!"

"But I didn't intend to take it," Father apologized miserably. "I had to have $500 right away or my option expired."

"So you had an option on it all the time!"

"I asked Hill if he could let me have the money for just a few days. I had a deal on so I thought I could pay him right back. And he said if I didn't, he'd not have enough to pay his board and . . . well . . . I said in that case he could just skip the board. And my deal fell through and I couldn't pay him.

"Anyway," propitiated Father, "I put the lot in both our names."

"So I own half that ditch. Isn't that fine! And I've got to feed that man free for 5 months!"

"But you're not feeding him free. He paid me the money."

"That's not paying it to me. I'm just going to tell him he'll have to find himself another place."

"Now," cried Father, "you're not going to put the Admiral out!"

"I suppose I can't, but I certainly feel like it. And I'm furious with both of you. It was a very poor trick to play on a woman."

"But I'm going to pay the money back to you."

"I've heard you say that before."

"All right," said Father, nettled, "if you want your $500 back I can get it for you today. In fact, I've already had an offer of $750 for our ditch."

"Now don't tell me fairy stories. Why should anyone want to pay $750 for it?"

"Because," gloated Father, "this morning the council voted to put in a culvert and fill in the Arroyo—that's why."

"Oh," gasped Mother, "and you knew it all the while."

"Knew it! I've been working on it for months, getting it all sewed up. Well, do you want to sell it for $750, or do you want to hang onto it?"

Mother cogitated. "Let's hang on to it," she said.

And hang on to it they did. And each year as the assessments were levied for that culvert, Mother would get furious at Father all over again and wish they didn't have the old lot. But later on when the assessments were paid up and they got increasingly larger offers for it, she'd think, my, wasn't I smart to buy that lot. They never sold it, and eventually Father built the new laundry plant on it. With the development of the town, the paving of Stone Avenue and the building of the subway, Father's ditch has become a very valuable piece of property.

But thereafter when Mother took in a new boarder she stipulated, "And you pay your board money to me and to no one else."

CHAPTER 9

Salvaging Miss Sally

MOTHER hadn't yet had the problem of someone who couldn't pay any board at all. She was going to get that with Mrs. Lynch. But Mother solved that one, too. She made Mrs. Lynch be our cook.

Mrs. Lynch—only she liked to be called Miss Sally because it was friendlier and made her feel younger—had the living room and the private bath. For in the summer after the Admiral left Mother put a bathroom off the living room. She had a little money in a savings account, and she thought she'd better get it off the money tree and into some plumbing before Father found out about it and bought another ditch.

Father said two bathrooms in one house were ridiculous, and if Mother had any money why didn't she lend it to him and he'd buy some stock in a new hotel that was going up.

Suggested Father, "Why not pay for a bathroom in this new hotel?"

But Mother said thank you, she'd put the bathroom on her own house, and that just once in a while she'd like to pick the fruit from the money tree herself.

So the new bathroom was built on to the west, just off the little hall between the living room and the next room. It could be used for those two rooms, or it could be a private bath just for the living room.

Dr. and Mrs. Merrill were going to take the room. They had been gone from Tucson for a couple of years but were coming back and of course wanted to stay with us. When Mother wrote them about the new bathroom they said they would like to have the living room.

But in the fall when they arrived Dr. Merrill said $50 extra a month was quite a bit to pay, and maybe they ought to save their money and take the second room and wash with the family just the way they had before—that is, if Mother didn't mind.

"Heavens, no," said Mother. "I think you're sensible. Using the bathroom with us is a very easy way to make $50 a month."

So Mother put an advertisement in the paper, and the very next afternoon a taxi brought Mrs. Lynch to the door. She was a large woman, wearing a huge beflowered hat and a light blue silk suit with a ruffly peekaboo waist. She had pale gold hair and a skin like peaches and cream.

After she'd spoken about three words, Mother said, "What part of the South are you from?"

"Richmond," replied Mrs. Lynch.

"I knew it," cried Mother, and then they had a regular love feast.

"Are you here for your health?" Mother wanted to know.

"It's just nerves. My doctor thinks the sun would do me good. At my age, you know . . ."

"Surely, it's not time for that in your case."

"I'm forty-seven."

"You don't look it. I'd say thirty-five at the most."

"Aren't you sweet! Well, I do my best. I feel women should try to keep their looks. Now may I see the room?"

Mother showed it to her, and Mrs. Lynch loved it. "Such a large room! And that private bath!"

"There's just yourself?" asked Mother.

"Yes, I've been a widow for 17 years."

Mother explained, "I planned on having two people in this room and getting two hundred for it. I couldn't let it go for less than a hundred and seventy-five."

Mrs. Lynch thought that was "right much," but she'd take it just the same. She said she'd go back to the hotel and arrange to have her baggage sent up.

The taxi soon brought her back accompanied by six bags and a hatbox. One of the bags was small and bright blue. Behind the taxi was a dray with three big trunks.

"It's a lot, isn't it?" Mrs. Lynch apologized. "But it takes just so much for me to get along."

"Can I watch you unpack?" I asked, for I was bursting to know what was in all those trunks, especially in the little blue bag.

"Now you're not to bother Mrs. Lynch," ordered Mother.

"Let her stay. I won't mind. And I wish you'd call me Miss Sally, the way they do back home."

So I stayed and watched her unpack.

"Open the little blue one first," I begged.

"Oh, that!" She snapped it open, revealing an amazing assortment of little bottles and jars and tubes. "I had that made up especially so I could keep all my things together. Here are my cold creams. Here are my manicure things. Here's the soap for my hair and the scalp tonic. In this box I keep soft linen cloths to take off my creams. Here are my powders."

Miss Sally had anticipated the later-day beauty kit.

It was fun watching her unpack. She had everything wrapped up in tissue paper or in little boxes. One trunk drawer was full of satin-covered hangers with little silk bags suspended from them.

"What are in the little bags?" I asked.

"Sachet, dear. Smell."

I smelled one, and it was lavender.

She put another one before my nose. "This is rose. And this is sweet pea. And here's carnation. I like variety in scents, don't you?"

"Oh, yes," I agreed, because it was fun to be consulted as if I were a grownup.

Miss Sally carried the hangers to the closet. "But where shall I put my shoes?" she asked.

"On the floor," I suggested.

"Not *my* shoes on the floor." She looked around the room. "What's in there?" she asked, pointing to the bookcases on either side of the fireplace. The bookcases had colored glass doors so you couldn't see through them.

"Why, books," I told her.

"Could you take them out?" asked Miss Sally, "and let me put my shoes in there?"

"Oh, yes," I said, and I went to ask Mother where to put the books.

"Shoes in the bookcase?" puzzled Mother.

"Because they're too nice to go on the floor."

"Oh, are they? I'd like to see them." And she came back with me to Miss Sally's room.

The shoes were now out of the trunk and unwrapped from their tissue paper. Lots of them were bedroom slippers—beautiful little things in blue and pink and green, with feathers on them or gold braid or little rosebuds.

"Looks like a shoe store," exclaimed Mother.

"Yes, doesn't it?" smiled Miss Sally. "Shoes are a weakness of mine. I find it rests my feet to change them often, and at night . . . well, don't you think it's nice to have your slippers match your nightgown?"

"Oh, yes, indeed," said Mother emphatically, which made me wonder, for Mother had only one pair of bedroom slippers and they were of dark brown felt.

"I always feel," Miss Sally went on, "that women should be just as beautiful going to bed as in the daytime."

"By all means," agreed Mother, and I saw her give Miss Sally a look.

But Miss Sally didn't see it for she was looking at the other bookcase.

"I'll put my sheets in the other case if I may."

"Sheets?"

"I always bring my own. And I like them changed every day. Of course I pay for the laundering."

Gasped Mother, "Clean sheets every day!"

"It is pampering myself, isn't it? But it's just one of the things I have to have. I suppose I can get a laundress for them."

"We own a laundry; you can send them there."

"But," said Miss Sally gently, "I don't like my things washed with other people's. I hope you don't mind."

"No, of course not. We'll get you a laundress."

"Another thing," began Miss Sally, and hesitated.

"Go on," urged Mother.

"It's just that I'm very sensitive to objects around me. And so"—waving her hand at the biggest trunk—"I always bring many of my own possessions with me. So you won't mind, will you, if I ask you to take certain things out of the room. It isn't that they aren't perfectly nice things, but I'd rather have my own."

"What things do you want me to take out?"

"Well, I have my own down comforter, and my own blankets, and pillows with special feathers, and lampshades—don't you think we women need softer lights after a certain age?"

"Oh, decidedly."

"And I have my own towels, of course, and bath mats . . ."

"Whatever you don't like," interrupted Mother, "put outside the door and we'll take it away." Then to me, "Come on and let Mrs. Lynch unpack in peace."

Reluctantly I followed Mother into the kitchen where she banged a few pots and pans around and said to Lizzie, "Lizzie, you're going to have a lot of extra work." And Mother shook her head. "I don't know about this." When she told Father about her, Father said, "Well, I hope we'll be clean enough for her."

"And," continued Mother, "she has about a dozen pair of bedroom slippers, all different colors, so they'll match her nightgowns. She thinks women should be just as beautiful going to bed as in the daytime."

"Well, shouldn't they?" asked Father, a gleam in his eye.

"She's forty-seven years old," snapped Mother.

"I didn't ask her age," said Father meekly.

"And she's so sensitive she has to have her own towels and blankets, and pillows with special feathers . . ."

"Is she going to use any of our furniture? Has she brought her own dishes?"

And just then in came Miss Sally looking perfectly beautiful in a pale pink dressing gown, carrying a little bed tray laden with dishes.

She put it down on the kitchen table and after Mother had introduced her to Father she said, "Aren't I a lazy one, having breakfast in bed? And I like it on my own dishes. You see, in the morning my energies are at such a low ebb. . . . Don't you find it so?" she beamed at Father. "It cheers me up to eat from my own dear little set."

It was a pretty set, too, of palest green, with little pink rosebuds for the handle of the cup and the cream pitcher and the knob for the top of the sugar bowl.

"I just have coffee and toast and fruit," said Miss Sally. "That won't be too much trouble, will it?"

"No," replied Mother shortly.

"Thank you. I know I'm going to be happy here." And she smiled and left us.

"Whew!" whistled Father.

"I told you she's forty-seven years old."

"I still say 'Whew!' " He grinned at Mother. "Well, honey, you picked her. I didn't."

"I thought I liked her. Maybe I still do. And think of getting $175 for one person in that room. But I don't know how it's going to work out. I don't think Lizzie's going to like changing the sheets every day and waiting on her hand and foot, and"—getting to her real worry—"for whom is all this beautifying, I'd like to know?"

But Mother needn't have worried. Miss Sally preferred to change her own sheets. "I'm like the princess who felt the pea under thirty mattresses," she told Mother. "No one makes a bed to suit me. It's the same with my room. Except for the weekly cleaning, I'd like to take care of it myself."

And as for the person Miss Sally was making herself beautiful for—that was none other than Miss Sally. She had not the slightest interest in Father or Dr. Merrill because they were men. In fact I think she preferred a compliment from Mother or Mrs. Merrill or even me, because we were women and should be more concerned with the problems of Miss Sally's skin, nails, hair, chin.

But once you gave Miss Sally a compliment you had to keep on with it.

Father would say, "Well, now, you're looking very nice today, Miss Sally."

And Miss Sally would reply, "Do you think so? I looked in the glass this morning and said to myself, 'Sally, you're a perfect hag.' "

And then Father would say, "Now, now, you couldn't be a hag."

From Miss Sally: "But look around my eyes; I'm getting crow's-feet—dreadful ones."

Father: "You haven't any crow's-feet, not a one."

Miss Sally: "And my neck, you can't say it isn't crepey."

Father: "Of course it isn't."

Miss Sally: "It's this water. It's terrible. I cream and cream, but just look at my elbows! Like nutmeg graters."

And so on until even Father's gallantry wearied.

Miss Sally's day was devoted entirely to Miss Sally and went like this: I took her tray in to her. She'd be sitting up in bed, mirror in hand, studying the ravages of the night. She'd usually consult with me. "I'm afraid I'm sleeping too much on my right side. Isn't my face getting lopsided?"

I'd put the tray down and study her. "No, Miss Sally, it isn't."

And she'd smile with relief and say it must be her imagination.

Then there was the morning she thought she was getting a mustache.

"Look," she cried, pointing to her upper lip.

"I don't see anything, Miss Sally."

"Hairs . . . hundreds of them."

I leaned close. There was a down on her lip, and two or three golden hairs.

"A mustache!" cried Miss Sally in the voice of doom.

"But, Miss Sally, you can't see a thing unless you're an inch away."

"But *I* know they're there. It must be that new cream I'm using. Go ask Dr. Merrill if that could be it."

Dr. and Mrs. Merrill were having their breakfast, and when I asked him he gave a guffaw and said it wasn't the cream making the mustache; it was something else.

"What?" I demanded.

"Age," Dr. Merrill announced. "Age makes us hairy,

Tell Miss Sally she'll soon have a couple of handle bars, but if they get in her coffee she can use a mustache cup."

"Allan!" scolded Mrs. Merrill.

After breakfast Miss Sally took a little nap—she said it helped her digest her breakfast—and then got up and washed the underwear she'd worn the day before. (She said it was too nice for anyone else to handle.) She hung this in the bathroom, and while it was drying she made her bed and straightened her room. Then it was time to do her ironing, which she did with infinite care. After this exertion she must have her morning bath and then cream and powder her face and dress for lunch. After lunch she undressed completely—the only way she could relax, she said—and had her afternoon nap.

She awoke from her sleep about four o'clock, took another bath, and began to dress for dinner. I usually came in about this time because I liked to watch Miss Sally brushing her hair and working on her nails and patting her chin. Then she often gave me little samples of cold cream and powder that she was always sending away for. Once in a while Phillip and Oliver came in, too, but they didn't care much for the samples, and Miss Sally never had anything else for them.

At dinner Miss Sally seemed to enjoy her food, and she said she didn't mind getting fat because when you got thin the wrinkles came. When she wasn't eating, her hands were busy in her lap, pushing back her cuticle.

Of course you can't take a bath too soon after a meal, so Miss Sally sat around with us for a while after dinner. She didn't say much, but smiled sweetly, and pushed at her cuticle and looked at her hands and at her elbows. If she did say anything it was usually about how dry her skin was getting.

When an hour had passed Miss Sally would excuse herself and go to her room where the evening ritual began. There was a long soaking tub, and then Miss Sally patted her chin and brushed her hair again and last of all cold-creamed herself all over from head to toe. No wonder she had to have her sheets changed every day.

The amount of time Miss Sally took up bathing and creaming herself was really fantastic.

"And who's it for?" demanded Father. "It's not even for us. She doesn't stay around long enough for us to admire her."

"It's for herself, Father," I told him. "She says a woman must keep beautiful for herself."

"At least it's a never-failing audience," laughed Dr. Merrill and said that personally he preferred Miss Sally who worshiped Miss Sally to the Woolleys with their hell-fire and damnation.

"I must say," said Mother, "that I've never had anyone who was so little trouble."

All Miss Sally ever asked for was a bowl of ice at night to rub on herself, or a lemon for the same purpose. And Sunday mornings when she washed her hair she had us beat up the white of an egg—it was supposed to make her hair glossy. And once she asked for a feather, a little soft feather.

"A feather?" asked Mother curiously.

Miss Sally said it was something she'd read that she wanted to try, but she wouldn't tell us any more. I went out to the chicken yard and found her a tiny, downy feather.

That evening Miss Sally went to her room right after dinner, and pretty soon we heard the strangest noises—a sort of scuffling and running, and then soft giggles and queer panting sounds.

"Is she chasing a mouse?" asked Dr. Merrill.

"Miss Sally," Mother called, "is anything the matter?"

"Nothing," she called back, "I'm just working on my chin." And there was more running and scuffling, and then the sound of a chair falling over.

"Go see what she's doing," Mother told me.

I opened the door, and there was Miss Sally in a lovely blue nightgown running around the room blowing at a feather. When she saw me she stopped and, reaching up, picked the feather out of the air.

"It's the new chin exercise I read about. You blow at the feather and keep it from falling. Want to help me?"

So we both ran around the room blowing at the feather, laughing and panting, bumping into each other and into the furniture.

"It's a splendid exercise," beamed Miss Sally, when at last we stopped. "And not boring like patting."

"Rosemary!" Mother called, and I realized this was the third or fourth time.

"Did you both go mad?" Mother demanded when I came out.

"We were blowing that feather," I explained. "It keeps us from getting a double chin."

"My God!" snorted Father.

"Isn't it fine you have a little playmate?" laughed Dr. Merrill.

Then Miss Sally appeared at the door. She'd put on her blue robe and she was still a little flushed, and her golden hair was tumbled.

She smiled at us and said, "Did you think I'd lost my mind?"

"Lost your *mind?*" Dr. Merrill repeated. "No, we didn't."

"But it *is* a good exercise. See how it makes you s-t-r-e-t-c-h!" And she blew two or three times at an imaginary feather. "We must all do it sometimes."

"Oh, we must," said Dr. Merrill.

"Well, I must get my ice now."

She came back with a great big bowl of it and said to Mother, "I'm taking so much I ought to pay you for it."

"It doesn't amount to anything," Mother assured her.

"It's doing my skin worlds of good. You see, after your hot bath your pores are all open, so you rub your creams into them—giving them a meal really—then you rub the ice on, and that makes the pores close tight on their nourishment. It's quite scientific, isn't it?" She looked over to Dr. Merrill for confirmation.

Dr. Merrill nodded gravely. "Oh, quite."

Miss Sally smiled lovingly at the bowl of ice. "It's making my skin like velvet, just like velvet all over. Well, I must get to it. Good night."

Dr. Merrill looked over at Father. "I wonder," he mused dreamily, "I wonder how we'd like it, if we had women like velvet, just like velvet all over."

"I'd like it fine," grinned Father.

Mrs. Merrill suddenly stood up. "How much cold cream have you?" she demanded of Mother.

"Oh, lots, a whole jar."

"So have I. Shall we rub it all over ourselves tonight?"

"Oh, yes," said Mother, catching on, "from top to . . . toe."

"We must use a lot. We can't get velvety with just a little."

"We'll use the whole jar. We'll be good and greasy."

"And you've lots of ice?"

"Plenty."

"Because we want our pores to close tight on their nourishment."

"Yes, indeed, so when we go to bed we'll not only be greasy all over, we'll be icy cold."

Dr. Merrill reached for Mrs. Merrill and pulled her down on his knee. "I'll be good," he grinned up at her. Then he started to laugh and sent Father another of those special looks. "But I'm sure Miss Sally would never suit either of us. Never in the world."

"Why wouldn't she?" demanded Mrs. Merrill.

"Because," said Dr. Merrill, "I'm positive that at most inopportune moments—and I repeat—at *most* inopportune moments, Miss Sally would be worrying about elbows getting rough!"

"Allan!" cried Mrs. Merrill, while Mother burst out with a shocked "Dr. Merrill!"

"You ought to be ashamed of yourself," Mother told him, and then to me, "Why aren't you in bed with the other children? Go along this minute."

I heard Dr. Merrill and Father snickering as I went out.

Miss Sally had not always led this pampered life. According to her for ten years she'd been a household drudge. She had been married very young, at seventeen, to a boy but two years older. They had practically nothing for a long time.

Said Miss Sally, "I know about cooking and dishwashing and scrubbing and all the rest of it." She held up her lovely hands. "These hands have done plenty of hard work."

But then her husband had come into money, and they had moved to a hotel.

"He told me," said Miss Sally, "that I'd done my share of work, that I didn't have to lift my hand again, that I was just to be an ornament for the rest of my life.

"But he only lived three years after things got easy for us." Miss Sally blinked her eyes very fast. "When I take care of myself and try to keep young and pretty, I feel I'm being faithful to his memory." A tear slid down her cheek, and she got up and went into her room.

We were all silent and embarrassed for a moment and then Father said, "She must be pretty well fixed. I wonder . . ."

And Mother, without waiting for him to finish, cried at him, "Now don't you dare try to get Miss Sally to put any money into your crazy schemes."

"But I just said . . ."

"And you heard what she said. She's an ornament. She's going to be an ornament for the rest of her life.

You need money for that. You can't go gambling with it."

"My God, I've got the most suspicious wife. I merely wonder if the woman is well fixed, and you think I want to rob her!"

"I don't think you want to rob her, but it'll be the same thing for her if she loses her money."

And privately Mother warned her not to invest in any scheme of Father's.

"All I have in the world is $28," laughed Miss Sally. "I just get my check each month, and I spend every cent. Why should I save when there's always another one coming?"

The next month her check came right on the dot. Miss Sally paid Mother and went downtown to buy some underwear.

When she got home there was a letter from a Richmond lawyer. Miss Sally read it and let out a shriek.

The letter informed Miss Sally that the insurance company in which her husband had invested his inheritance had suspended payments. The check Miss Sally had just received was in all probability the last.

"But it can't be true!" cried Miss Sally. "Someone's playing a horrible joke on me."

Father made investigations. He sent wires. He talked to the lawyer long distance. It was true. The company was bankrupt.

Miss Sally lay on her bed and wept. "I can't believe it. I won't believe it."

"You've got to believe it," Mother insisted, "because you've got to do something about it." But Miss Sally only buried her head in her pillow and wept the more.

"Hasn't she any money at all?" asked Father.

"I'm giving her back her rent, and she can return that underwear she hasn't worn. She'll have about $300. That'll get her home and give her something to start on."

"Whatever will she do?"

"I can't imagine. But she'd better go where she has friends and relatives to help her."

But Miss Sally said it was no use to go to Richmond, that her relatives couldn't or wouldn't help her, that she hadn't any friends.

"But how can a person not have any friends?" demanded Father.

"How many people do you meet in a bathtub?" asked Dr. Merrill.

"And she won't take back her rent money," Mother went on. "She says her board's paid until the end of the month and she's going to stay here."

"And then what?"

"I don't know. And neither does she."

"Could she take a business course?" suggested Father. "Do office work?"

"Would you want her in your office?" asked Mother.

"No, I wouldn't."

Mrs. Merrill had an idea. "She irons nicely."

"That's right," said Father hopefully. "I'll ask Russ Logan. . . ." He stopped. "You couldn't put her in a laundry."

Mother shook her head. "She'd never stand that work. No, the only thing I see for her is to be a cook. She's at least done that."

Asked Dr. Merrill, "Is that insurance company absolutely finished?"

"Absolutely," groaned Father. "She won't get a nickel."

But you couldn't make Miss Sally believe it. She kept writing to the lawyer and to the company asking if there wasn't some mistake. Each morning when I brought in her tray she snatched at the mail. There was never anything but samples. "But it will come tomorrow," she'd say to me, "I know it will. And I won't worry; it makes wrinkles."

"She can't go on like this," said Mother. "She'll have to face it. We aren't helping her when we let her act this way."

She went into Miss Sally's room. "You've got to go to work," she told her.

"What can I do?" wailed Miss Sally. "I've never done anything."

"You ran a house for ten years."

"What do you mean?"

"I mean you could be a cook."

"Work in somebody's kitchen!"

"Work anywhere to earn a living."

"My hands in dirty dishwater!"

"If you scrape your dishes carefully, the water won't be dirty."

"It's not the end of the month yet," Miss Sally cried. "I don't have to decide until the end of the month."

"I'm trying to get you into something while you still have some money. And why haven't you taken that underwear back?"

Miss Sally got out of bed. "While I still have some

money I'm going to stay here and live just the way I always have, and when I haven't any more money . . ." She stopped. "Please excuse me. I'm going to take my bath."

"Well?" said Father, when Mother came out.

"She won't lift a hand to help herself."

"We can't put her out on the street."

"No, we can't. But we can't keep her here for the rest of her life either. And I'm frightened."

"She wouldn't be that foolish."

"I don't know."

Lizzie came in to clear the table. "My mother is going to have a baby," she announced.

"For heaven's sake," cried Mother, "this is the thirteenth!"

"Fourteenth," corrected Lizzie. "I have to go home to help her."

"Now, Lizzie," moaned Mother, "of all times . . ." Then she stopped as if something had struck her. "All right, Lizzie, you can go, and go right away.

"This is going to kill or cure," she promised Father.

"Now what?"

"You'll see!"

And Mother went into Miss Sally's room and right into the bathroom where Miss Sally was sitting weeping. She'd left both doors open so we could hear her talking clear out to the dining room.

Said Mother, "My cook is leaving, and you're going to help me out. I'll pay you what I pay Lizzie. You stop that crying and get out of that tub and get dressed. Right now!" It was just the way she talked to us children.

We all looked at one another.

"Great jumping grasshoppers!" gasped Father.

When I got back at noon Miss Sally, in one of Mother's aprons, was setting the table. Mother came in and said, "You haven't set a place for yourself."

"Cooks eat in the kitchen, don't they?" sniffled Miss Sally. "So I'll eat in the kitchen."

Mother didn't argue with her. "Very well. Perhaps it will make it easier with the serving."

Miss Sally waited on us, and it was dreadful. I mean it was dreadful having Miss Sally do it. Oliver kept saying, "Where's Lizzie? Why is Miss Sally doing that?"

"Miss Sally has to learn how to make a living," Mother told him, "and it's better for her to learn on us."

So Miss Sally was our cook and had a terrible time. She was all out of practice. She burned up food, she burned herself. She dropped things and spilled things. She cut her fingers on the knives. She took forever to get anything done. When Mother made suggestions she burst into tears.

The rest of us tried to act as if having Miss Sally for our cook were perfectly natural. We ate everything she made, even when it was awful, and, when we couldn't eat it, we wrapped it up and hid it in the fireplace until we could take it to the garbage.

"Why are we doing all this?" asked Dr. Merrill one day as he worked his jaws on a tough piece of meat.

"Because," said Mother, "we can't just throw Miss Sally away. I mean it's like having something in the icebox, and you can't put it on the table, but you don't throw it out. You add something to it, and work with it, and cook it over, until . . . well, until you can put it on the table."

"I know what you mean," grinned Dr. Merrill. "We're going to salvage Miss Sally. We're going to trim off the self-pity and self-admiration and stir in a little gumption and self-confidence, and maybe someday we'll have a decent person."

"Yes," nodded Mother, "that's what I mean."

Miss Sally told Mother she shouldn't keep the living room, that Mother should rent it to someone else, and that she'd take the servant's room.

"No, Miss Sally," said Mother, "you keep your room. You've paid me plenty for it, and you're entitled to it now. Besides I wouldn't be renting it this late in the season anyway." And privately to Father, "Imagine any new people putting up with her."

But after a while things got easier for Miss Sally. She didn't cringe every time she picked up bits of food from the sink. And she could sweep and mop and scrub without getting utterly exhausted. She even did things she didn't need to, like polishing andirons that we never polished and wiping behind picture frames, and things like that.

Mother kept looking in the advertisements and asking at the employment agencies to find just the right job for Miss Sally. "She's not a bad cook," said Mother, "and when she cheers up she'll be pleasant to have around."

Miss Sally took but one bath a day now—at night—and cold-creamed herself only then. But except that her face was swollen from crying, her skin was just as nice as ever. Of course her hands weren't quite so nice. And she was always looking at them and bursting into tears.

One day Mother brought her home a pair of rubber gloves. "These will save your hands," Mother told her. "I don't know why I didn't think of it sooner."

"I can put cold cream in them," exclaimed Miss Sally, "and give my hands a treatment while I work." She smiled for the first time. "I've got some wonderful hand cream."

And after that Miss Sally seemed much happier and would look at her hands and say, "That cream is marvellous. You'd never know I was doing housework, would you?"

But still it was an arrangement that couldn't go on forever. After all you couldn't let the cook have the best room in the house. And it was still pretty awkward. Besides, Lizzie was ready to come back.

It was Father who solved the situation. He came home one day beaming all over. "I've got it! I've got it!"

"What have you got?" asked Mother.

"The perfect job for Miss Sally."

And it was. An old codger had come into Father's real-estate office to rent a house, and he also wanted a housekeeper. Some pleasant, middle-aged woman to run things and read to him—since the old codger had poor eyesight—and to do the shopping and boss the cook.

"There's to be a cook, too?" asked Mother.

"Yes," gloated Father, "the housekeeper is to hire a cook. Miss Sally won't have to do any kitchen work."

Said Mother, "It hurts you having Miss Sally work in a kitchen, doesn't it?"

"Yes," admitted Father, "it does."

"Well, it hurts me, too," laughed Mother, "and I'm glad she won't have to do it."

So Miss Sally became Mr. Bentley's housekeeper. Lizzie came back, and we all breathed a sigh of relief.

"I wonder how she'll get along," said Father.

She seemed to be getting on all right. She telephoned us every day or so. She said she had a nice little maid, that she liked Mr. Bentley, that everything was lovely.

Then one day Father came home and said he'd run into old Bentley on the street for a minute and he was a damned, dirty skunk. "I asked him about Miss Sally and he said she was the cook now as well as the housekeeper."

"But what could have happened?" wondered Mother.

"Suppose he thought it was too much money."

"It is a lot, sixty for Miss Sally and thirty for the cook, but that was the arrangement and I think it's a mean trick to play on her."

We all felt blue that Miss Sally was a cook again.

"He's a skunk," repeated Father, "and I'd like to tell him so."

That evening we were all out for a ride, and we drove by the old codger's house. There on the porch were Miss Sally and Mr. Bentley, and she was reading to him.

She saw us and called, "Come on in for a while."

So we stopped and went on up to the porch and sat down. Miss Sally looked as happy and pretty as you please, and the old gentleman was in a white suit and all spruced up, and he looked happy and handsome, too.

We talked for a while, and then Mother said to the old man, "So you fired your cook, did you?"

"Me fire her? No, Miss Sally did."

Said Miss Sally, "It doesn't take two women to look after one man. I can do it all myself."

"I told her not to," said Mr. Bentley, "but she insisted. So what could I do? She's got me wrapped right around her little finger."

"Now, Mr. Bentley," scolded Miss Sally, "you know that's not so."

But you could see it was.

On the way home Dr. Merrill said to Mother, "Nice bit of salvage work, Mrs. D."

But Mother looked worried. She spoke to Father, "You didn't tell me if he had a wife back East."

"No," said Father, "he's a widower."

"Then that's all right," said Mother.

And it was. We all went to the wedding.

CHAPTER 10

Back-door Boarders

OUR BOARDERS were not all confined to the front of the house. We had plenty in the back—the ones who ate free.

A steady stream of tramps came to the door asking for meals.

"It's your Mother's fault," complained Father. "If she wouldn't feed them they wouldn't come."

"Don't talk to me," retorted Mother. "You're the one who's always passing out money to them. I make them work for what I give them."

And she did. Or at least she wouldn't feed them unless they offered to work. If the request was, "I'm hungry, will you give me something to eat?" there was no food forthcoming. It had to be, "I'm hungry, may I work for something to eat?" Often there wasn't any work to do but she wanted them to show a willingness to work. Mother placed great emphasis on willingness.

One winter when the traffic to our back door was particularly heavy, Father said, "I think our place is marked." We all went out to investigate, and, sure enough, on the cement coping we found a row of red chalk marks.

"Want me to read them?" asked Father. "I'm sure

they say, 'Soft-hearted woman; good cook.'" And he rubbed them off.

Protested Mother, "Those tramps make a beeline for this house before they ever see those marks. I've watched them. Two blocks away they start heading right here."

"They've heard about your cooking from the others," Father told her.

And that must have been it, for, even with the chalk marks gone, our back-door boarders still kept coming, and after a while the marks were on again.

I remember being in the yard with Mother one day, and far down the street we could see someone coming.

"That's a tramp," said Mother, "and he's coming right to me."

And without looking to the right or the left, straight to Mother he came, tipped his hat, and said, "I'm hungry, ma'am. May I do some work for one of your good meals?"

"How do you know my meals are good?" demanded Mother.

"Oh, ma'am," he grinned, "I heard about you down in Houston, Texas."

I was fascinated by tramps and planned to be a lady tramp when I grew up. Sometimes I could hardly bear it when some obviously hungry hobo would fail to ask Mother for work, and she would turn him away. Once I ran after one and told him the formula. "Ask for work," I whispered, "then you'll get a meal."

Once two broke into the house, but I gave them a meal and wasn't in the least bit frightened. I was alone in the house that afternoon and heard a noise on the

back porch. Being about eight, with more curiosity than sense, I went to investigate and on the porch saw two men with their heads in our icebox.

"Are you looking for something to eat?" I asked.

They nearly jumped out of their skins. "Yes," said one, "we're hungry."

Said the other, "Is there anything we can do for something to eat?"

Since they'd ask for work I could feed them. I said, "No one's home but me. I don't know what work there is. But I'll give you something to eat."

I hacked up the cold roast, gave them some tomatoes and a bowl of custard. I felt terribly proud of myself.

"If you wait until Mother comes home, she'll tell you if there's any work."

My guests said they didn't want to eat and run, but they thought they'd better not wait for Mother.

One of them looked longingly at the remains of the roast and said it would be nice for sandwiches.

The other muttered something about candy and kids.

Argued the first one, "Candy I can leave, but it's different with a nice piece of pork."

"I'm sure Mother would want you to do something for so much meat," I told them.

"Well, look, we'll come back tomorrow, first thing in the morning, and work all day. How's that?"

I felt that was all right and wrapped up the roast and gave it to them.

Mother was very cross about the matter when I told her. She said if I ever heard anyone breaking in the house again, I was not to go out and feed them but run out the front door and tell the neighbors.

Father said what else could Mother expect, that I'd inherited a love of hobos from her.

Sometimes a whole family would come to us for help, some poverty-stricken group on its way to the coast, whose jalopy had broken down or who had no more money for gasoline. And we would have grownups and five or six kids camping out by the woodshed, with the man doing jobs for Mother and for the neighbors until he could make enough money to move on.

"What could I do?" Mother would say to Father. "Those children were hungry."

And Father would fuss and fume about Mother's being such a sucker and then go out and slip the man a couple of dollars.

Both Father and Mother were push-overs for sob stories, but each suspected the other's charities. Yet each was always sending out an S.O.S. to the other in behalf of someone down on his luck.

"Mother," Father would call up, "there's a Mexican boy here—his father and I were kids together—have you got any work he could do around the yard?"

"The last one you sent out here left the weeds and pulled up the flowers," Mother would complain. "But send him along and I'll find something for him to do."

Or it would be Mother telephoning, "There's an old man here—well, he's not so very old—and he's walked clear from El Paso, and he says he knows laundry work. I'm going to send him down to Russ."

"Good night, Russ can't take in all the down-and-outs. The laundry isn't an old people's home."

"But this man is in desperate need."

"Give him a dollar then and get rid of him." Father could be very brutal over the telephone.

"He doesn't want charity; he wants work."

"Oh, all right. Send him down to the laundry. I'll phone Russ."

Father's hand was always in his pocket, but Mother wouldn't give out cash. Giving money to people, she felt, ruined their characters. Lending it to them was quite different—at least in her mind.

For the good of Mother's pocketbook she got too interested in those who worked for her. She always wanted to know where they were from, where they were going, about their families and troubles. And once she knew about them she couldn't help being sympathetic. Instead of an anonymous Mexican cutting our lawn, it was poor Juan with the tubercular wife in bed at home and the nine-year-old daughter who was trying to take care of the younger children, run the house, and go to school. So Mother would say, "Here's a jar of soup to take to your wife and here are some clothes for the children." And when Juan needed $4 for medicine Mother would lend it to him.

She'd write it down in the back of her cookbook—that catch-all record. "Now you owe me two days' work. You can come next week."

Sometimes Juan came and sometimes he didn't. Like the others she lent money to he meant to come back and "work it out," but it was only human for him to postpone Mother's chores to work where he could get cash rather than just a penciled note in the back of a cookbook that he now owed $2 instead of $4. Tasks around our house and garden were always waiting for laggard debtors to put in appearance.

"I should think you'd learn," Father snorted, "that when you lend them money, you kiss them good-by. Give it to them, if you must, but don't lend it. I don't see why you can't get a regular gardener like other people."

But a regular gardener wanted more than Mother was willing to pay. So she depended upon itinerant workers, the once-in-a-whilers, who weren't much good, who were always in financial difficulties and borrowing money from her, and then nine times out of ten disappearing forever.

Other back-door boarders were our former cooks, temporarily out of jobs, who would come and stay with us for a while until they landed something else. They would sleep on a cot on the back porch, eat in the kitchen, do a little work around the house in return for the food or shelter, or often not do any work at all.

"You'd think they were invited guests," Mother would sometimes complain.

The reason we had so many ex-cooks was that Mother never paid her servants enough to keep them long. And yet she had a great feeling of responsibility for them. If they were sick she took care of them as she did us children. She paid their hospital bills, lent—that is, gave —them money to get errant sons out of jail, always had a place for them while they were hunting for other jobs. Perhaps it was the old Southern tradition. You took care of your slaves, but you didn't pay them.

"I do all the cooking," Mother would protest. "Just house cleaning and dishwashing isn't worth a big wage." And it wasn't. But competent cooks, kept from cooking through no fault of their own, naturally went to other places where their cooking skill was desired and paid for.

Yet they all loved Mother and depended on us to tide them over lean periods. It was seldom that an ex-cook wasn't staying with us.

There was Della, for instance. Della was a scrawny old war horse, who was brown and wrinkled and had three unlovely moles on her chin. She was one of the best cooks we ever had—Mother would even let her prepare a meal by herself sometimes. Off and on Della worked for us for years, and, when she wasn't working for us, she was back-door boarding while she landed something else. Della might have been a permanent retainer except that Della had Ocky—full name, Oscar—who in Mother's estimation was the "no-'countest, laziest, good-for-nothingest male who ever walked on two legs."

Ocky was supposed to have a bad heart. Whether he had or not I don't know, and, anyway, Mother said that plenty of people with bad hearts earned a living. He was a chubby, smooth-faced little fellow, blond, not bad looking, always a certain spruced-up look about him, his hands clean, his hair trimly cut. Quite happily he tagged after Della and let her support him.

Each time Della came back to work for us Mother would warn, "Now I want you to understand I'm not having Ocky."

"Ocky has a job," Della would say proudly. "He's rented himself a room."

"All right. Just so he doesn't come here."

Inevitably Ocky lost his job—if he ever had one—got lonesome for Della, and at night would be sneaking into her room.

Mother always heard him. "There's that Ocky again!"

"Why do you care?" Father would ask. "What harm does he do? Why can't you put up with him?"

And for a while Mother would try not to see Ocky sliding out in the morning or Della wrapping up sandwiches and taking them out to Ocky, lounging across the street under a tree. Then Ocky would get tired of sitting on the curb and would stay in Della's room all day while she slipped his meals in to him.

"It just gets my goat," said Mother, "that woman working as hard as she does and that lazy man lying in there waiting for her to bring his food."

"Now, now," Father pacified her, "wouldn't you bring me my meals if I were in there?"

"If you were as good-for-nothing as Ocky, I'd have got rid of you long ago."

And so Mother and Della would come to the parting of the ways. Della would get another job, lose it because of Ocky, come back to us until she got the next one, and always Ocky was hovering in the background, sneaking in at night, waiting across the street for a handout.

Once Mother asked her, "Della, why *do* you hang on to such a worthless man?"

Demanded Della, "Do you think I'm beautiful?"

"Why, n-o-o, I don't."

"Of course you don't," snapped Della. "Because I'm not. I'm an ugly old bag of bones. I've only got to look in the mirror to know that. But Ocky loves me. When he's around he makes me feel like I'm the youngest, the loveliest, the most beautiful woman in the world. That's why I hang onto him."

When Mother told this to Father he gave a guffaw and said, "If Ocky makes that old battle ax feel like that, she ought to support him. He's cheap at the price."

Angelita was another one of our cooks who was always coming back to us. She was the prettiest little thing, living up to her name of "little angel," just sixteen when she first came to us, a blonde, which is rare in a Mexican, with velvety brown eyes and a clear olive skin. Ours was the first place she'd worked, and Mother taught her everything she knew. She was just like one of the family. Then she had to fall in love with Manuelo, a good-looking scamp who had a job of sorts in a poolroom.

"He's another Ocky," Mother sized him up and tried to persuade Angelita not to marry him. To no good, of course.

So Angelita got married and we got another cook. It must have been about two weeks after the wedding that late one night we heard a knocking at the back door.

"Who on earth at this hour?" exclaimed Mother.

It was Angelita run away from her husband who had got drunk and beaten her. Her face was a mass of bruises, and there were great black marks on her neck where he'd tried to choke her.

Yet next morning when he appeared Angelita forgave him and, despite Mother's protests, went off with him.

"He ees my hosband. He weel not do eet again."

But he did. And each time poor battered Angelita fled to us. Mother wanted her to get a divorce, but of course that was against her religion.

"Then don't divorce him," said Mother. "But leave him. Don't stay with him until he kills you."

"He ees my hosband," Angelita would repeat.

As time went on Nature took its course.

"Now you've got to leave him, Angelita. Suppose he beats the baby."

And the next time Manuelo went on the rampage Mother took things into her own hands and with the help of a friendly policeman she had Manuelo arrested and run out of town.

Because Angelita would have to stay home and mind

her baby Mother bought her a sewing machine and got her started as a seamstress. She really sewed quite well. With Mother's help she got customers right away, and since she was a hard-working, thrifty little soul, by the time the baby came she had the money to pay for it.

But back into town came Manuelo, sober and repentant, and Angelita took him in again. A few weeks of reconciliation—"He ees a good man now"—and Manuelo was drunk once more and abusing Angelita and the child. Once more Mother had him arrested, once more run out of town. Once more Angelita was pregnant. And this story was repeated until Angelita had six children in seven years, and the slim pretty girl changed to a middle-aged, shapeless woman.

"Someone ought to kill him. Someone ought to operate on him," raged Mother. But since both were out of the question, Mother tried to relay a little birth-control information to Angelita. "Since you will have that man around, you at least can take precautions."

But Angelita was horrified. "Eet ees a sin! Eet ees a sin!"

"It's a sin to bring children you can't take care of into the world."

"And she's only twenty-five," Mother mourned to Father. "She may have another twelve or fourteen children."

"Good God!" cried Father.

But Angelita didn't have fourteen more children. She didn't have any more children. Appendicitis and Mother intervened.

When the cousin phoned Mother they'd taken Angelita to the county hospital to be operated on, Mother thought fast and asked who the doctor was going to be. It was Dr. Rolland, our own doctor.

Mother called him up. "I can't speak over the phone, but I'm coming right down to talk to you."

So Angelita had her appendix out and some further ministrations from the doctor that she never knew about.

And after that she had no more babies.

"You and Dr. Rolland took a lot on yourselves," Father said when she told him about it.

"Someone had to do it."

Angelita never knew. She thought it was the appendicitis. "Eef you don' want babies," she'd say, "have appendicitis. Eet cures you."

Colored people seemed to gravitate to Mother, and she got along very well with them. We were "folks" to a dozen or so. There were two in particular—Alonzo Reece and Bart Buggs—who did chores for us for years.

Alonzo was an engaging, dapper little fellow who had once worked on a Pullman-car diner. Mother used to have him help in the kitchen and wait on table at some of our parties. Then he was good at house cleaning and gardening, too.

The reason he didn't have a steady job was that he liked his gin too well. When he was sobering up he'd come to Mother and talk himself into some work. He could always find something to do.

I remember once Mother said to him, "Alonzo, Bart has been here for three days. There's not a thing you can do. But if you're hungry I'll give you a meal."

"I find something to do," Alonzo promised, and he went all around the house and through the garden.

He came back to Mother. "That Bart sure one shiftless, lazy nigger. He's gonna let you-all be stung to death."

And Alonzo took Mother and showed her several big wasp nests under the eaves.

"Half a dollah to get 'em down."

"Those wasps have never bothered us."

"That don' mean they ain't gonna bother you. Half a dollah?"

"Twenty-five cents and your dinner. You need food."

"You're a hard trader, but it's a deal."

Very gently Alonzo took down the wasp nests so he wasn't stung, and Mother gave him a quarter and a meal.

Then Alonzo got sick. He said he didn't know what was the matter with him—although of course he did—that he just felt "dragged out." His gait changed. He didn't seem steady on his feet. He was forever waving his hand before his eyes. "Spots," he said.

"Why don't you go to a doctor?" Mother asked.

"I go down to Dr. Leery"—he was the city health officer—"he's fixin' me up."

"He's not fixing you up very fast," said Mother. "You're getting worse all the time. Maybe you shouldn't be working."

"Don' feel any worse workin'," and Alonzo went on with his waxing.

Mother went and called up Dr. Leery about him. I'll never forget her face when she came from that telephone.

"Alonzo," she cried, "you leave this house! Don't you ever come back."

Then she called Father and told him to come right home and to bring a bottle of—I can't remember the name—it was a disinfectant.

Mother paced up and down the room and wrung her hands, and when Father drove up she ran out to meet him. When they came in she was crying, "Dr. Leery says it's in the worst stage, the most contagious. And he's been working here for days!"

"See what you get for picking people up!"

"I didn't pick him up. We've had him for years. You got him first. He swept out your office. It was you who sent him up here. It's your fault if we get it."

"What are we going to get, Mother?" asked Phillip.

Mother tried to control herself. "Nothing. Nothing. Your Father and I are just talking."

But she told Lizzie to bring in a dishpan of water, and she poured the bottle Father had brought into it, and then she and Lizzie went over the whole house, washing everything that Alonzo had touched—woodwork, doorknobs, broom handles, mop handles, everything. And out in the yard she went over the handles of the shovel and the rake and the wheelbarrow.

Even so she worried and got the boarders worried, too—I think it was old Mr. and Mrs. Myles who were with us then—and so one morning Father came up and all of us drove down to Dr. Rolland and he stuck needles into us and took our blood—we children cried, too—and he said it was a lot of damn nonsense; people didn't catch it from wheelbarrows.

Of course the reports were all right. Mother could stop worrying.

Alonzo never came around again. We saw him on the

street occasionally, shuffling along, looking woebegone and bedraggled. Mother always looked the other way, but we children would wave to him.

Once we ran into him just as we were coming out of the movies. Mother gathered up us children and walked ahead, but Father stopped to speak to him and I saw Father reaching in his pocket.

"Why did you give him money?" Mother demanded when Father caught up with us.

"The poor devil needs it; he's sick."

"He's sick because he's sinned. When you sin you get punished."

"Sinners have to eat, too. If all who sinned like Alonzo got punished like him, God help the health of this nation."

"What I can't forgive is he worked for us while he knew he had it."

"Well, let's not talk about it."

Bart Buggs was just the opposite to Alonzo, a steady, sober, hard-working colored man with a wife and four children. He made a fair living as a janitor for several offices that he cleaned at night, and for doing occasional jobs of carpentry and painting in the daytime.

It was because of Bart that Mother tangled with the local painters' union and, I regret to say, came off second best.

Bart was an awfully good worker, but, after Mother lent him $22 to pay a doctor's bill, he didn't come around so much.

"I'm going to have to get after that Bart," Mother said, and when one of Father's stores had to be painted for a new tenant, she told Bart to do the job—about a 4-day one—and she'd mark off the debt. Father, incidentally, was down in Mexico at the time.

About an hour after Bart started to work, he stopped and came up to the house.

"A union man, he came by. He say I can't paint down there."

"I never heard of such a thing!" cried Mother. "Of course you're going to paint that store. You go right back to work."

Pretty soon up came a man from the union. I don't recall his name, so let's call him Mr. Brown. Very politely he asked Mother to fire Bart and hire a union painter.

Just as politely Mother refused, explaining that Bart owed her $22 and this was the way she was getting paid.

Mr. Brown said that was too bad, but of course the financial relations of Mother and Bart were of no concern to the union. Then he began a long story of what the union had done for the workingman through the years.

Mother said it was all very interesting, she was sure the union did a lot of good, and if the union would pay her the $22 owed by Bart she would have a union painter.

No, the union couldn't do that.

"Well, then, I'll just keep Bart." And Mother said to excuse her for she was very busy.

The union man took his leave, and Mother thought that was all there was to it.

Then up came our prospective tenant, the printer, and he was in a state. "Mrs. Drachman, if that colored fellow paints that store, the union is going to picket me!"

"That's ridiculous," said Mother. "You have nothing to do with it." And she telephoned Mr. Brown.

"You're making a mistake," she told him. "I'm the one to be picketed. Send your men up here. They can walk around my house all they want. But if they step on my verbenas I'll turn the hose on them."

Mr. Brown came to see her again. He said no, the union hadn't made any mistake. It would be the printer they'd picket, not Mother.

"But that's not *fair,*" Mother accused.

Mr. Brown said anything was fair in love and war, and that the workingman had been at war for years, fighting for his rights. And he was off on another long discussion about capital and labor and how the laboring man had been exploited.

"I'm sure you don't want to exploit your fellow man," he concluded.

Mother said no she didn't, but neither did she want her fellow man to exploit her.

"And when the union keeps me from getting my $22 I'm being exploited. Right is right," Mother wound up. "Bart is going to do that painting."

Mr. Brown again said good day.

Another visit from the printer, desperate now. "Let that colored man go, and I'll pay you that $22."

"But you don't owe the money to me."

"If I'm picketed, I'm ruined."

"Right is right," Mother stubbornly insisted.

Luckily Father came home to break this impasse. And did he blow up! "You run the house," he told

Mother, "and I'll run my business." He fired Bart and put on a union man.

"It's not *fair*. Bart owes me that money. He should be allowed to pay me."

"Get the money from Bart some other way. We're not going to buck the union. And for God's sake," cried Father, "why do you make these loans?"

Bart worked out $5 of his debt, and then he got a job in Bisbee. He promised to send Mother the other $17, and he did send her $4. Then I guess it was out of sight, out of mind, for the remittances stopped.

Mother didn't blame Bart. "Bart would have paid me," she said, "if the union hadn't stopped him." And in her cookbook she crossed out where she'd written "Bart owes me $13" and put "Union owes me $13."

CHAPTER 11

New Teeth for Jeffrey

IT WAS funny about Floyd Cook.

He started out as a back-door boarder, but he soon worked his way up to become a front-door boarder—at least, almost. And in the process he rescued Jeffrey. I'm sure if it hadn't been for Floyd, Jeffrey would still have those two terrible teeth of his, would still be tied tight to his mother's apron strings.

Jeffrey and Mrs. Lawson took their meals with us but lived in the little house in the rear. (For it was a complete little house now since Mother had turned the garage part into a kitchen. As Mother had said when she did it, Father never put his car in there anyway, not even when he owned a whole car instead of just a third of one. So what was the use of that waste space?)

In the big house we had two mining men in the living room, but they were in Mexico most of the time. However, they said it was worth Mother's price just to have a home-cooked meal when they did come in.

Mrs. Lawson liked the little house, for she and Jeffrey could each have a bedroom, and Jeffrey could write his poetry in the kitchen.

Jeffrey wrote poetry. He wrote several poems a week. And Mrs. Lawson sent them back to a St. Louis paper where they were published—Father said he'd like to

bet a wooden nickel Jeffrey's father owned stock in that paper—and then she cut them out and pasted them in a scrapbook. He had really written quite a few, and most of them were sad.

Jeffrey was twenty-three, although he looked eighteen. He was thin and stooped, and his looks were spoiled by two terrible teeth, his two front ones, which stuck out from his mouth like two diverging tusks. They caused his upper lip to curl back and made it hard for him to close his mouth.

"Why on earth didn't she have those teeth straightened when he was a child?" I once heard Father ask Mother.

"Because the braces made him cry and she couldn't stand it."

"Lord! So she lets him grow up looking like a rooting hog."

We all felt sorry for Jeffrey because Mrs. Lawson clucked over him all the time. "Jeffrey, take your nap." "Jeffrey, eat your egg." "Jeffrey, drink your milk." And endlessly we heard how delicate he was, how he could never play with other children, how he couldn't go to school but had to have private tutors, how he nearly died with croup, and whooping cough, and bronchitis, and grippe, and quinsy, and last winter double pneumonia.

"He'll never be able to work," mourned Mrs. Lawson. "But we have enough for him. Besides"—and she'd smooth his hair or pat his hand—"Jeffrey has his poetry."

You would have thought there was no escape for Jeffrey. But Floyd Cook was on his way to our back door.

He came on a Sunday afternoon while Mother and Father and Mrs. Lawson and Jeffrey were out driving in the car. I don't know why we children weren't with them. Maybe we were being punished for some reason. Anyway we were alone in the house when we heard a knocking at the back door, and all three of us went to investigate.

There stood a curly-headed, blue-eyed boy in faded levis and a white shirt. He asked for the lady of the house. He said he had a very embarrassing question to ask.

"Mother isn't home," I told him .

"What's the embarrassing question?" demanded Phillip, while Oliver put in, "If you want something to eat you must ask to work."

"I'm not hungry," the boy answered, "but there's something else. . . . You see . . . when you haven't much money you sleep where you can. I got a place last night for fifteen cents. And . . . well . . . I got lice there. . . ."

"We got lice, too," Oliver piped up.

"We have *not,*" I cried.

"We did, too, have them," he insisted.

"We *had* them, but we *haven't* them." I explained to the boy. "Last summer at the beach. From the children next door."

Oliver went on, "We had our heads shaved right to the skin. But not sister. Mother combed them out of sister."

"Mine are in my clothes," said the boy. "So I want to boil my clothes. I saw the washtub in the yard. If you could give me something to put on while I did it."

The tub was for our Mexican washerwoman. (Mother still wouldn't send certain things to Father's laundry.) It sat on some bricks, and the wood was all laid under it for Monday morning.

"No," said Phillip, "you can't use that wood because there's no more short wood." (We bought our wood in long lengths from the Indians and then hired men to cut it. For weeks Mother had been telling Father the short lengths were getting low.)

"I'll cut some more," promised Floyd. He suddenly scratched himself. "There they are again! Please! I could undress in the woodshed. If you'll just lend me something to put on."

So we went and got him Father's overalls. While he

changed in the woodshed I brought matches and Phillip filled the tub from the hose.

Floyd came out with his clothes and dumped them into the water. He looked funny in Father's overalls. They were so big he'd yanked up the straps until the pants came right under his armpits. His skin was so white and he looked sort of thin and young.

Oliver peered into the tub. "Where are the lice?"

"Getting drowned, I hope," laughed Floyd. "Now let's have the ax."

We found the ax for him, and he started chopping the long wood.

The water was just beginning to boil when I heard our car stop out front. Pretty soon Mother came out from the back porch.

"What *are* you children doing?"

"We're boiling his clothes," I nodded over at Floyd who was chopping away.

"Because they've got lice," explained Phillip.

Floyd turned and came toward us. He did look strange in those overalls with his hair tumbled over his face, and carrying the ax.

Cried Mother, "Oliver! Quick! Go get Father!"

Floyd tossed back his hair and smiled at her. "I hope you don't mind. The children said I could. I wanted to kill the lice. . . ."

"You . . . you . . . came here to get rid of your *lice!*" Mother got out at last. "You took advantage of children. . . ."

By this time Oliver was flying out the back door followed by Father, Mrs. Lawson, and Jeffrey.

Father strode over to us. "What's all this? What

under the sun? Oliver says you're killing lice and for me to hurry. Who's this boy? What's he doing with our ax? And, great jumping grasshoppers!" yelped Father, "he's got on my overalls!"

"I just borrowed them," protested the boy; "I had to wear something." He swallowed and went on with a certain dignity. "I only have two dollars. I got a bed last night for fifteen cents . . . and got lice. So I'm boiling my clothes to get rid of them."

"Lice!" cried Mrs. Lawson. "Lice in that tub! Stand back, Jeffrey, in case they jump." And she jerked him back.

Floyd appealed to Mother, "You had lice; so you know how it is."

"I never did," snapped Mother.

"Oh, yes, Mother," Oliver corrected. "Remember at the beach?"

Mother looked furious and humiliated and Mrs. Lawson, horrified. Father began to laugh.

"Sure the kids got 'em; had a time getting rid of them, too."

"From some awful children next door," Mother explained to Mrs. Lawson.

"She had the barber shave our heads," Oliver went on, "but she combed . . ."

"Stop talking about it," Mother screamed at him. Then she turned to Floyd. "Well," she said crossly, "since you've started I suppose you'd better finish."

Floyd said, "I'd like to work to pay for the wood I've burned."

Mother's face cleared immediately. "You haven't used much. Keep on chopping those long lengths if you like.

And I'll give you a basin and a fine-toothed comb. You take a bath in the woodshed and wash your hair. And then comb it. If any have got in your hair you want to get them out before they lay their eggs."

We wanted to stay with Floyd, but Mother took us inside and she said next time, for Heaven's sake, when someone came with lice we were not to wash his clothes.

Mrs. Lawson and Jeffrey came in, too, and Mrs. Lawson said she was sure something was crawling on her, and for Jeffrey to shut his mouth, and didn't he feel things crawling on him, too?

Jeffrey said no, he didn't, and hunched himself down in a chair and let his mouth fall open again.

Mrs. Lawson asked us if we'd like to hear Jeffrey's latest poem.

Of course we said we would. (As Father once said to Mother, "We're lucky he doesn't write novels.")

Jeffrey went and got his poem and Mrs. Lawson read it to us. It was called "Oh, Let Me Be Awake," and began,

Oh, let me be awake if Death does come,
The final great adventure of them all,
And not in sleep unheeding meet the call . . .

and then went on about how wonderful life was but death was wonderful, too, and how awful it would be to die in one's sleep and not know what was happening. I remember the last line was

I've loved my life, why should I miss its end?

"Isn't it powerful?" Mrs. Lawson asked. "I'll read it again." And she did with all of us listening politely, and then Mother said, "Why, that's fine, Jeffrey." And Father nodded, "Yes. Yes, indeed." And then no one spoke for a minute until Father put in, "But as far as I'm concerned, when I'm dying I'd just as soon be asleep."

"But you've missed the whole point," complained Mrs. Lawson. "This poet loves *life,* so he doesn't want to miss a moment of it, not even the final one."

"I still feel," insisted Father, "that when that old man with the pitchfork comes after me, I want to be snoring."

Suddenly Oliver looked up and began to cry. "Is a man with a pitchfork going to get my Daddy?"

"Of course not," soothed Mother. Then to Father, "You see. 'Little pitchers have big ears.' He's getting too old for you to talk like that."

"That's right," agreed Father, "pretty soon I won't have any baby." He got down on the floor on his hands and knees. "Come on, son, ride the bucking bronco." And Oliver climbed on his back, and they went galloping around the room.

Mrs. Lawson looked put out at the way Father had forgotten the poem and Mother said to Jeffrey, "It's a nice poem, Jeffrey. And I think when my time comes, I'd like to be asleep."

Mrs. Lawson got up and told Jeffrey to close his mouth and come take his nap, and Mother said she'd go see how the boy in the yard was getting along.

Phillip and I went with her, and we found that Floyd had not only cut up a lot of wood but he'd carried out a big heap of trash to the alley, and he'd found a piece of wire and was mending a hole in the fence.

His clothes were on the line and he'd poured the water out of the tub.

"I'm afraid," said Mother, "those clothes won't be dry tonight."

"Then I'll wear them damp, for I'm catching the six o'clock freight for California."

"You'll catch your death of cold," warned Mother. Then, "Why did you leave home, son?"

"Oh . . . Dad got married again. And she and I didn't get along. Dad had a little lunch counter in Topeka. I helped him with it. But after she came I was one too many. So I cleared out. I always wanted to see California."

He finished the fence and offered to fix the gate hinge if we'd give him a hammer and nails.

"Go get them," Mother told Phillip. Then suddenly to Floyd, "You seem like a handy person. I've got several days' work around here. If you want to stay and do the odd jobs you can have a cot in the woodshed and I'll give you your meals and a dollar a day."

"Suits me fine," grinned Floyd.

When Mrs. Lawson and Jeffrey came over for supper that night and Mother told them what she'd done about Floyd, Mrs. Lawson was horrified.

"Taking someone into your home that you know nothing about! Someone with lice!"

"But I'm not taking him into my home, but into my woodshed, and he hasn't lice now."

"And putting him right next to us!" wailed Mrs. Lawson. "How do we know he won't break in and cut our throats!"

During the next few days Floyd accomplished wonders in the way of wood chopping, grass cutting, tree pruning, window cleaning, floor waxing, chimney sweeping. He was amazingly quick and thorough, and all the time he worked he either sang or whistled. "Honestly," marveled Mother, "I never saw anyone enjoy working the way he does."

But Mrs. Lawson complained that Floyd kept Jeffrey from concentrating. "He starts to write," she said "and then he hears that singing and gets all out of the mood."

So Mother spoke to Floyd and after that he sang and whistled under his breath.

I remember one afternoon Floyd was up in the umbrella tree sawing off the dead branches when Jeffrey came out and watched him.

Apologized Floyd, "Guess this saw makes so much noise you can't do your writing."

"No, I don't write in the afternoon."

"What do you do then?"

"Oh, take my nap, read, or go to the library."

Floyd went on sawing and Jeffrey stood watching him, his mouth wide open and those two terrible teeth pointing straight up.

"Watch out this sawdust doesn't go down your throat," warned Floyd.

Jeffrey closed his mouth but still stood there.

"Do you like to write poetry?" Floyd asked, trying to be polite.

"No."

"Why do you do it?"

"I don't know what else to do." His mouth had dropped open again.

There didn't seem to be any more to say, so Floyd finished up the sawing, Jeffrey watching him enviously all the time. Then Floyd climbed down from the tree and started gathering up branches. We children picked up some, too. So did Jeffrey.

"You don't have to help me," smiled Floyd.

"I'd like to."

At this moment Mrs. Lawson came out of the little house and, seeing Jeffrey with the branches, cried out, "Jeffrey, what *are* you doing?"

"Carrying branches."

"Well, come in and take your nap. This minute!" she cried sharply because Jeffrey started to take his load to the alley first. So Jeffrey dropped the branches and went meekly into the house.

Floyd made a face. "Gol-lee! That's the way the woman Dad married used to yell at me. It must be worse when it's your own mother. What's the matter with him?"

"He's delicate," said Phillip.

"He's never played with other children," I explained.

"We call him rabbit," Oliver summed up.

After about a week all the odd jobs were done and Floyd said he'd be pushing on.

"I hate to see him go," Mother told Father. "He's a good boy."

"I'll speak to Russ," Father promised. "Maybe there's a job down at the laundry."

Russ said yes, they could use a presser, so Floyd went to work at $12 a week. Mother said, "Now you must get yourself a room." But Floyd asked if he couldn't still stay on in the woodshed and do chores after work and on Sunday for the rent. "I figure sleeping in that shed is an easy way to save money."

"That's the way I'd figure it," Mother approved. "Well, you don't need to do chores for the rent of that shed but if I can count on you for odd jobs you can still have your meals here."

Because Floyd went to work so early he came in and got his own breakfast, doing it very quietly and cleaning up after himself. He ate near the laundry at noon; and at night, because he got back late, the cook left his dinner in the oven.

Mrs. Lawson was appalled by Floyd's new freedom in the house, but she said she was certainly glad he was to be gone all day. "I don't know what's got into Jeffrey but he hasn't written a single poem since that boy came here, just wants to follow him around and watch him work."

But even with Floyd away Jeffrey couldn't settle back to literature. So he said for a while he wouldn't try to write, he'd just go to the library and study. And he left right after breakfast and was gone until noon, and then after lunch he left for the library again.

Mrs. Lawson said any study was mental enrichment, but she preferred Jeffrey to do creative work.

Down at the laundry one of the drivers quit and Russ gave the route to Floyd. Floyd worked so hard and got so many new customers that he was soon making over $20 a week.

"Now," insisted Mother, "it's time you got out of that woodshed and had a little comfort."

"I don't want to leave here," Floyd protested.

"Take the little back room then. I'll charge you $30

a month for it and your meals as you've been having them. And you don't need to do the chores."

We all felt very proud of Floyd's success, but Mrs. Lawson was cross because he was still around, for Jeffrey hadn't yet got back to writing and was still going to the library.

One day Father said to him, "Jeff, you're getting quite a tan on you."

Maybe that's what made Mrs. Lawson suspicious, for the next noon she came home in a dreadful state. She'd dropped in at the library and Jeffrey wasn't there. And, infinitely worse, Jeffrey hadn't been in the library for weeks. "I talked to the librarian," wailed Mrs. Lawson. "She told me she couldn't remember *when* she'd seen Jeffrey! Maybe not for a month."

She appealed to Father. "But where did Jeffrey go? Where *do* men go when they don't go where they say they're going?"

"Well," answered Father, pursing his lips, "some of them go to saloons, some of them go play poker, some of them go to . . . ah . . . women. . . ."

Mrs. Lawson wrung her hands. "Oh, why doesn't he come home?"

Just then we heard Jeffrey's step on the porch. He slouched in with his usual preoccupied air.

"Close your mouth," Mrs. Lawson ordered automatically and then, "Did you get a lot of studying done this morning, Jeffrey?"

I saw Father shaking his head violently behind her back, but of course this didn't mean anything to Jeffrey.

"Yes, Mother, I did."

"You're lying, Jeffrey, you're lying!"

Poor Jeffrey, he tried to concoct some explanation, but he was no match for his mother, who soon learned what he'd been doing.

It seemed that Jeffrey had been driving around in the laundry wagon with Floyd.

"I might have known it," cried Mrs. Lawson. "That awful boy! But why, Jeffrey? Why would you do such a thing?"

"I like the horse," muttered Jeffrey miserably.

"You like the horse!"

"Yes. Floyd lets me drive sometimes. And . . . and I like it. And we talk . . . and we sing. He's taught me a lot of songs. And I see the town . . . and I help him."

"Help him?"

"Well, if the clothes aren't ready, I count them and tie them up while he's going to the next house."

That last sent Mrs. Lawson into hysterics. Jeffrey, her son, handling dirty clothes!

"I've handled dirty clothes," put in Father.

"Dirty clothes may be all right for you," she snapped. "I mean . . . you're a big strong man, but Jeffrey is delicate. For twenty-three years I've struggled just to keep him alive, and now he exposes himself to all kinds of germs in people's soiled clothes. Aside from the moral part of it, the lying to me, the sneaking out of the library to ride in a laundry wagon . . ."

"Just hope he never does anything worse than ride in a laundry wagon," advised Father.

Mrs. Lawson shook her finger at Jeffrey. "Tomorrow morning, the very first thing, you sit down at that typewriter and you write a poem. And don't you ever go in that wagon with Floyd again. Do you hear me?"

"Yes, Mother."

"All right. Close your mouth. Lunch is on the table. Forgive this family scene," she apologized to us.

"Poor little devil," Father said to Mother after lunch. "Probably the first bit of fun he ever had and now it's all over."

But it wasn't.

The next day Jeffrey got up early, ate breakfast with Floyd in the kitchen and was off before any of us were up.

"He's gone again," Mrs. Lawson told us tragically at breakfast. "He's gone with that tramp."

"You mean," asked Father, looking pleased, "he actually had the gumption . . ." Father stopped and took a gulp of coffee. "You mean he went away with Floyd."

"He did. And he swore at me."

"Floyd swore at you!"

"Not Floyd—Jeffrey."

"*Jeffrey* swore at you!"

"When I told him he wasn't to leave the house he said he'd . . . damn well go where he damn well pleased."

"Jeffrey said that to you!" gasped Father, frowning hard.

"Now you see what that Floyd is doing to him."

"I certainly do."

"He's ruining my son. Making him into a sneak and a liar, making him give up his writing, making him swear at me. And yet you still keep him in the house."

"Now, now," soothed Father, "it could be a lot worse."

And so it could.

And so it was.

Jeffrey came home without his two front teeth. Floyd had knocked them out.

Of course it was an accident. They had stopped in front of a house; Floyd had flung down the weight to hold the horse. They had both gone inside. Coming out Floyd was ahead. He stooped to pick up the weight and heave it into the wagon. Behind him Jeffrey also stooped to pick up a dropped pencil. The weight in Floyd's upswinging arm caught poor Jeffrey right in those two front teeth. C-r-a-c-k! And there they were down in the dust.

Mrs. Lawson acted like a mad woman. She wept and wailed and raged and blamed everyone indiscriminately, Mother and Father for taking in a tramp off the street, Floyd for being so criminally careless—or was it carelessness?—and Jeffrey for disobeying her.

Floyd felt dreadful. He had the teeth in his pocket and kept bringing them out and asking, "Look, I picked them up. Don't you think maybe a dentist could stick them back on?"

But of course the dentist couldn't, and poor Jeffrey had to have what was left of his teeth dug out by the roots and was in excruciating pain for days. Mrs. Lawson carried on dreadfully about how he was suffering, how his looks were now ruined, and what an awful handicap having false teeth would be to Jeffrey's career.

"God!" cried Father, "did the poor dub need those tusks to write his poems?"

Floyd was wretched about it. "I wish I'd never let him come along with me. I wish I'd never egged him on to stand up to his old lady. But I felt so sorry for the poor little shrimp. He'd never had any fun."

"Stop blaming yourself," Mother bade him. "It was an accident. And you're paying the bill." For Floyd had arranged with the dentist to pay him so much a week. "And," comforted Mother, "it isn't as if they'd been good-looking teeth."

For a while Jeffrey went around with a gaping hole in his mouth and was thoroughly cowed and back on his mother's apron strings again. Once more he tried to write poems. But as Mrs. Lawson said, "It's hard for him to get back into the mood after having had his mind on dirty clothes."

One evening just before dinner while Jeffrey was still at the dentist's, she came in holding a piece of paper between her thumb and finger.

"I found *this* under Jeffrey's blotter."

"What is it?" asked Mother.

"I'll read it, and you'll see. It's called 'The Laundryman's Lament.' " Whereupon Father put down his paper and was all attention.

Holding the sheet at arm's length because she was so farsighted, Mrs. Lawson read,

Miss A. sleeps in a single bed
But the sheet we lost is double.
Young Mrs. B. has too well fed
With hips she's having trouble.
But 'tis we who've shrunk her dress,
Not she whose size is double . . .

"So you see where my son's mind is!"

"Go on," approved Father, "read the rest of it."

"That's all there is."

"Well, he ought to finish it. That's just the way people are. When the laundry loses a sheet it's always a double one, even though there's not a double bed in the house. And when some woman gets so fat she can't get into her clothes, then that's the laundry's fault, too—we've shrunk the dress. And ties," continued Father, warming up, "it's always a favorite tie we lose. Not once did we ever lose a tie that someone didn't like. . . ."

"I'm not interested in the laundry's failings," Mrs. Lawson interrupted coldly, "but in my son's mind and what ideas are going into it. . . ."

And then we heard Jeffrey on the porch, and in he came in that quiet way of his. Mrs. Lawson started to say, "Close your mouth," but Jeffrey's mouth was closed. He came on into the room, with his eyes wide, watching us expectantly. And then he smiled.

Jeffrey had his new teeth in.

"Why, Jeffrey!" we cried.

"I didn't know it was today you got them," said his mother.

We all crowded around him while he smiled and smiled. His new teeth were marvelous. They matched his others almost perfectly. And he could close his mouth. He was a different person, a nice-looking boy. I realized I'd never really seen his face before. I'd always been looking at those two terrible teeth.

"I want to see the teeth," clamored Oliver. So Jeffrey knelt down and smiled for Oliver. And Oliver patted the teeth with his finger. "Now, we won't call you rabbit."

And then Jeffrey stood up and looked in the mirror over the mantel, and we all looked in with him.

"Jeff, they're wonderful," praised Father.

Even Mrs. Lawson had to admit they looked fine, but she said of course it was always better to have your own teeth.

Floyd came home and Oliver ran out and brought him in. "Gol-lee," cried Floyd, and again, "Gol-lee!" He clapped Jeffrey on the shoulder. "Never saw a guy get so good looking having his teeth knocked out. I should have done it sooner."

"Indeed!" gasped Mrs. Lawson, and drew Jeffrey back.

"Well, excuse me," Floyd apologized. "I'll go make myself a quick sandwich. I've got a lot of deliveries to make before dark."

"I'll grab a sandwich, too," offered Jeffrey, "and come with you."

"Jeffrey!" ordered Mrs. Lawson, "you're not to go out this evening."

Jeffrey turned and smiled at her, and answered her quite pleasantly, "But I am, Mother."

Mrs. Lawson got purple. I thought she was going to burst. "Did you hear him? He *defied* me! He *deliberately* defied me. Well! Well, there's but one thing to do. I didn't want to go back home. It's still cold there. But a boy's soul is more important than his health. I must get him away from this evil influence."

"Now, Mrs. Lawson," appeased Father, "you're taking this all too seriously."

"Taking it too seriously, am I? When he lies to me and defies me, sneaks out of the library to go riding in a laundry wagon. And that poem, all about a woman in bed and a woman's hips. Are those the things for a young man to be thinking about?"

"Lots of young men do," said Father, and—rolling his eyes around toward Mother—"and some older men, too." Father could get the silliest look on his face sometimes.

Shaking her head at Father, Mother said quickly to Mrs. Lawson, "I don't think it's fair to Jeffrey to take him back in the cold when he's gained so much here in Arizona, and it's not fair to me. You said you'd stay until May and I've counted on it."

"You haven't been fair to me. Keeping that evil boy here when I told you what he was doing to my son. So we'll go as soon as we can get packed, possibly tomorrow."

"I'd like to hold her trunks," Mother told Father after dinner. "She promised to stay till May."

"Now, let's not have any fight. Let her go. But I feel sorry for the kid."

It must have been a half hour later that we heard Mrs. Lawson's heels clicking up the walk.

"Now what?" groaned Father.

Mrs. Lawson pulled open the door and marched in.

"You'll have to fire Jeffrey," she flung at Father.

"Fire Jeffrey?"

"Because he's working for you—down at the laundry."

"I don't know what you mean."

"Don't tell me you don't know what Jeffrey's been doing in that laundry wagon."

"I haven't any idea. Tell me."

"Working!" Mrs. Lawson hissed out. "Working for Floyd and getting two-fifths of what they make."

"Well, well," grinned Father, "Russ told me Floyd had worked up a whale of a business. So that's how he did it. I wouldn't worry about the split. It'll probably be fifty-fifty later on."

"I don't mean that," she cried impatiently. "I mean Jeffrey has his own money now. He thinks he can do as he pleases. He says he won't go home with me, that he's going to stay here and move in with Floyd. And when I told him that if he stayed he'd not have one penny of allowance, do you know what that insubordinate boy said to me?"

"Tell me."

"He took out his bankbook and said, 'Well, Mother, then I'll just have to use my own money.' "

"Er—er—hem," gurgled Father, and began to cough violently.

"So you see why you must fire him."

"How can I fire him?" Father choked through his coughs. "He's not working for me; he's working for Floyd."

"Then you'll help my son defy me?"

"Good God! Mrs. Lawson, Jeffrey is over twenty-one. He can do what he likes."

"I shall phone my husband. He'll see about this. He'll bring Jeffrey to heel." She went to the telephone in the hall and we heard her telling central to get Henry Lawson of St. Louis and to reverse the charges.

"Call me when it comes through," she told Mother,

And out she flounced, not exactly slamming the door, but almost.

Father could at last have his laugh. "Lord, it's wonderful! I wish I'd been there when he took out the bankbook. 'Well, Mother, then I'll just have to use my own money.' So that's why the little son of a gun's had all this spunk. He knew he had that money. Nothing like a little money in the sock to give you self-confidence."

"You're right," agreed Mother meaningly, "that's why I like to keep a little in my sock."

"The lamb kills the butcher," chortled Father. "Boy! Oh, boy!"

"I hope Mr. Lawson doesn't make him back down," worried Mother.

"Can you hear the phone ring in the little house?" asked Father abruptly.

"Of course not."

"Then when it rings I'll answer it. Before she gets in her lies, I'm going to give the old man an earful."

Pretty soon the telephone rang, and Father answered it and, as he'd promised, gave Mr. Lawson an earful. He must have talked for 15 minutes.

"I'm glad the charges are reversed," said Mother.

At last Father was through, and I went out to call Mrs. Lawson.

Jeffrey came with her and he was saying, "Mother, I'm going to talk to Father, too."

"After I've had my say," she said grimly, and they both went into the hall and shut the door.

We all listened as hard as we could but could make

nothing out except once in a while a wailing, "Now, Henry. . . ."

"Don't worry," grinned Father, "I got him lined up."

At last Mrs. Lawson gave the telephone to Jeffrey and came out. She was a wilted woman.

She sank into a chair and put her hands over her face. "I can't fight both of them. My son has deserted me and now my husband."

Said Mother, "No one has deserted you, Mrs. Lawson. Your son has just grown up."

She shook her head. "My son . . . a laundry driver!"

"Don't be foolish," advised Mother. "Jeffrey isn't going to *stay* a laundry driver. It's just a way of earning a little money, standing on his own feet. After all, he's twenty-three. The birds have to leave the nest sometime."

Mrs. Lawson stood up and drew a deep breath. "Unlucky the day I came to this house!" And out she walked blowing her nose.

Mother stared after her. "Poor woman!"

We heard Jeffrey saying, "Good-by, Father, and thanks," and in he came looking awfully happy.

"It's all right," he told us, "Dad was on my side."

"That's good," approved Father.

"Usually if Mother gets to him first, I'm licked before I even start, but this time it was just as if I'd got to him first. Wasn't that strange?"

"Very," nodded Father.

"Guess I'll go tell Floyd. You don't mind my moving into that little room with him after Mother goes?"

"We'll be glad to have you."

So Jeffrey went back to talk to Floyd, and Father

looked over at Mother. "We sure don't mind our own business, do we?"

"We sure don't," Mother agreed.

As Mother had predicted, Jeffrey didn't remain a laundry driver. He went back to St. Louis in the fall and went to college. Floyd stayed with us for a couple of years until he married a girl in the laundry office and set up a home of his own. He now owns a little laundry in Los Angeles.

CHAPTER 12

Mother's Little Helpers

MOTHER used to say, "My children are spoiled rotten," and I'm afraid we were.

Certainly we didn't do very much around the house. But Father said he'd had such a terrible childhood, having to go out and start earning money at six years old, that by God his children were going to have some fun.

Mother, on the other hand, had had a childhood "as free and happy as a little bird's," and she wanted her children to have the same kind. She felt her poor Arizona offspring were already sufficiently penalized by not having been brought up in Virginia.

She was always telling us about those halcyon days on the old plantation: The things to do! The things to see! The things to eat! Sliding down wheat stacks. Riding on the fat old horse's back to the spring. And never was water more delicious than from that spring. Hunting wild-partridge eggs. Shooting squirrels. Trapping rabbits in the early morning and coming back to those Gargantuan breakfasts. Hickory and butternut time in the fall. The glory of the maples and the sumac. Ice-cutting time and the great barbecue that followed. Skating on the pond. Finding the first arbutus under the snow. Dogwood in the spring and the wild anemones and the little white violets. The lusciousness of wild plums and ripe papaws. The mouth-wateringness of ash cake and poke salad and hog jowl.

And Mother would shake her head sadly over our hard luck in being Arizonans.

And we'd protest that maybe we had missed a lot but she'd never built wigwams out of greasewood, never had a horned toad for a pet, never hunted garnets in the little sandy washes. Arbutus and dogwood might be wonderful, but what about our saguaros with their spring crowns of waxy flowers? What about the paloverdes? And the yuccas? And the ocotillos? And the little fluffy yellow balls on the catclaws? What about the smell of the desert after a rain and overnight the grass coming up like green velvet? What about our Arizona moons and our Arizona stars?

But still Mother felt sorry for us. No childhood had ever been so wonderful as hers at "Birchlands" in Halifax County. No little girl had ever been so happily carefree, with old Mammy and the other Negroes—free now but still on the place—seeming to exist for the sole purpose of waiting on young Miss Ethel. (Mother's mother had died when she was ten.)

Mother was fond of telling a story of how one of the younger Negresses tried to teach her tidiness. It was Mother's practice to walk out of her nightgown and leave it on the floor. The maid told her it was high time she learned to pick it up. Mother flew down to report to her Mammy. Whereupon big, black Mammy puffed up the stairs and beat hell out of the maid.

"The very ideah," gasped Mammy, in between slaps, "the very ideah! No Claiborne don' nevah yit picked up after theirsel's and they ain' gonna start with Miss Ethel."

Probably as a result of Mammy's attitude, Mother, as I have already said, was a very poor housekeeper. We children, taking our cue from her, were no better.

We made our own beds, but how we made them! In the morning as we slipped out we yanked up the covers after us. If it were an especially cold morning we didn't stop to pull and smooth but came back after we were dressed, if we remembered. I'll admit the results of our yankings were more tousled than smooth, with bumps here and there where we'd left the flatiron we'd slept with or our slippers or possibly a dressing gown we'd worn to bed and then taken off.

And yet, when we didn't have a servant and we children helped Mother make the boarders' beds, we always did them very carefully, with all the covers taken off and put back on one by one, the sheets tucked under at the corners, the blankets pulled just so. Because some people liked their beds that way. We felt a little contemptuous of finicky souls who couldn't sleep with a few bumps and wrinkles.

The same way with the bathroom. If there weren't any boarders it looked like a cyclone. But when others used it with us it was as tidy as could be.

We were supposed to keep our rooms clean or whatever space was allotted to us. Since we had lots of closets and shelves, this was easy, for our conception of tidying was to get things out of sight. In the dining room, along the length of the five bay windows, was a window seat. It could hold a world of newspapers, magazines, toys, shoes, whatever had to be got rid of for the moment.

When we couldn't find anything we looked first in the window seat, pulling out the stuff and spreading it all over the floor, sometimes—until he got too big and wouldn't fit—sending Oliver crawling clear to the end to retrieve some toy that had got pushed far back.

"Let's throw out that junk," Father would plead. "Take it to the alley."

But, no, some of the magazines had recipes Mother was going to cut out when she got around to it; the newspapers were good for wrapping up rugs in the summer or for fires next winter; the toys could be mended either for us or for some poor children. Back into the window seat it all went.

The only time we ever parted with any of it was when the lid wouldn't go down, not even when we jumped on it. Then we'd take out a few armfuls and—no, not throw them away—carry them up to the attic or down to the cellar.

Father, unlike the rest of us, was a tidy person. Whenever he had a closet to himself it was very neat. The same with his bureau drawers, shirts and handkerchiefs and underwear, all in careful piles. But Mother's bureau drawers were fun to go through. We could find all sorts of things in them—a couple of mints, hard now and stale, but still good, brought home from some party to give to us, or a few pecans in a little nut basket, or half a stick of gum, or some Mexican coins someone had slipped to her when she wasn't looking, or little bottles she was saving, or pieces of gold cord and ribbon from candy boxes, or—lovely find—a long flexible corset steel, splendid for catapulting pebbles and nearly putting out one another's eyes.

Occasionally Mother's conscience warned her that we were undisciplined little brats and we ought to do a little work. So, the odd-job man not appearing, she'd make us help her with some extra menial task like raking out the cowpen, washing the garbage pails, or cleaning up the chicken yard.

But then of course she didn't want us to get the idea that we'd come down in the world.

"Ladies and gentlemen can do *anything,*" she'd tell us, and likely as not she'd get out and read to us the Claiborne family tree, a typewritten document of about twenty pages which some relative had sent her. (As a matter of fact Mother was an Edmunds, since that was her father's name. Her mother was Mary Jane Claiborne.)

According to that manuscript our ancestors were certainly wonderful. The first one came to England with William the Conqueror. His name was Alan Fitz-Herve, but after William gave him Claiborne Manor he called himself Claiborne. Other Claibornes were earls and judges and admirals and generals—a surveyor general, too—and ministers and members of Congress and somebody who was hanged for starting a rebellion. (One of the first Virginia Claibornes married Lord Delaware's daughter, and subsequent Claibornes allied themselves with Spottswoods and Dandridges and Carringtons and Ravencrofts. In some way, too, we were related to Pocahontas.)

"Always remember what nice people you come from," Mother would admonish us, and then, "Phillip, you'll have to scrub your hands again. You've still got manure under your nails."

Father, I suppose, had as many ancestors as Mother, but no one had typed them up for him. Father's father came to Arizona in the sixties, his mother in sixty-seven. She was the second American woman to come to Tucson. We used to love to hear Father tell stories about those early days.

Father didn't make fun of the Clabornes—exactly—but he said a family shouldn't be like the potato vine with the best part underground.

Mother got in the habit of saying, "I go back to William the Conqueror," which was not strictly true, of course, but since she "went back" to him, we children "went back" too.

We boasted to the little boy across the street whom we didn't like, "Ya-ah! We go back to William the Conqueror and who do you go back to?"

Since he didn't know, he couldn't tell us, but the next day he had his answer.

"Ya-ah, yourselves," he screeched over to us, "I heard my father tell my mother your William the Conqueror was nothing but a b-a-s-t-a-r-d!"

When we brought this news to Mother she said of course William the Conqueror wasn't what that horrid boy called him, he was a king. And anyway our ancestor was Fitz-Herve.

And Father snorted that a man's being a king didn't keep him from being something else and maybe she ought to look up what the word "Fitz" stood for.

Mother pretended not to hear and asked us if there was any wood in the wood box. Filling the wood box was another of our chores. We were supposed to keep it full, with both wood and kindling. We often forgot, of course, and then Mother or the cook would have to go out and get it.

"They're having so much fun playing, I hate to bring them in," was her excuse for not calling us.

When Mother had the cow we churned the butter. I can see us now, dish towels around our necks, sitting on a high stool, pushing the dasher up and down, up and down, from time to time peering in to see if the butter had come.

Father didn't like the cow, for she was continually disturbing his sleep. The Harris', who lived just back of us, had two driving horses and had their back yard in alfalfa. Mother was always afraid the cow would break out of her pen—which was on the vacant lot to the west of the Harris'—break through their fence, and eat so much alfalfa she'd bloat herself.

When Mother was a little girl, one of the "Birchlands" cows had bloated herself on alfalfa and, big as a balloon, had come staggering up to the house for help. Mother's father not being there, nor any man about, old Mammy had got the butcher knife and stabbed the cow in the stomach. And then to the accompaniment of a loud whistle and an awful smell, old Bossie went down to her natural size.

When Mother heard strange noises in the night she was sure it was our cow breaking out of her pen and into the alfalfa, and she'd tell Father to get up and see.

Father would groan, "Now, Mother, you're always hearing noises."

"I hear that cow in the alfalfa. If we don't get her out, she'll bloat, and if she bloats, you'll have to stab her."

Father would get up, put on his pants and shoes, but

swear he'd be damned if he was going to stab any cow in the stomach.

"You'd let her die?"

"I'd get the vet."

"He's 'way out in the country; he couldn't get in here for an hour."

"Well, I'm not going to stab her."

"Then I will," promised Mother.

We thought it would be terribly exciting if Mother had to stab the cow, and we were always disappointed when Father reported the cow safe in her pen.

"You worry more about that cow than you do about me," Father would fume.

"I'd worry about you, too, if you ate alfalfa."

One dawn—the light was just beginning—Mother heard a noise and got up and looked over into the Harris' yard. "Oh," she cried, "there's the cow!"

We all got up and looked, and sure enough, we could see the cow lying over there in the yard.

"I'm afraid she's gone," moaned Mother.

Father struggled into some clothes and raced out.

When he came back he stamped in and demanded, "Where's my gun?"

"Do you have to shoot her? Can't we stab her?"

"I have to shoot her," cried Father, "because if I don't shoot that cow I'm going to shoot you." He pulled off his clothes and got back into bed. "What you are looking at," he said coldly, "is not the cow at all, but an old wooden tub. Now will you *please* not do any talking and let me get some sleep."

A little while after that the cow went away to have her calf, and we did not get her back. We missed her grand rich milk, but Father said he could stand not missing his sleep.

We children were good at helping Mother steal things. Maybe "loot" would be the better word, although the effect was the same.

For instance, there was our kindling. Loads of new houses were going up all around us. After the workmen left in the afternoon we took our little wagons and went over and gathered up the odd pieces of wood and shavings and brought them home. Why should Mother pay for kindling when we could get it free?

Father said we ought to leave it for the people who were going to live in the house.

"Was there a stick around our place when we moved in?" demanded Mother. "What we don't get the little Mexican kids will take."

And it was true. Our dark-skinned fellow looters came with sacks over their shoulders and lugged away a whole lot more than we ever took.

We also helped Mother take soil from vacant lots. In our part of Tucson the topsoil was very thin, only two or three inches deep, and then began the hardpan or *caliche*. If you wanted flower beds you had to have this *caliche* dug out and then the beds filled in with good soil—bought from a nursery if you were a scrupulously honest person, or else scraped off the adjoining lots if you weren't.

So far as I know the only ones who came under the first category were late-comers to a neighborhood, who, finding their own property scraped bare and lots around them already built upon, had willy-nilly to put out good money for dirt.

Since we were first-comers in our district, we had lovely soil. Buckets and buckets of it we children had brought home, scraping it up with hoes and shovels. Especially good soil was found under mesquite trees, where it was soft and loamy. Mother would usually come with us and help us.

One of the places Mother liked to loot best was our own laundry, in the room where the "overs" were kept. "Overs" were the articles which for some reason or other got into the wash unmarked and so could not be sorted into the bundles. Also in this room were the damaged articles—those faded, torn, ink-stained—that people wouldn't accept and the laundry had to pay for.

You never saw such piles of things as were on those shelves. Stacks of sheets, pillow slips, towels, washrags, tablecloths, odd doilies and napkins, children's dresses, men's shirts, pieces of underwear, socks by the hundreds, usually not mated, handkerchiefs by the thousand, everything under the sun.

Some of it eventually got back to its rightful owners; and some of it Mother appropriated. If some poverty-stricken family needed clothes Mother made a beeline for the "overs," grabbing up what she could despite Russ Logan's protests that some of the things she was taking had only just come in, and they might still find the owners.

"These children are almost naked," Mother would answer; "they've got to have clothes."

For our own house Mother annexed towels, sheets, tablecloths, pillow slips. Our linen was a hodgepodge of different styles, different colors, and with different initials. Once Mother brought home four lovely pillow slips with A.M.B. on them, but Russ came up and took them away from her, saying he'd found out who owned them.

Privately Russ told Father, who told Mother, that he surely wished she wouldn't take things quite so soon.

"At least leave them in overnight," Father begged.

"Those pillow slips were down there for months," Mother retorted. "I thought I might as well have them."

Mother was particularly keen about handkerchiefs and would run through the piles and pick out the nice ones for herself.

Mother didn't mind the handkerchiefs having initials or even whole names. She had several very beautiful ones with "Amelia" embroidered on them.

"Some of these days," warned Father, "you're going to be sitting next to Amelia and she'll see you've got her handkerchief. Why can't you buy your own like other women?"

"But why should I buy them," demanded Mother, "when I can get such nice ones for nothing?"

Something for nothing—how that satisfied some quality in Mother's nature. It no doubt went back to those lean days in Virginia when if you didn't get something for nothing, you didn't get it at all.

If Mother were in a market and saw a clerk pulling off the outer leaves of a cauliflower her eyes would gleam, and she'd ask, "What are you going to do with those cauliflower leaves?"

"Throw them away."

"May I have them?"

"Why, certainly, ma'am," and the clerk would wrap them up for her.

Mother would take them home, cook them as cauliflower greens—very good they were, too—and boast, "This vegetable cost me nothing."

Now we know those outer leaves are full of vitamins, but Mother wasn't thinking of nutrition. It was getting something free.

"My wife is the doggonedest looter!" Father would snort. "She'd rather save a penny by bringing home a few old cauliflower leaves than make a thousand dollars."

Mother said that wasn't true, she'd much rather make a thousand dollars any time, but there were so many more opportunities to save pennies.

"It's those pennies they took away from you as a child," he'd gibe at her; "you're still trying to catch up on them."

Father loved to tell this story about Mother, and I thought it was rather tragic.

A few years after the War a stranger rode up to "Birchlands" one nightfall. As was the custom, he and his horse were housed and fed. But in the morning this stranger outraged Southern tradition by offering to pay for the hospitality. As if that weren't enough, when Mother, eight years old, opened the gate for him so he could ride through without dismounting, he reached into his pocket and threw her a handful of pennies.

Mother picked them up—so many her two hands could hardly hold them—and ran, terribly excited, to show them to her mother.

"Where did you get those?" her mother demanded.

"From that man. He threw them to me when I opened the gate."

"*Threw* them to you!"

And she snatched the pennies out of Mother's hands, wrapped them up in a piece of paper, and gave them to a Negro servant, ordering him to get on a horse, overtake the stranger, and give him back the money he'd dared to throw at a daughter of a Claiborne.

"It was the most money I'd ever had," mourned Mother. "I never will forget how badly I felt at having to give it up."

"I'd hate to try to get any pennies from her now," laughed Father.

Mother was not only a penny-saver, but a penny-earner. She always had something to sell, and we were her salesmen. We adored doing it, for she always paid us a commission, and we greatly enlarged her scope.

Though Mother was a lady and there was nothing honest a lady couldn't do, still even Mother couldn't ring doorbells with a basket of figs over her arm or shout to someone in the street to come in and buy flowers, but we children could and did.

We had a most gorgeous Maréchal Niel rosebush at one corner of our porch. When it was in full bloom it was magnificent, and people would stop to admire it. I used to wait on the porch, and when they did stop I'd step out brandishing a pair of scissors.

"The roses are 25 cents a dozen," I'd say. "Mother lets me keep 12½ cents, and the other 12½ cents goes into the rose envelope. Of course you can't divide a penny, so one time I get 12 cents and the next time 13. This is my time to get 13 cents."

Few people could resist me.

I certainly sold a lot of roses, and Phillip and Oliver wanted to sell flowers, too, so Mother said we could have a little stand. She helped us make one out of a couple of orange boxes—what would Mother have done without orange boxes? We had lilacs, snapdragons, larkspurs, daffodils, and roses in cans of water. After school we stood there, calling to people to come and buy.

Once we nearly kept Father from borrowing some money by selling roses to the wrong person. For we didn't know the gray-haired man with the walrus mustache was the bank president. He was just a customer to us, and we shouted at him as he drove by in his car. So he stopped and came up to our stand.

"Want to buy some?" I asked. "Twenty-five cents a dozen."

"We could sure use a little piece of money," said Phillip, exactly mimicking Father's tones.

And Oliver piped up, repeating what Father was always saying, "My Daddy's broke. We gotta sell 'em because my Daddy's broke."

That night when Father came home he was perfectly furious. "Mr. Fowler said I must be in pretty bad shape if I had to have my children sell flowers on the street."

"All children sell things," soothed Mother, "and I'm glad he wouldn't lend you money. You're borrowing too much."

"Oh, he lent it to me finally, but he didn't want to. Why do our kids have to sell things? Why don't we give them an allowance like other children?"

"Oh, Father," we wailed, "we like to sell things."

"It's good for children to earn their own money. You sold plenty of things as a child."

"But I had to do it; we needed the money."

"If we don't need money, why are you borrowing it?"

Father couldn't answer that, so he told us about the first job he ever had, which was ringing a big auction bell for a shoe sale. Up and down the streets of old Tucson he went, ringing his bell, and crying, "Zapatos! Zapatos! Muy baratos! Muy baratos!"

That struck us as an excellent idea, and we got an old cowbell from somewhere, put our flowers in a basket, and went around our neighborhood ringing our bell and yelling, "Flow-ers! Flow-ers! Chee-eep! Chee-eep!"

The boarders, too, were sources of revenue. For a price we shined their shoes, ran errands for them, took their books back to the library. We also found it profitable to have our banks much in evidence. If we shook them ostentatiously and wondered loudly how long before they'd be full, we'd often get a nickel or a dime or sometimes even a quarter. I'm afraid we were awful little chiselers.

Yet chisel from them though we did, we had a great feeling of responsibility for our boarders. They were our guests; we must make them happy. If the boarders had children, they were our special charges. Perhaps we were of more help to Mother in this way than in any other.

The children were sometimes spoiled brats and usually delicate, but we tried to be nice to them. We slowed down our play to their limits; we let them use our toys; we took them to movies and to dancing school with us. Fat little girls were dutifully lugged around the floor by Phillip and Oliver. (Not without some protests in private, I'll admit.)

One reason for this nobility was mercenary. Our bump of finance was well developed and Mother would warn, "If that child isn't happy, her mother will take her someplace else. I'll lose two people's board, and you know how hard up your Father is now."

With no one did we do a better job than with little Deanie Mathews.

Deanie was a sad little picked bird of a child, whose pipestem legs were helpless from the effects of infantile paralysis. She had to stay in bed all the time.

Mother felt so sorry for Deanie and wanted us to be particularly nice to her. She did something rather clever. She said Deanie was our boarder and that we could have her board money and put it in the bank.

I remember how exciting it was when we went into Deanie's room and she gave us each $25. Mother was charging her $75 and Mrs. Mathews $125. Mrs. Mathews paid Mother by check, but they had arranged that Deanie pay us in cash.

"You must give Deanie a receipt," Mother told us.

So I wrote out, "Deanie paid us $75," and all three of us signed it.

Then Mother took us down to the bank and opened up accounts for each of us and said we could start to save for our college education.

"Is she going to give us this much every month?" asked Phillip.

"Every month. She's your boarder. I hope she'll be happy and stay a long time."

"Gosh, yes," said Phillip, "we want the money."

So it was up to us to keep Deanie happy. We racked our brains to think of things to amuse her. We brought her books and toys. We organized games right outside her window so she could watch. We dug a lake and sailed boats on it, and she managed her boat with a long string. At night we went in and played cards with her—casino and slapjack and Canfield. We tried to let her win, but she caught on and said, "There's nothing the matter with my hands." And there wasn't, for she often beat us even when we were trying to win ourselves.

Because Deanie couldn't leave her bed, she and Mrs. Mathews had their meals on trays in their room. But Deanie had no appetite, and each time when her plate came out just barely touched Mother would feel so badly.

Of course Mrs. Mathews felt worse.

"I don't know what to do," she cried to Mother. "I tell her she'll die if she doesn't eat, but still she won't touch a thing."

"Heavens," said Mother, "that's no way to talk. What else do you say to her?"

"I don't say anything. I just start crying."

"No wonder she doesn't eat. Well, we'll have to think of something."

And the next evening Mother said to us that since Deanie was our boarder we ought to eat with her and let Mrs. Mathews eat with the grownups.

She put Oliver's little table and chairs by the bed and set it with some bright red china she'd got that afternoon at the ten-cent store.

"Now you're not to mention eating to her," Mother

warned us, "but eat a lot yourselves—as if I need to tell you—and say how good everything is."

She apologized to Della, "It'll be more steps for you."

"Do you think I care if we can get that child to eating?"

So we were all at our little table. It was fun being by ourselves. Deanie looked happy and excited. We dived into our food, loudly praising it, and covertly watching Deanie. But she was just picking at things, not really eating at all.

I remembered how Mother had got Oliver to eat one time. I piled a load of potatoes on my fork. "My fork's a train," I said, "and my mouth's a tunnel. Choo, choo. Down the tunnel!"

Phillip and Oliver, catching on, picked up their forks and loaded them with food. "We've got trains, too. Choo, choo. Down the tunnel." Oliver missed his mouth and got it all over his face.

Deanie laughed out loud. She picked up her fork, slid it under some carrots. "I've got a train of carrots. Choo, choo. Down the tunnel."

And so we played the game, gulping and giggling.

"Mine's a train of meat."

"My train is bigger than yours."

" 'Tis not!"

" 'Tis!"

"Choo, choo. Down the tunnel."

Deanie's food disappeared along with ours.

When Della came in and saw her empty plate she started to say something, then closed her mouth. But I saw her stop at the dining-room table and proudly show the plate.

From then on Deanie's appetite picked up, and pretty soon she was eating almost as much as any of us. Her cheeks began to swell, her eyes got bright. The nurse who came to rub her legs in the morning said she could see the pounds going on.

"She just needed to have a little fun with her food," said Mother, "instead of all that weeping."

Mother had another idea to keep Deanie amused. Oliver got very poor grades. He was bright enough, but he wouldn't study. Deanie was smart as a whip and romped through her lessons. She had a tutor in the afternoons.

"Deanie," Mother asked her one day, "how much would you charge to tutor Oliver in the evenings? He needs some help with his lessons."

"Why, she won't charge anything," Mrs. Mathews began, but Mother silenced her with a look.

Deanie and Mother finally agreed that 10 cents the half hour would be fair, and every evening Oliver brought in his books and papers and Deanie worked with him. For her sake he studied, and she was so proud when his grades went up and so cross when he made mistakes. "You know seven and four is eleven," she'd scold. "You know 'wagon' isn't spelled with an e!"

After lessons Phillip and I came in for our evening card game.

I'll never forget the day she got her braces and with their aid and her crutches took a few tottering steps.

We had a celebration that night. Della made a freezer of ice cream and Mother had a cake with two candles on it.

"It's not your birthday," Mother told her, "but your

walkday, and the two candles are for your two legs that are going to get big and strong."

When the Mathews' left the last of May Deanie's legs were lots stronger, and with her crutches she was getting all over the place.

Mr. Mathews came out to take them home, and Mrs. Mathews told him, "It was those children who really made her better. I don't know how to thank them."

Mr. Mathews said he knew how, and the next day he took us to Steinfeld's toy department and told us to choose anything we wanted.

"Do you mean *anything?*" Phillip asked.

"Anything," Mr. Mathews assured him, "just anything."

We took him literally. Oliver chose a tricycle. Phillip took a little automobile almost as big as himself. I said I'd like the desk and the blackboard. They must have cost him a pretty penny.

Mother was terribly embarrassed when she saw all our plunder. "I just thought you were going to get some little toy. You'll have to take those back."

"But, Mother, he said *anything,*" protested Phillip.

"I said anything, and I meant anything," insisted Mr. Mathews. "Nothing is going to be taken back."

We went to the station to see the Mathews' off. As the train pulled out they stood on the observation platform. Deanie waved to us as long as we could see her.

"She sure was a nice boarder," said Phillip. "When are we going to get another one?"

"Maybe next year," Mother told him.

But next year all the boarders were grownups. We were terribly disappointed.

CHAPTER 13

We Save the Women

IT WAS Miss Kennedy and Miss Cable who got Mother into the hot tamale business.

Of course Mother had made Mexican food for years—we scarcely ever served anything else at our parties. But it wasn't until after Mother had cooked the benefit dinner for the Y.W.C.A. and the Y. made over $100 from it that Mother saw what she was missing by not selling Mexican food herself.

Miss Kennedy and Miss Cable had the living room, and were two spinsterish, not so young ladies from New York. Both had been national officers in the Y.W.C.A.

They weren't beautiful, and after Father met them he told Mother he could see they were fine, noble women.

"Next time," snapped Mother, "I'll try to get some chorus girls for you."

And Father put on his grieved look and appealed to Mr. and Mrs. Myles who had the room next to the living room, "Why does she start talking about chorus girls? All I said was they were fine, noble women."

And Mr. Myles, who was very, very old, but had a twinkle in his eye, said a chorus girl would be a novelty in the house and that he agreed with Father. Miss Kennedy and Miss Cable *were* fine, noble women.

Besides being old, Mr. and Mrs. Myles were quite frail. Mr. Myles had only one-quarter of a stomach because the doctors had taken out the other three-quarters years ago. And in her husband's words, the doctors had also "nipped into Abby," for Mrs. Myles had only one kidney.

Because Mr. Myles's quarter of a stomach could hold so little food he couldn't eat enough at meals to last him; so Mother kept milk and sandwiches in the icebox, and he went and helped himself every hour or so. Mrs. Myles, with her one kidney, had to have bland, smooth foods like puréed vegetables and custards, and nothing highly seasoned.

So of course they couldn't eat Mexican food. They did taste it once and smacked their lips and said they wished they'd met it before they had their operations.

But Miss Kennedy and Miss Cable could eat anything, and they were crazy about Mexican food. They could eat as much of it as Father, who'd had chili dishes all his life and swore he was weaned on frijoles.

Mother had learned how to make the stuff from an old Mexican woman who used to work for us. The "señora" we always called her. She taught Mother how to make tamales and enchiladas and frijoles and chicken pipián and albóndigas and tacos and all the rest of it.

The one thing Mother couldn't learn was how to pat out those great wheat-flour *tortillas*. Again and again the señora showed her, taking a little piece of dough, rolling it into a ball, starting to pat it with the ends of her fingers, at the same time pulling at it and stretching it. Larger and larger the *tortilla* would grow, and thinner and thinner, flipflopping back and forth over her arms, and you wondered how it could possibly stay together. Finally, when it was big as a wagon wheel—well, anyway a yard across—and thin as tissue paper, the señora, with a single deft movement, would fling it on top of the red-hot wood stove, where it would toast to brown and white crispness.

Then along with the señora Mother would take a piece of dough and, watching her like a hawk, try to imitate her slightest movement. Pat, pat—just so. Stretch your fingers and pull—just so. But always, when Mother's *tortilla* was big as a dinner plate, it would begin to tear and either fall on the floor, or Mother would squeeze it disgustedly back into a ball again, while the señora giggled and said *"Zompa, zompa,"* which means clumsy.

"What is there about it?" demanded Mother. "If she can do it, why can't I?"

"You didn't start soon enough," consoled Father. "I've seen the little Mexican kids patting out *tortillas* when they weren't as high as the stove."

Preparing Mexican food was an awful lot of work, and the whole family got involved in it. We started days ahead of time. Washing and drying the corn shucks for the tamales. Cleaning the chili—that is, taking out the veins and seeds from the pods so it wouldn't be too hot for gringo throats. Cooking and grinding the chili for the sauce. Grinding the corn to make the masa, the paste that's spread on the corn shucks. Sometimes, though, we could buy this already ground. Cooking and cutting up the meat for the chili con carne which goes in the heart of the tamale. Patting out and frying the enchilada cakes. Cutting up onions and green olives, and grating cheese to sprinkle over the enchiladas. Cooking and mashing and frying the frijoles, Mexican beans. Roasting and skinning the long green peppers for salza, a Mexican salad. Frying in deep fat the little corn *tortillas*—tostados—which most people liked better than the big wheat-flour ones.

In those days there were no Mexican restaurants in town that I can remember. If you wanted Mexican food you went through the above labor to get it, or you bought it from a Mexican family whose cleanliness you trusted.

The compensation for all this work was that it was simply scrumptious and that it was very cheap. Mother figured that when she gave a Mexican dinner she could serve each guest for about 15 cents apiece.

"It's easy on the pocketbook," admitted Father, "but hard on my hide." And he'd hold up his hands to show the blisters he'd got from grinding chili.

It was the food's being so cheap that gave Miss Kennedy and Miss Cable their wonderful idea.

They sprang it on us one evening at dinner.

Remarked Miss Kennedy very casually, "If you can serve a Mexican dinner for 15 cents, then if a person paid you 50 cents, there'd be 35 cents' profit."

"Is someone going to pay me 50 cents?" asked Mother.

Miss Cable smiled mysteriously. "Lots of people might."

"The Y.W.C.A. is trying so hard to raise money," Miss Kennedy said. "Now if you gave a benefit Mexican dinner and we sold tickets . . ."

"We could have it here," put in Miss Cable. "People like to come to a home and . . ."

Father gasped, "Serve dinners here!"

"*Benefit* dinners," Miss Kennedy soothed him, and said to Mother, "The Y.W.C.A. ladies would do all the work. You'd just direct. And take out your expenses, of course."

"Now see here," sputtered Father, "I don't like the idea of selling meals in my home."

"But it's for the Y.," placated Miss Kennedy. "Think of the good the Y. does, all the women it helps."

Father said that was fine, he was all for helping women, but why not have the dinner in the Y. building?

"It wouldn't be large enough."

And this was true, for the Y. was then housed in a small ramshackle dwelling on Alameda Street.

"You say it's so cheap," Miss Cable continued, "so it would be almost all profit. We thought if we charged 50 cents and sold 250 tickets . . ."

"Two hundred and fifty tickets!" yelped Father. "How under the sun can you get 250 people in here?"

"They won't all come," Miss Kennedy assured him.

"If they aren't coming, why will they buy tickets?"

"To help the Y.W.C.A. You can't just ask people for 50 cents, but they'll buy a ticket and not come."

"I wouldn't count on it," warned Father, "not anyone who's had our Mexican food."

"Well," calculated Mother, "if we took down the beds in three of the rooms, we'd have the parlor, hall, dining room, those three rooms–six in all. We could probably set up 30 card tables. That would be 120 places."

"Then just sell 120 tickets," begged Father.

"That would be only $60," scorned Miss Kennedy,

"while 250 tickets would give us $125. Less your expenses," she added to Mother. "How much do you suppose they'd be?"

"If we don't have tamales, we won't have to buy meat. We could serve enchiladas, frijoles, salza, tostados, and coffee. I think I could do that for $25."

"The work!" groaned Father.

"The Y. ladies will do it all," Miss Kennedy promised. "She won't do a thing; she'll just be boss."

"I know that kind of bossing. Well, I've been meaning to go up to Globe. Tell me when you're going to have it so I can be out of town."

"Now you stay here," Mother ordered. "I'll need you."

"But if you're not going to do a thing, why do you need me?"

"There'll be something for you to do. Something will come up."

"You bet something will come up!" predicted Father. "And I know what it'll be! Grinding that chili! Well, I'm not going to do it." Father took out two silver dollars and passed them over, one at a time, to Miss Kennedy. "Here's helping the women, and here's helping me. You hire some big husky to do that grinding. Let him wear the skin off *his* hands."

Miss Kennedy took the money and said the Y.W.C.A. would send him a note of thanks.

"My thanks will be not having blisters," said Father.

"We can help with the work," offered old Mrs. Myles. "Not anything very strenuous, but anything sitting down we can do."

"I'll put you in charge of grating the cheese and cutting up olives and onions," said Mother.

"There'll be lots of things to borrow," she went on, "chairs, tables, dishes, silver . . ."

"Don't forget water pitchers," Father interrupted. "You know how people drink when they eat chili. And ice! Don't forget to order extra ice."

"We'll remember the ice," Mother promised. "Stop worrying."

They talked over the date and decided on a Thursday night—maid's night out—3 weeks from then.

Mother made a list of things to borrow: card tables, chairs, silver, sugar bowls, cream pitchers, water pitchers, large coffeepots, big pots and pans, tablecloths, glasses, plates, cups and saucers, bowls for salza, platters for tostados. She engaged the señora for two days and her grandson to do the grinding.

Miss Kennedy and Miss Cable said they'd clean the chili. Mother had bought four big strings of it. Mother showed them how to go about it, how to hold the pods at arm's length and turn their heads when they slit them open to pull out the seeds and veins so they wouldn't breathe the chili dust. She told them to be sure not to get their hands near their eyes.

Poor women! Their arms weren't long enough. They didn't turn their heads away fast enough. The chili dust got into their noses, their throats, down their lungs. They began to cough and sneeze. Miss Cable forgot and rubbed her eyes, causing them to burn and water until she couldn't see. Miss Kennedy's sneezing and coughing brought on an attack of asthma, which she hadn't had in 28 years.

"You'll have to quit," Mother ordered, "or you'll both be in the hospital."

"We're so ashamed," wept Miss Cable.

"Never mind," Mother comforted them. "Rosemary and Phillip can do it after school. There's plenty of time."

"We'll pay them," offered Miss Kennedy. "We'll give them a dollar each."

"That's too much," Mother demurred.

"Oh, Mother, it isn't," I cried. "I mean," I added, "there's an awful lot of chili."

"Two dollars is little enough," wheezed Miss Kennedy, "not to have to touch that stuff."

So Phillip and I tackled the chili. It didn't bother us. I guess our lungs were used to chili dust. Besides we automatically turned our heads when we slit the pods and never touched our faces with our hands. In spare moments Mother and Lizzie helped us.

The Y.W.C.A. sold all its tickets. The Great Day approached.

Women drove up with card tables, and baskets of dishes and glasses and silver, which were stacked all over the house. "I hope they can sort it out afterward," worried Mother. A hotel supplied us with big pots and pans. Mr. Eales, the undertaker, sent up his folding chairs. Some of them had his name on the back: "E. O. Eales, Undertaker." Mother said we'd put them where it didn't show.

Bright and early Wednesday morning the señora and her grandson appeared, also Miss Kennedy and Miss Cable with six helpers from the Y.W.C.A.

"Now we girls will do everything," beamed Miss Kennedy. "Just show us how."

As tactfully as possible Mother told them Mexican food required a special technique difficult to learn, that it would be better if the Y. ladies confined themselves to putting up and setting the tables and serving the food when it was time to serve it.

They were all for getting to the tables right then, but of course the beds couldn't come down until Thursday morning, because we had to sleep in them Wednesday night.

"It'll be better if you come back tomorrow," Mother suggested.

Quite happily the ladies departed.

However, when old Mr. and Mrs. Myles came out, she put aprons on them and set them down at a table and gave them the olives and onions and cheese.

"I hate to have you do the onions," said Mother, "because they'll make you cry."

"No, they won't," chuckled Mrs. Myles. "Because we'll hold matches in our teeth." And they did, and it worked. They didn't weep a tear. Something about the sulphur in the matches disarmed the onions. (Try it and see!)

So the two old people sat at their table, aprons tied around them, matches gripped in their teeth, and cut up hundreds and hundreds of little green onions and then—without the matches—quarts and quarts of big green olives, and then they grated up mountains of strong yellow cheese.

In the kitchen Mother, the señora and Lizzie roasted peppers, patted out enchilada cakes, fried tostados, while the grandson ground away at the chili.

The grandson's name was Jesus—pronounced Hehsōōs, of course—and when old Mr. Myles found out his name he thought it was awfully funny. "Never thought I'd be working in the same kitchen with Jesus," he cackled to his wife.

"It would sound better if you pronounced it 'Hehsōōs,' " Mother reproved.

But of course that wouldn't have been any fun for

Mr. Myles. Every few minutes he'd call over to him: "Well, Jesus, my boy, how are you getting along?"

And Heh-so͞os would grin and answer, "Bueno, señor."

Which was a gross exaggeration, for Heh-so͞os was putting the chili into the grinder too fast, and that's one thing you can't do with chili. You have to put it into the hopper pod by pod, a slow and uninteresting process, but if you try to hurry it the chili backs up on you and spurts all over the place.

"Heh-so͞os," scolded Mother, after wiping up the third chili mess from the floor, "you're putting in too much at a time. Just one or two pods. Tell him, señora."

The señora jabbered at him in Spanish, and he nodded his head and said, "Sí, sí."

But the minute they took their eyes off him he grabbed up a fistful of pods and tried to poke them down with his fingers.

"A-i-i-e!" Heh-so͞os suddenly yelled, jumping up and down with his finger in his mouth. He'd caught it in the grinder.

"Serves you right," cried Mother unsympathetically.

Heh-so͞os sucked at his finger. "I go home now."

"But the skin's not even broken," protested Mother, "and you're grinding with the other hand."

"I hurt," insisted Heh-so͞os. "I go home."

Mother knew it was useless to argue. "Is there anyone else who can come?" she asked the señora.

There was another grandson, Segismundo.

"You tell Segismundo to come right up here," Mother ordered.

"I tell him," Heh-soos promised, and went out the back door.

"So long, Jesus," called old Mr. Myles.

Segismundo didn't appear until late in the afternoon, and then he was so slow that by eight o'clock when he said he had to leave there was still a lot of chili unground.

"It's got to be done tonight," Mother worried. "What am I going to do?"

"You know very well what you're going to do," fumed Father. "Only it's what I'm going to do. Where are my overalls?"

Father put them on and started in. He ground and ground. Phillip and I stood by, feeding pods into the hopper one by one, also putting in an occasional kernel of garlic which went through with a satisfying crunch and a grand smell. We all loved garlic.

"It's fine to help the women," panted Father, "but the way I feel now they can all lie in the gutter."

Thursday dawned. Miss Kennedy, Miss Cable, the Y. ladies with two of their husbands were all over the house pulling beds apart, moving out furniture, setting up card tables. Our sleeping porch became a jungle of bureaus, rocking chairs, lamp stands, while on the beds themselves were stacked the other bedsteads, the springs and mattresses, the bedding and pillows. "Shove it on the porch," was the word.

Mother, the señora, and Lizzie were of course carrying on in the kitchen.

We children helped set the tables, folded paper napkins, filled sugar bowls. Oliver had sugar all over his face.

At noon we had milk and sandwiches, and there were more sandwiches and milk for dinner.

Father said sandwiches weren't going to be enough for him.

"All right," snapped Mother. "Busy as I am, I'll fix you some eggs."

"No eggs for me. I know what I'm going to eat." He went to the stove and dished himself up a big plate of frijoles.

"Pretty good," he grinned at Mother, after he'd tasted them.

Mother said what she always said, "I'm afraid they're not quite as good as I usually make them."

"All I say is I'm sorry for the poor guys who come too late tonight to get this food."

"I've made enough for 175 people," Mother told him. "If there's any left over we can have a party Saturday."

"Party! You're a glutton for punishment." Suddenly a look of horror spread over his face. "The ice!" he cried. "Did you get the extra ice?"

Mother put her hand to her head. She'd forgotten the ice!

So Father took a dishpan and went off to the plant. While he was gone Miss Kennedy plugged in an electric hot plate she'd borrowed to heat the coffee water—there wasn't room on the stove—and it must have been defective, for it blew out the lights.

Just as Mother had at last located a candle, in came Father carrying his 50-pound cake of ice in the dishpan.

"What have you done to the lights?"

"We've blown them out; you'll have to go get a fuse."

"Jesus!" cried Father, and he didn't pronounce it Heh-sōōs.

Finally Father was back with the fuse and the lights were on, but we didn't dare try the hot plate again and decided to make the coffee at Mrs. Harris' who lived just back of us. Mother also asked Mrs. Harris if she could put Oliver to bed over there as the beds on our sleeping porch were piled high with things.

The first customers arrived, a party of eight, but only four of them had tickets. The other four had planned to buy their tickets at the door.

"I'm sorry," Mother began, "but if you haven't tickets . . ."

"Oh, there'll be plenty," Miss Kennedy interrupted, and took the additional $2 gleefully.

Next came two young men accompanied by—there's no other word for them—two painted hussies.

"What kind of women are they?" asked Mother of Father under her breath.

"What do you expect, opening up your home to the public?"

"I've never had anything like that in my house."

"Their half dollars are as good as anybody else's."

Other people began to come. Cars drove up. Streetcars stopped at our corner, and out piled customers. They came on bicycles. They came on foot. Soon every seat was taken, and they were waiting on the porch. Miss Kennedy and Miss Cable and the Y. ladies served like mad. Father and Phillip and I couldn't keep up with the demands for water. That was a cry that kept up continually: *"Please,* may I have another glass of water?"

Even old Mr. and Mrs. Myles tottered around with pitchers.

Lots of people wanted second helpings, and Miss Kennedy was serving them and taking the extra money until Mother stopped her.

"Nobody can have seconds until those people waiting on the porch have had firsts."

It was a madhouse. A Y. lady dropped a laden plate. A wobbly card table collapsed, and what a mess that was! The two men and the hussies produced beer bottles and began getting noisy. Mother wanted Father to tell them to leave but Father said, "The Y. brought 'em, let the Y. bounce 'em." So Miss Kennedy had to get rid of them. In the midst of it all Oliver wandered home from the Harris', crying because he'd waked up in a strange place and immodestly wiping his eyes with the bottom of his nightgown. There was literally no place for him to sleep, so Mother pulled out a quilt from the mess on the back porch and made up a bed for him in the bathtub.

"But suppose someone wants to use the bathroom?" protested Father.

"No one's going to mind a little boy. Besides, he'll be asleep."

And still the people came. There must have been three hundred who planned to eat Mexican food that night. It was dreadful.

By watering the chili sauce toward the end, serving one enchilada cake instead of two, giving minute portions of beans, Mother managed to serve two hundred people—we figured that out afterward. But finally the cupboard was bare, there wasn't another spoonful of anything, and the people waiting on the porch and sitting on the curb had to be told it was all gone; there wasn't any more.

Miss Kennedy said of course the Y.W.C.A. would give them their money back, but she said it in such a way that no one took it.

"I've never felt so disgraced," lamented Mother, "people going hungry from my house!"

"Serves you right," Father told her, "selling more tickets than you had food."

Finally the last customers, fed and unfed, had departed.

We were all ready to collapse. But there were the dishes to do, the tables to take down, the beds to set up.

"Do the Myles's room first," Mother ordered, for the old people looked about to drop.

The Y. ladies were jubilantly counting up the returns. "One hundred and forty dollars!" Miss Kennedy squealed delightedly. "That's one hundred and fifteen for the Y."

"Just dandy," grunted Father, at this moment helping to maneuver a big double mattress through the door. "but the next time you ladies want money, please let me know. I'll pass around the hat; it'll be much easier."

"Yes, sir!" agreed Mr. Myles on the other end of the mattress.

Out in the kitchen two women were quarreling over their silver. Both had identical patterns and had tied it with white string. They were so tired and cross it looked like a hair pulling.

"Do you absolutely have to have that silver for breakfast?" demanded Father.

Oh, no, they had enough for breakfast.

"Then for the love of Mike, leave it here, and sort it out tomorrow!"

At last the beds were up, the dishes washed, the last helper gone. Mother got Oliver out of the bathtub, Phillip from off the window seat. We started undressing.

Our beds—how good they felt!

Father heaved a sigh of relief. "Well, we saved the women. Thank God that's over."

"Think of it," marveled Mother, "all those people coming to eat my food. It makes me proud."

"Ye-ah," yawned Father.

"Of course we had too many."

"Too . . . damned . . . many."

"But about twenty," mused Mother, "wouldn't be too many."

"What do you mean twenty wouldn't be too many?"

"Well, you could put five tables up in the parlor very easily. Oh, I don't mean every night, but say once a week, on Thursday. I could give a little more food, say a tamale and a taco, and charge a dollar. That would be $20, and at least fifteen would be profit."

Father sat straight up in bed. "So help me God," he thundered, "so help me God, if you sell any meals here I'll leave! I won't stay! I'll go live at the club! I'll . . . I'll . . ."

"Oh, hush. I'm not going to sell any meals here."

Mother probably meant it when she said it.

But the next morning the Worthy Matron of the Eastern Star called up and said my, but she'd certainly enjoyed Mother's food at the Y. dinner and did Mother think maybe she could serve fifty Eastern Star ladies on next Thursday night?

Fifty dinners! Twenty-five dollars!

Now I ask you, could Mother turn that down?

"I can't serve you here," said Mother, "but I can make the food for you and you can take it away."

CHAPTER 14

More Sin at Midnight

OUR boarders were likely to come two by two rather than one by one. Two people in a room meant more profit, and Mother usually made the price for one person almost as high as for two. This discouraged a lot of people, of course, and then, if the lone person were a woman, Mother didn't want her young and pretty. Our lone female boarders usually brought forth from Father the comment, "Gosh, you can sure pick the sour old maids!"

"You have plenty of pretty ones coming into your office," Mother told him.

Father said as far as he was concerned he'd do all his business with men, but sometimes women wanted to buy property, too, and once in a while one of them was pretty.

"Maybe," snorted Father, "I ought to say to her, 'Sorry, my beauty, I can't take your money. But send in your crippled old mother and I'll do business with her.' "

"I've noticed," accused Mother, "that when it's a pretty woman you're selling to, it takes you a long, long time to close the deal. You've got to do a lot of traipsing around the country showing her properties. But you find something right away for an ugly one."

"Sure," agreed Father. "A pretty woman's more particular; it takes her longer to make up her mind. I know one pretty woman who took 4 years to make up her mind about a certain proposition. If she'd been ugly, I'll bet I'd have put the deal over in a lot less time."

"You're hopeless," scolded Mother, but she looked pleased.

Nevertheless no unattached woman with what we today would call "oomph" got into our house.

Except Rita Vlasak, nee Rita Martin.

Mother slipped up there, all right!

The year we had Rita Vlasak we had another lone woman, Miss Russell. Miss Russell had the living room and from Mother's point of view was the ideal female boarder. She was a retired chemistry professor, about sixty-five, quite crippled with arthritis, with a mind as keen as a knife blade. She was a prodigious reader, and two or three times a week I went down and changed her books at the library. They were always big heavy ones with titles that didn't make sense. Then she received a lot of books and scientific magazines by mail. She was keenly interested in politics, too, and she loved to argue with Father. She hated Teddy Roosevelt, and Father, despite the fact that he was a Democrat, was a great admirer of Teddy. They used to have grand fights about him. Father, before he cut off his mustache, used to look a lot like Teddy.

Rita Vlasak came to us through some friends of friends of ours. She had just divorced a husband in Wisconsin and had come West to get away from it all. She was a blond little thing, about thirty, thin to scrawniness, listless and washed-out looking, with a receding chin and eyes that were slightly popped. Not Father's type at all, Mother thought.

Rita said she could afford Mother's price, and Mother put her next to Miss Russell, the two of them sharing the bath.

Rita told Mother about her husband—through overhearing Mother talk to Father, it filtered down to us children—how shamefully he'd neglected her, how he was out every night until two and three in the morning.

"Women, I suppose?" clucked Mother sympathetically.

"Women! Don't make me laugh. He's in love with fertilizers."

"Fertilizers?"

"Yes, fertilizers! It's too humiliating."

It seemed that Dr. Vlasak, a naturalized Hungarian, was a chemist with a big chemical company and was deep in the problem of how to treat sewage so it could be put on the land.

"It sounds horrid," said Mother.

"He finds it fascinating. Naturally I got tired of being by myself all the time."

"Naturally," Mother agreed.

"So one night I went to the movies with an old friend, and then what do you think he did?"

"What?"

"He beat me."

"Good heavens!"

"With a stick."

"You should have had him arrested."

"No, I left him the very next day, and I filed suit for divorce."

"You poor little thing," sympathized Mother. "We'll try to make you forget."

Rita Vlasak started forgetting that very night. Just as soon as she met Father.

You never saw such a change in a woman the minute he came into the room. I don't know how else to describe it except to say that it was like Colonel when someone picked up the car keys. One second he was a sleeping dog, dead to all the world, and the next, with just the faintest tinkle from those keys, he was an electrified bundle of joyous yelps and wriggles.

Father—any man—was to Rita what the car keys were to Colonel. She came to life; she sparkled; she grew pretty right before your eyes. It was unbelievable.

Father, of course, ate it up. All through that meal he was just too, too gallant. He hung on Rita's words. He pressed food upon her. Wouldn't she have this? Wouldn't she have that? Miss Russell's attempts to renew an argument of the night before were almost rudely ignored. Toward the end his manner became nothing less than protective.

"Mother," he said, "we've got to fatten this girl up, get some roses in her cheeks. Now see that you give her enough to eat."

Mother replied coldly that she'd never been known as a stomach robber, that Mrs. Vlasak could have all she wanted to eat and more.

After dinner Father had to go to a meeting of the chamber of commerce, which he couldn't get out of because he was the president.

As soon as the door closed behind him Rita sank back in her chair and went dead doggo, just like Colonel after the car left without him. She sat there staring into space drumming her fingers up and down.

"Would you like a book to read?" Miss Russell asked. "I have several in my room."

"No, thank you. I'll go to bed, I think." She got up and left us.

Mother looked at Miss Russell, and Miss Russell looked at Mother.

Miss Russell shook her head. "My dear," she said.

And that's the way it went—Rita lying around the house all day, bored and listless, and coming dramatically to life the minute Father stepped in the house. Even if Mother hadn't been a jealous woman—and she was one, somewhat—it was extremely irritating.

"I object," I heard her say to Miss Russell once, "I object to being found so uninteresting that all day long I'm not even worth a smile."

Rita, of course, told Father about her husband.

"When I think of that brute beating that little thing," fumed Father to Mother, "I just see red."

"We don't know his side of it."

"When a man beats a woman with a club, what side can he have?"

"She told me it was a stick."

"Stick or club, what difference does that make? The point is that he beat her. We must try to make it up to her."

And Father did his best.

It was bad enough for Mother to see this flirtation going on under her very eyes, but then Father and Rita, in Mother's phraseology, began "traipsing" about the country. Oh, they had a perfectly good reason to "traipse." Rita wanted, or said she wanted, to buy a few acres upon which she could build a little ranch house. "I feel the need of the primitive," she explained.

Naturally she and Father had to spend a lot of time looking over various pieces of property, for Rita had quite definite ideas about this site for the future "Rancho Rita." It must not be too near town or too far from it. It must be on a hill to have a view, yet she mustn't have to go too deep for water. It must be thickly covered with greasewood, have a few ocotillos on it, and at least one tall saguaro.

Nearly every day Father had a new location to show her and would drive out to the house to pick her up.

"She's certainly taking up a lot of your time," complained Mother. "If she ever does buy, your commission will be all spent on gasoline."

At last Rita decided on a certain 10 acres in the foothills just north of town. But she still wanted to think about it and to see how the land looked early in the morning and at high noon and at sunset. Then she wondered how it would be by moonlight.

Suggested Mother, thinking fast, "Let's have a picnic supper out there. Then we'll build a fire and sit around it and wait for the moon to rise."

But when the evening came Rita had a headache and we didn't go. Father remembered, too, that he had to go to an Elks' initiation.

That was the evening Mother got a new slant on Rita. For Mr. and Mrs. Gibson dropped in. Mr. Gibson had quite a deep voice, and it must have carried to Rita's room, where she was nursing her headache or whatever was wrong with her. Out she came, expecting

Father was back, I suppose. Instead it was Mr. Gibson. But Mr. Gibson was a man, wasn't he? Rita turned on the charm and was the most sparkling, vivacious creature you ever saw. She had Mr. Gibson eating right out of her hand. So much so that Mrs. Gibson, who had intended to spend the evening, soon protested they must be leaving and took her husband home.

Whereupon Rita went back to her room.

It was then, I think, that it dawned on Mother that Rita wasn't interested in Father as Father, but in Father as the Male, that Rita was one of those women who liked anything in pants.

Well, then, why not introduce her to that Male of Males, Hamish Cole? Hamish had been divorced by two wives and was now at liberty, very much so. If it was anything in pants for Rita, it was anything in skirts for Hamish. Even as a little girl I knew that the way Mr. Cole looked at me was different. There was something exciting about it, and something not quite nice.

Hamish had a real-estate office not far from Father's. The problem was to get Rita into it and introduced to Hamish. It took a bit of maneuvering, but Mother was good at that. She managed to go downtown with Rita on some errand, and, as they passed Hamish's office, she said, "Come in here a minute. I want to phone Della."

Mother introduced Rita to Hamish and went over to the telephone that was on a desk where a secretary sat typing.

"Don't stop typing," Mother told her. "I can hear all right." With her back turned and her little finger holding down the receiver hook, Mother had a long conversation telling Della how to make a meat loaf. Then she changed her mind and said no they wouldn't have meat loaf, they'd have stuffed shoulder of lamb, and she went into lengthy instructions about that. Out of the corner of her eye she could see that Rita and Hamish were getting along nicely. So in the minutest detail she took up the rest of the menu. Should they have mashed or escalloped potatoes? What was there in the icebox for a salad? Should Della make some more mayonnaise? What about a batch of light biscuits, or would it be better to make some spoon bread? She was just taking up the matter of dessert when the secretary interrupted.

"I'm sorry but this is a business phone. It must be kept open for incoming calls."

"Just one more minute," Mother begged sweetly, and told Della most elaborately how to make a lemon pie. At last she hung up. "I have such a stupid maid," she explained, "I have to tell her everything."

She went over to Rita and Hamish. "I'm afraid I've kept your phone busy," she apologized.

"Not at all! Not at all! It has given me opportunity to get acquainted with Mrs. Vlasak."

"I hope you'll have many more opportunities. Mrs. Vlasak plans to build here."

"So she told me. I'm glad of that."

He escorted them to the door.

"Hamish," invited Mother, "drop around and see us sometime."

"Yes, do," seconded Rita.

"I most certainly will," promised Hamish.

They walked off, and after a minute Rita said, "Isn't he charming?"

"He's known as a lady killer," warned Mother.

"That's the kind I like," admitted Rita. And then, "Do you suppose your husband would mind if I looked around a little more before I bought that property? Mr. Cole said he could show me some acreage, and I feel I should see everything before buying."

"I think you're entirely right," Mother agreed. "Hamish may have just what you're looking for."

Of course Father was furious about it, although to Rita he said, "Fine. Fine. Look around until you're sure my place is the best bet." Privately he fumed to Mother, "But how did she meet him?"

"We ran into him downtown," said Mother a little inaccurately. "I had to introduce him, didn't I?"

"Of all the luck! He'll spoil the sale."

"If he has something that suits her better, let her have it."

Father was decidedly out of the running after that. Attractive as Father was, Hamish had a lot more of what Rita wanted, and he was unmarried. So although she still turned on the charm for Father's benefit, it was with Hamish she now did the traipsing, seeking the site for "Rancho Rita." And Hamish took to dropping around in the evenings and from time to time took Rita out to dinner and to the movies.

One Sunday Rita and Hamish were going to spend the whole day in their quest for acreage. Mother packed a lunch for them.

"I've put in enough for your supper in case you don't want to come back early," she told them.

After our own Sunday dinner, our family and Miss Russell went for a ride. When we came home late in the afternoon, there was a man sitting on our porch smoking a big cigar.

"Now who is that?" Mother wondered.

When we came up to the porch he stood up. He was short and thickset, dark, with a high color in his cheeks, and he had the most piercing blue eyes I'd ever seen.

"I'm Paul Vlasak," he announced. "I am looking for my wife." He had a nice voice with just a suggestion of an accent.

"Wife!" exclaimed Mother.

"Yes. Does not my wife live here?"

"But . . . but . . . is she your wife? Aren't you divorced?"

"Oh, that!" He dismissed it with a wave of his hand. "But we will be reconciled. We will be married again."

Somewhat embarrassed, Mother fell back upon the conventions. "This is my husband," she said.

"How do you do?" Dr. Vlasak put out his hand which Father took and dropped immediately.

"And this is Miss Russell."

Suddenly Dr. Vlasak smiled, showing very white teeth. "Winifred Russell? I heard you lecture at Cornell once."

"Did you?" exclaimed Miss Russell, looking pleased.

"A very good lecture it was."

He turned back to Mother. "And where is my wife?"

"Your wife—Mrs. Vlasak—is out looking at some real estate. I don't know when she'll be back."

Dr. Vlasak looked at the sun. "One cannot see much in the dark. She should return soon."

"N-o-o. But it was going to be a sort of picnic. They were going to build a fire, cook their supper. She probably won't be back until late. Perhaps you should come to see her tomorrow."

"I prefer to wait and see her tonight. You will permit me to sit on your porch?"

"But it's cold out here," said Mother uncertainly, her sense of hospitality overcoming her prejudices. "If you are going to wait you had better come inside."

Dr. Vlasak accepted unhesitatingly. "Thank you. I shall."

I noticed as he went in that he had a paper-wrapped parcel under his arm.

While he and Father hung up their overcoats Mother and Miss Russell went to take off their wraps. We children were flinging our coats on the window seat.

Father and Dr. Vlasak sat down. Father cleared his throat.

"A frog?" asked Dr. Vlasak politely. Then, "Is my wife going to buy property here?"

"She's been looking at property lately," admitted Father.

"She always wanted a house in the West. It is not too bad an idea."

Mother and Miss Russell came in. We all stared at Dr. Vlasak. This was the wife beater. He looked so nice.

Oliver edged over to the parcel that Dr. Vlasak had left on the floor.

"What are you doing, Oliver?" asked Mother. "Leave that package alone."

"Is it candy?" demanded Oliver hopefully.

"No, I'm sorry," said Dr. Vlasak, "it's not candy. I did not know there were children. However," he added to

Mother, "I should be grateful to have you put it on ice."

"Certainly," said Mother, and took it out.

She came back in, and for a while they sat and made conversation until finally Oliver wailed, "I'm hungry, Mother."

Dr. Vlasak jumped to his feet. "It is your supper hour. Please go ahead and do not mind me."

"We're just going to have what's left of the chicken," said Mother. "Won't you have some with us?" She looked at Father and I could see she was flashing at him, "Well, what else could I do?"

"I will eat with you on one condition," smiled Dr. Vlasak, "and that is that you allow me to contribute."

"But we have plenty of food."

"This will not be food. You will see."

When Mother called us to the table he asked if he could go to the icebox. He came back carrying a bottle.

"Champagne!" he announced. "We will celebrate the reconciliation with my wife."

"But . . . but," Mother started to protest.

"Glasses!" demanded Dr. Vlasak, and seeing the China closet, began rummaging in there without as much as a by-your-leave to Mother. He brought out some goblets we used for desserts. "These will do."

He did something to the bottle; out popped the cork with the loveliest pop; into the glasses went the bubbling golden liquid. He slid them over to Mother, to Miss Russell, to Father.

Firmly Mother shook her head. "I don't drink. I haven't had alcohol since I nursed Oliver, and then it was only beer."

Miss Russell said she couldn't touch it because she had an ulcer.

Scowling, Dr. Vlasak turned to Father. "And you, is there anything the matter with you?"

"My health is perfect," Father assured him, and picked up his glass.

"To my wife," toasted Dr. Vlasak.

"To your wife," said Father.

They drained their glasses. Father gave a sneeze.

Dr. Vlasak reached for the other two glasses.

"To my wife," he toasted again.

"To your wife," repeated Father.

The golden liquid disappeared.

"Shall we sit down?" invited Dr. Vlasak as if he were the host.

Said Mother severely, "In the first place she isn't your wife, and in the second place, if you brought that champagne to celebrate, you should wait and celebrate with her."

"Is it my fault she is not here when I am ready to forgive her?"

"Forgive her!" cried Mother. "What have you to forgive her?"

"Many things. But she will drink nonetheless. I have another bottle for her." He refilled his and Father's glass. "This is my wedding night. Let us drink again."

"This is *not* your wedding night," Mother contradicted. "Even if your wife forgives you and marries you again, you can't get married until tomorrow. So this can't be your wedding night."

"A mere technicality. I do not like technicalities."

"Have some sandwiches," offered Mother. "The top

ones are egg and onion. The bottom ones are roast beef."

"I will not eat while I drink, and certainly I will not eat onions on my wedding night."

"You seem very sure you are going to get her back. And after the way you treated her!"

"How did I treat her?"

"You know."

"So she has told you things."

"She has."

Dr. Vlasak put down his glass. "Look!" he said. He tensed his arm and a great bulging muscle sprang up. "See. I am a powerful man, and she is a little woman. Am I not a brute to beat that little woman? And with a club, too!"

"You are a brute," Mother told him.

"Shame on you," accused Father, and hiccuped.

"Did it ever occur to you that I did not beat her?"

"But she said . . ."

"Lies. Lies. She has told you many things. Now I will have my say. Listen!" And he leaned forward, his blue eyes holding Mother's. "It is night, very late, perhaps two o'clock. I come home from working in my laboratory and she is there on the porch with a young whippersnapper. I tell him to leave. Perhaps I am rude. Two o'clock is late to find one's wife with a whippersnapper. Is it not so?"

Put in Father, "No whippersnapper comes on my porch."

"If you came home nights yourself," countered Mother, "she wouldn't want other company. A man owes something to his wife."

"A man owes something to his work."

"Chemists shouldn't marry," said Miss Russell drily. "I didn't."

"Chemists' wives should understand. But we were talking about how I beat her. So the young man departs. Perhaps I help him a little. But I am not particularly angry. I just want him to leave. We go inside, when suddenly a wildcat springs at me. My shins are kicked, my face is clawed." He leaned toward Mother, pointing to his cheek. "You can see the scars."

"I don't see anything."

"Then you are blind. Do you see them?" he asked Father.

"Sure, I see them," answered Father loudly.

"Do you allow your wife to scratch?"

"No, sirree!" cried Father, banging the table with his fist.

"Would you not punish her for scratching?"

"Yes, sirree!" shouted Father, and banged the table again.

Dr. Vlasak grinned. "Have some more champagne. So . . . my shins ache, my face is bleeding. There is a yardstick there on the table. I take it. I use it three times. Whack! Whack! Whack! It breaks. So then I smack a few times with my hand. Would you not do the same?"

"Certainly," agreed Father.

"So that is the end, I think. I have a few scratches. She has a few smacks. What is there to it? The next night I come home early to take her to the movies, and she is gone. Gone, bag and baggage. And I am served papers. I read that I have beaten her with a club, that

I have made bruises from head to toe. How can she have bruises from head to toe when I have smacked only in one place?"

" 'Diculous," said Father in a funny thick voice, "can't be bruises."

"No, it was not those few smacks that made her leave me. The real reason was that I was unfaithful to her. I betrayed her . . ."

"Just a minute," interrupted Mother. "You children go on out. . . ."

"I betrayed her with my work," Dr. Vlasak kept right on talking, "I let my work come first. But now she can come first, or if not first, at least what you call, 'even Stephen.' "

"Are you going to give up your work?" asked Miss Russell. "That would be a pity."

"No. But my company has now made my work entirely research, my own research. No longer do I have to boil the pot in the day and do my own work afterward. Now I work for myself in the day. At night I have time for my wife, like other men."

"I think you should have come out here a little sooner," warned Mother.

"I could not come sooner. If I did, a year's work would have gone for nothing. But now I am here, I can be a proper husband to her."

"If you're not too late."

"I am not too late. You have not fooled me. She is out with a man tonight. What of it? We are not married. But now she has me she will not want that other man. For I am the one she loves. Shall I tell you why?"

But we were never to know, for at this interesting point Mother suddenly stood up, and said since we children had finished eating we could go and play with our toys. She hustled us into the back room and then left us. I suppose she didn't want to miss anything. Neither did we and sneaking around through Miss Russell's room we tiptoed up behind the curtain that hung between the entrance hall and the dining room. But the fuzz on the curtain tickled Oliver's nose and he gave a loud sneeze. So Mother hustled us out again and this time she made us go to bed even though it was still light.

I lay in bed thinking over what I'd heard, and I was on Dr. Vlasak's side. Rita deserved what she got, I decided, for scratching his face.

I dropped off, and the next thing I knew it was dark and Father and Mother were talking.

"Just this once," I heard Father say, still in that funny, thick voice. "Just this once. I never asked you before."

"But you haven't told me yet what you want me to do."

"Untie my shoelaces," begged Father.

"You ought to be ashamed of yourself."

"It's my head. When I stoop over it goes off somewhere."

"Disgraceful! The way you two drank—that whole bottle."

"Celebrating the wedding."

"She won't take him back."

"How much'll you bet?"

"Ten dollars." (Mother was always very glib about betting because when she lost she never paid Father. However, she made him pay up when he lost.)

"She'll take him, if I know women."

"You don't know women. Go to bed."

When Mother came out she stood looking through the screen toward the street. "That man's not gone back to his hotel at all. He's still out there. I can see him walking up and down on the sidewalk. He's waiting for them."

"Glad I'm not Hamish," mumbled Father.

"You'd better be glad you're not out showing her real estate."

"Don't show real estate in the dark. Les' go to sleep."

"I hope there's not going to be any trouble."

"Hamish is used to that kind of trouble. She should've come in sooner."

Said Mother, who was now on Rita's side, "She's not married to him. She has a right to go out with Hamish if she pleases."

"Oh, les' stop talking," mumbled Father.

It seemed as if I'd been asleep for hours when I was suddenly wide awake. All sorts of noises were coming from the front of the house.

Mother was sitting up in bed trying to rouse Father and getting no more out of him than a few grunts.

The noises kept on, and there was a woman's scream.

"Mother!" I cried, "what's the matter?"

"I don't know, and I can't get your Father awake."

Phillip and Oliver were sitting up now too.

The scream came again.

"I'll have to go see what it is."

"I'll go with you, Mother. You come, too," I told Phillip and Oliver. My bravery was half curiosity and half wanting to protect Mother.

We scrambled into our robes and ran down the hall toward the dining room. We could see that the light was on.

Mother pulled open the door. There was Rita on the floor. A chair was turned over. Miss Russell was standing in the door of her room. Dr. Vlasak was coming in from the front porch. His hair was rumpled, his tie pulled to one side, and he was breathing hard.

He grinned at Mother. "I am sorry for the noise. I had an argument."

"Leave this house this minute!" ordered Mother, "or I will call the police."

"No need for that," soothed Dr. Vlasak, and walked over to Rita and started to pull her to her feet.

Mother flew at him.

"Leave her alone, you . . . you wife beater!"

"But I did not throw her on the floor. It was the real-estate man because she scratched him."

"Leave her alone," Mother repeated, pulling at her other arm.

But Rita flung her off. "You go away," she said, and turned to Dr. Vlasak and buried her face in his shoulder and started crying.

Dr. Vlasak put both arms around her and rested his chin on her head. "See," he grinned down at Mother, "she doesn't want me to leave."

"Well!" gasped Mother, "Well!" And she stared at them open-mouthed.

Rita cried harder, and she put her arms around his neck.

Dr. Vlasak looked from Mother over to Miss Russell. "What do you think? Am I not the man for her?"

"The evidence does point that way," she admitted.

Dr. Vlasak took out his handkerchief and wiped Rita's eyes. "Don't cry, my dear, we are going to have champagne."

Falling back on her favorite remedy for any crisis, Mother asked, "Would you have those sandwiches you didn't eat at supper? But they've got onions in them."

"Will you eat onions, darling?"

Rita moved her head up and down.

"Fine! Bring them on. We will have the wedding supper."

Suddenly Mother stopped dead in her tracks. "But you're not ma . . ." she began.

"A technicality," Dr. Vlasak put in quickly, "which can be remedied tomorrow."

Mother still stood there in frozen horror, and Dr. Vlasak suddenly laughed. "I am a fool, a fool. We *are* married. The decree is not final until the fifteenth, and this is the eleventh." He prodded Rita. "Isn't that right, sweet? Tell her we are married."

"We're married," said Rita.

Mother went out and brought in the sandwiches.

When we got back to bed Mother tried once more to wake Father.

"I owe you ten dollars," she said, shaking him.

"Uh, uh," muttered Father.

"Listen to me," ordered Mother. "They say they're still married. I have to take their word for it, don't I? It isn't up to me to make them prove it, is it?"

More mutters from Father.

"If there's any sinning being done, it's on their conscience, not mine, isn't it?"

Father's voice came from a long way off. "Uh . . . huh." It really did sound as if he were trying to say "yes."

Mother relaxed and lay back on her pillow. "That's what I think, too."

CHAPTER 15

Keep It in the Family

DID MOTHER get cross when any of our boarders sent their clothes to another laundry!

Father, however, didn't care. "Let 'em go somewhere else," he'd say. "Then I can eat my meals in peace, without hearing how a button's off their pants or they've lost a sock or something. Anyway, I wish they'd take their troubles to Russ. The laundry isn't my business any more."

"It is too your business," Mother would scold. "It pays you a nice check every week, so you ought to feel responsible."

Mother was very much Mrs. Laundry Owner when anything went wrong with the boarders' wash. She'd call up Russ and tell him he'd have to make it good and ask what was the matter down there that they did such poor work. But if the boarders changed to another laundry—for there were several in town now—how she would fume and fret.

"You've got their board money," Father pointed out, "so let someone else have their wash. Why must you always get their last nickel?"

"I don't want their last nickel," Mother retorted, "but I think their business should stay in the family. Besides, how does it look to have another wagon drive up here and take clothes out of this house? People will think our laundry is so bad we won't even go to it ourselves."

"They think that anyway," said Father, "when they see your wash hanging on the line every Monday."

"That's different," Mother hedged. "I'm certainly not going to send my good linen down there for you to ruin. And you know what Russ does whenever there's something lost from a bundle; he just replaces it with something of mine. But they ought to be able to wash a shirt without tearing it to pieces. You should speak to Russ."

"He's doing all right. I'm not poking my nose into things because of an old torn shirt."

Of course if the boarders' business amounted to anything—if they were buying property, investing in ranches or mines—then Father wanted to be the salesman and he didn't like it if they went elsewhere. But he was much more philosophic about it than Mother.

"Sure, lots of people you think ought to come to you, don't. But others who maybe should go someplace else, come to you. So it evens up."

Mother had her eye out for any profit, however small, and, Father now being in so many businesses, she was constantly on the alert for any trade that should come our way. Father was now in the banking business. He and some friends—none of whom knew much, if anything, about banking—had bought a bank. Father was a vice-president and proud as Punch. So our boarders must do their banking in "our" bank. Father had bought—or owed money on—a fourth interest in a wholesale grocery store which, in order to have an outlet, had bought five retail stores. If a boarder wanted to send a box of Arizona oranges home or a sack of piñones, these must be bought from one of "our" grocery stores. Father was also part owner in half a block of shops up by the depot, and among his tenants were a barber, a shoe repair man, an Indian curio dealer, a jeweler. Mother steered the boarders in this direction whether their need was a shave or a new sole, an Indian basket or an alarm clock.

I think sometimes the boarders resented this "steering," and occasionally they sneaked off to make their purchases where they pleased.

Mother always was cross about this, but Father said for Heaven's sake to let people buy where they wanted to buy.

But if Mother had let Mr. Latham buy where he wanted to buy, Father wouldn't have had that nice profit, and it would have been pretty sad for Mr. Latham, too.

Mr. and Mrs. Latham were from New Jersey. He was a retired hardware merchant, a plump little man with white hair and very pink skin. Mrs. Latham looked just like him. She might have been his twin sister.

They had no children of their own but had devoted most of their lives to bringing up the seven children of Mr. Latham's brother—who, with his wife, had been drowned when the children were small.

"Six girls and a boy," Mrs. Latham told us. "They're all married but the boy. He's the oldest and he's doing fine as a civil engineer. So our responsibilities are over. We've sold our business; we've sold our big house, and now we're going to enjoy ourselves. I think we deserve it."

"You certainly do," agreed Mother.

"You'll laugh when I tell you what I'm going to do," said Mrs. Latham. "Jigsaw puzzles! All my life I've loved to do them, and I've never had time. Now if I want to I'm going to work at them all day long."

And that's exactly what she did. She must have had about fifty or sixty boxes of puzzles. Some of them were enormous. One I remember was almost as large as the dining-room table. The whole family started on it after dinner, and at nine o'clock, when Mother insisted we children go to bed, it wasn't nearly done. The grownups worked at it until midnight, but it still wasn't finished.

Next morning we ate breakfast in the kitchen. And lunch. And dinner. All day long, whenever we could, we worked at the puzzle. Even the cook and an electrician who came to fix a light switch couldn't resist it. It wasn't finished until nearly ten o'clock. My, what a satisfaction when the last piece went in, and there was Admiral Nelson dying in the cockpit of the *Victory* and all his officers standing around.

Mother said unless we wanted to eat in the kitchen all the time we'd better not start another one on the dining-room table.

"That's the only really large one I have," said Mrs. Latham. "The rest will fit on a card table." And she had a card table set up in her room and always had a puzzle going. We children used to go in and help her, but Mother, after doing that first one, said she didn't have time.

"Save it up for your old age," laughed Mrs. Latham, "just the way I have."

All day long she worked at her puzzles. Sometimes

she made things extra difficult by turning the pieces over and trying to put them together just from their shape without help of the colors.

"Such a waste of time!" said Mother to Father.

There was also something Mr. Latham had wanted to do all his life, and he was busy about doing it, though what it was he never would say. He left the house right after breakfast each morning and then was gone after lunch, too.

"Wonder where he goes," puzzled Father. "I never see him around town."

Tactful questions by Mother elicited nothing from Mrs. Latham other than, "Oh, Eldred likes to get around and see people."

"But what people?" asked Father when this was repeated to him. "He doesn't know anybody."

Then one day Mother saw Mr. Latham being driven up to the house by Tom Bonny.

"God help him!" cried Father, when Mother told him this.

"That's what I say."

"We'll have to warn him."

"Bonny can rob him for all I care."

"What's got into you?"

"I know when I'm sat on, and no one sits on me twice."

"Who sat on you, for the love of Mike?"

"Mr. Latham. I asked him, 'Wasn't that Mr. Bonny who drove you home?' and he just looked at me and said, 'It's a grand morning, isn't it?' and went into his room. Telling me to mind my own business."

But Father felt differently. Bonny was a crook. Mr.

Latham should be warned. Besides, if Latham had money to invest, why didn't he come to Father?

He appealed to Mother, "Women are supposed to be such good snoopers. Can't you get it out of her?"

"No, I can't. I wasted a whole morning working one of those puzzles with her, and hinted and hinted, but never a word."

I was the one who found out what Tom Bonny was trying to sell Mr. Latham.

They didn't see me sitting on the grass hunting four-leaf clovers when they drove up, or if they saw me they didn't think I mattered. So they went right on talking, and, of course, I listened.

Tom Bonny was talking about a gold mine. I couldn't hear all of it, but that gold mine was surely rich. In some places you could go in and pry out the gold with a pocketknife. It was in big chunks, just like raisins in a cake. And it wasn't only the gold ore; there was one tunnel chock full of gold altar ornaments from the missions, hidden by the Spanish padres to keep them from the Indians back in the early days. There was an old map, too, which would show them where this tunnel was. And over and over again Bonny said how secret they must be, because other people were after that mine, too.

I told Mother what I'd heard, and she told Father.

"Lord," cried Father, "the old map and the lost tunnel again! That's the one he got Clara Winters on."

"I'd like to let him buy his old gold mine, but I suppose we'll have to tell him."

"No, we won't," said Father. "We'll let Clara tell him.

Have her over to dinner. If we can just get her started talking!"

"*If* we can get her started! When does she talk about anything else?"

For Mrs. Winters, instead of being comfortably fixed as Harry Winters had intended her to be, now had barely enough to live on, for which she could thank Tom Bonny.

So she came to dinner, and she talked. Her story was the same one I'd heard Bonny tell Mr. Latham, only Clara made it more vivid.

"Harry was hardly cold in his grave before that old vulture was after me. Coming up to the house and handing me that envelope with that little bit of gold wrapped up in tissue paper. Saying maybe I'd like to have it for sentimental reasons, since, just a few days before he died, Harry had dug it out of the mine with his pocketknife."

"Pocketknife?" Mr. Latham leaned forward tautly.

"Pocketknife," repeated Clara. "Because the mine was so rich all you had to do was go in there, take out your knife, and pry it out. The gold was in chunks, just like raisins in a cake."

"Raisins in a cake?" echoed Mr. Latham in a small, still voice.

"And besides the gold, there was a tunnel full of a lot of stuff the priests had hidden. And he showed me an old map and made me promise I wouldn't breathe a word about it; but he thought I'd like to know, for it was one of the last things Harry was doing."

"But," asked Mother, "didn't you wonder that Harry had never mentioned it to you?"

"Yes, I did, but Bonny, the old buzzard, said Harry didn't want to get my hopes up. And then it had to be such a secret, and of course you know how I talk. Well . . . What's the use of crying over spilt milk? Guess I've bored you all to death."

"On the contrary," Mr. Latham told her, "it's been intensely interesting. Intensely. I've always been fascinated by mines. When I was a little boy, there was an old miner, a forty-niner, who hung about my father's store. I used to listen to his stories by the hour, and I decided then that someday I was going to do some mining, too."

"All I can say is don't do it with Tom Bonny."

"I won't," he promised fervently.

"I could tell you plenty of stories about that one. Widows are his game. Widows, grieving their hearts out, and a little insurance money just come in. And he hangs around hotel lobbies and picks up tourists and fleeces them. You wouldn't believe it."

"Oh, yes, I would," Mr. Latham agreed sheepishly. "I could tell you a story about him myself."

But before he could unburden himself, there were heavy steps on the porch and three long rings of the doorbell.

"Uncle Brad!" cried Phillip. We children scrambled down from our chairs and ran to the door.

There he was, big and jovial and laughing, and grabbing all three of us for an enormous hug.

Uncle Brad wasn't our uncle, but that's what we called him. His name was Bradbury Watkins and he was an old, old friend of Father's.

Father introduced him to Mr. and Mrs. Latham—he

already knew Clara Winters—and I heard Father say under his breath to Mother, "This is sure going to look like a put-up job."

Uncle Brad pulled up a chair to the table, refusing food because he'd eaten downtown, and we children looked at him expectantly, for we could see his pockets were bulging as they always were when he came to see us.

"Well, how is everybody?" he asked noisily, for he was partially deaf and talked loudly enough to hear himself, which was too loud for everyone else.

We all said we were fine, and waited. So he said, "Well, well, well," and began slapping his pockets. "Seems to me I had some little thing. Wonder if I left it at the hotel? Nope, here it is." And he drew out a big bag of Mexican *panoche*—candy. We took it and thanked him and looked at the other bulges in his coat.

"Oh, yes. Maybe I've got something else." This time he drew out a box of chocolates. Then from another pocket he brought out three little Mexican lariats, from still another some Mexican dolls and three tiny Mexican serapes. By the time he'd gone through all his pockets the table was littered with presents and Mother said, "Honestly, Brad, you're spoiling those children."

"Haven't got any kids of my own," grinned Brad, "so why shouldn't I spoil them?"

"How's the mine, Brad?" said Clara, not noticing Father's negative signal.

"Still buying my beans."

Mr. Latham lifted his brows. "Are you a mining man?"

"Sort of," admitted Brad. "I've got a little hole in the

ground down in Sonora. I call it 'The Beanpot' because it pays for my beans."

He was still slapping his pockets although the bulges were gone. "Seems to me I had one other thing. Yep, here it is." He drew out a long white envelope. He waved it at us. "Now what do you think's in here?"

"Gold, of course," Mr. Latham put in coldly.

"Yes, but how did you know?" asked Brad. He reached into the envelope and drew out three folded tissues, and handed them over to us. "For a good girl. For a good boy. For another good boy."

When we unwrapped them, they turned out to be three little nuggets. We "oh'ed" and "ah'ed" over them delightedly and passed them around for the others to see.

"I presume," volunteered Mr. Latham, "you pried these out of the rock with your pocketknife."

"Pocketknife!" Brad roared with laughter. "Mister, that's placer gold. You get it out of a stream."

"And the gravel's so rich, I suppose it's more gold than gravel."

Brad guffawed again. "Mister, I wish that was true. I didn't even find them. I bought them off a Mexican. Guess those three nuggets represent a week's work. Slim pickings in those streams down there. Not much water most of the year, and when there is you can't pan much. I've bought all that's been picked up for the last 5 years. Don't think I've got over 10 or 12 ounces. Nope, I make mine out of 'The Beanpot.' I've got a little pay streak. She's thin, but so far she's steady, and I'm following her right along."

"And you haven't got any gold in chunks, like raisins in a cake?"

"Raisins? I don't hear too well . . ."

Clara gave a snort of laughter. "He thinks you're another Tom Bonny." And she was off on her tirade again, telling Brad all about her loss.

"The old sidewinder!" Brad swore. "Someone ought to string him up."

Mr. Latham was still looking suspicious. "Are you looking for someone to buy your mine, Mr. Watkins?"

"Listen, mister, nobody gets my little beanpot. What'd I do with the money? Just blow it in. Nope, I stay away from the promotion end. I've seen plenty of places where a little capital and a little work would mean a profit—maybe. It's the 'maybe' that holds me back. When it's other men's money I want a sure thing, and there's nothing sure in mining. Why, if I were after dough, there's an old dump not far from me . . . Gosh, she's rich! Someone could come down there and clean up. But me, I'm leaving it alone."

Mr. Latham suddenly relaxed. "Tell me about this old dump."

"Nothing to tell. They must of worked her in the eighties or nineties, got all the gold out then, but now the tailings are plenty rich."

"But," asked Mrs. Latham, "if all the gold was got out, how can it be rich now?"

"New processes. Rework the tailings and pick up the gold which they couldn't get thirty years ago. Like a broom that sweeps up a lot of dirt, but then along comes this newfangled vacuum cleaner and it gets up a whole lot more."

"Why, yes," beamed Mrs. Latham, "I see perfectly now."

"Where is this mine of yours and this dump?" Mr. Latham seemed eager.

"Two days from San José de Gracia. Two days by mule right up the side of a mountain. Come down and pay me a visit sometime."

"I'd like to."

"You're welcome any time," boomed Brad conventionally, not thinking that Mr. Latham was serious.

"But, look here," he protested, after Mr. Latham had at last convinced him he really did want to come, "you're not a mining man. If you're interested in the property don't waste your money coming yourself. Send an engineer and get a report from him."

"But that wouldn't be any fun for me."

"Oh, it's fun you're after. Sure, come along. You can take some samples from this El Tigre dump, see how they run."

"I'd like to send for James, my nephew. He's an engineer. We'll both come down."

"I'll go, too." Father's voice had that excited ring in it which I was starting to recognize whenever a "proposition" was in the offing.

"They certainly don't need you," protested Mother warningly.

"Maybe I want some fun, too," Father retorted.

"Well," Brad told Mr. Latham, "when your nephew comes, let me know. It takes a week for a letter to reach me. I'll arrange to have mules for you at San José."

At the end of January we went down to the train to meet James. He was a younger edition of his uncle, chubby and pink, and already a little bald, although he was only about thirty.

James's manner to us was decidedly *not* cordial. He oozed suspicion. To him we were all Tom Bonnys, birds of prey trying to get his uncle's money—money that one day should rightfully come to him and his sisters—into some worthless mining scheme.

He tried to talk his uncle out of going. When that failed, he urged him to take along an engineer.

"What did I send you to an engineering college for?"

"I'm a civil engineer, not a mining one, Uncle Eldred."

"You'll do to take samples."

So James went up to the university and interviewed professors in the department of mines. He talked to assayers and engineers in town. He got himself a book called *The Prospector's Handbook,* which he studied all the time, particularly a chapter entitled How Mines Are Salted.

While James pored over his handbook Mr. Latham had a perfectly elegant time buying an outfit. You would have thought he was going to be away for 6 months from all the things he had to have—all kinds of camping clothes, a tent, a sleeping bag, a large mosquito net, special gadgets for cooking, a long list of tinned food.

"You don't need all that stuff," advised Father. "We'll only be where we can't buy things for a couple of days. We'll get some grub at San José, and Brad will have plenty for us at the mine. We can live off the country as we go along."

"Eat those *tortillas* you were telling about, I suppose."

For Father had been pretty explicit about the *tortillas,* telling how the Indian women sat on the ground before their little fires, rolling out the dough on their thighs.

"No *tortillas* for me," said Mr. Latham. "I take my food with me."

"Oh, they don't all make them like that," grinned Father. "Most of them pat them out with their hands."

"With nice *clean* hands, too, no doubt. No, sir, not for me!"

Mr. Latham had a book, *The Perfect Camper,* or something like that, and he was learning what to do in any emergency. He said he could purify water by dumping ashes into it, and the next morning the ashes would have sunk to the bottom and carried down the impurities.

Father said that was fine but wouldn't it be simpler just to carry enough extra canteens?

Then Mr. Latham told us what he'd do in case of tarantula bite or scorpion bite or snake bite and his wife began to worry.

"Don't worry," Father told her. "I've never been bitten, and I only know personally one man who was. And it was in his own back yard while he was chopping wood. A rattler bit him right on the thumb, so he just took his ax and chopped off the end of his thumb quick and never had any ill effects. At least not from the bite. Of course the thumb bled a lot."

"Oh, but Eldred does so hate the sight of blood," Mrs. Latham flurried. "He'd never be able to cut off his thumb."

"All right, I'll chop it off for him," promised Father. "If he's bitten, just leave it to me."

James kept on reading about how mines were salted. Each mealtime he'd tell us some different way it could be done. One way was to fill shotgun shells with little gold nuggets instead of pellets and shoot them into the area to be tested.

"But," he warned, "I'll just remove a few inches of the surface before I start sampling."

"He sure thinks Brad and I are a couple of crooks," I heard Father complain to Mother later.

James read in his book how samples might be tampered with after they were taken, so he got some special canvas sacks with seals on them.

"See, after I've filled them, I lock them up," he told us. "What I've put in there is what's going to the assay office, not anything else."

"That's fine," agreed Father; "you can't be too careful."

Then James read that even in sealed-up sacks, gold in solution could be needled through the canvas into the samples by means of a hypodermic needle.

But he figured that one out, too. He got a large tin money box with a padlock on. "My samples go in there. Nobody's going to give them a shot of gold."

Next he wanted to know if Brad chewed tobacco.

"I think he does," said Father.

"That's another way they can fox you. A man chews up a lot of gold dust in his tobacco and then spits where you're taking samples."

"Now see here," began Father, "I'm getting tired . . ."

"You know," Mother interrupted hastily, "I think Mr. Latham's idea about sleeping caps is a fine one. They'll keep the dirt out of your hair."

So Father didn't say what he intended to. Instead he said, "There's lots of room to spit down there in Mexico, James. So if anyone comes up and spits where you're working, you've sure got a right to be suspicious."

"That's what I think," James agreed smugly.

At last word came from Brad that the mules would be at San José de Gracia on a certain date. So off the men went, with the car loaded down like an immigrant's wagon.

"We'll have to leave most of it with the car, in San José," Father told Mother. "We can't take it on the mules. But Latham had fun getting it."

We had a telegram from San José, and then we knew we wouldn't hear from them for about a week. Then came another telegram saying they were back in San José and then two days later the telegram from Nogales saying, "Have plenty of hot water ready."

I never saw three such tired and dirty humans. They looked happy though. Especially James.

Yes, they'd had a wonderful trip. No trouble of any kind, except one night they'd had what they thought was a little touch of ptomaine from some of their canned goods.

"The thing to do is live off the country," Mr. Latham admitted. "When we ate beans and *tortillas* we were all right."

We were all crazy to hear their story, but they said they had to have their baths first.

James did say, "The others think they've got something in that El Tigre dump, but look what I have." And he took out of his pocket a little bottle half filled with nuggets.

"Let me see! Let me see!" We children fought to get hold of it, but he snatched it away and put it back safely in his pocket.

He took one bathroom and Mr. Latham the other, so Father had to wait.

He sat down and pulled off his boots.

"Did James really find all those nuggets himself?" asked Mother.

"Sure he found them. He was meant to find them."

"What do you mean?"

"They were put in his pan. Our little friend James got salted good and proper."

Mother just stood there looking at him. "You didn't . . . I can't believe it." Her face was tragic.

"Don't look like that. We didn't do it. It was Miguel, Brad's foreman."

"But if you knew he did it. . . ."

"Afterward we knew. Brad got it out of Miguel."

"But . . ."

"Now let me tell it. You know how this greenhorn was going to be so careful and not get salted. Well, he starts out that way, making us all stand back when he takes his samples and giving Brad a dirty look every time he spits. So he gets his samples, seals them up in those bags, locks up the bags in that tin trunk of his, hangs the key on a string around his neck. His pocket isn't safe enough. One of us might be a pickpocket, see.

"All this time he's shooting off his mouth while old Latham isn't saying a word. Miguel gets the idea it's James who's the boss, not the old man.

"A big rain comes up and pretty soon there's water in the stream. Now James wants to do some panning.

"Miguel thinks it will help the deal if James finds some gold in his pan. He helps himself to Brad's nuggets, and every time James washes out a pan of gravel Miguel slips in a little gold."

"But didn't he see him?"

"You don't know Miguel. Of course James is ready to burst with excitement, and so is Latham. And I don't mind telling you I'm excited, too, but Brad tips me the wink, and I know something is wrong. Afterward we work on Miguel and get the truth out of him."

"And you didn't tell James?"

"No, we didn't. We told Latham. The old man nearly split his sides laughing. He says it's such a good joke on James he's willing to pay Brad for the gold. But he says not to tell James, because it would break his heart if he knew he'd been salted. As far as I'm concerned, I'd tell him and take the wind out of his sails."

All through dinner James had his bottle of gold right by his plate. He kept pouring the nuggets out on the tablecloth and turning them over with his finger. He wouldn't let any of us children touch them.

"There's a whole river full of gold down there," he said. "Why they want to bother with that old dump, I don't know."

"There isn't any river full of gold," Father told him. "You just happened to strike a little pocket. Besides there's no water there. You hit the only time the stream's been full in two years."

"Then build a dam to save the water when it does come. Get in a dredger. You can afford it when the gravel's that rich."

Put in his uncle drily, "When we send the engineer down, his report will tell whether the gold's in the stream or in the dump."

According to James panning gold was the most fun he'd ever had. After dinner he called for a pie pan, some dirt from the back yard, and told us to gather around the sink.

He put the dirt in the pan, threw in four or five of the nuggets and stirred them into the dirt.

"Now watch!" He ran some water into the pan and began rocking it back and forth, gradually letting the water and dirt slip over the edge. When almost all the dirt was gone there were the nuggets left behind in the fine silt.

James picked them out. "It does it every time. It's because the gold is heavy."

"I want to do it," demanded Oliver.

So we all took turns panning gold. We had to quit when Mother came out and said, gold or no gold, all that dirt going down the sink would stop it up and we'd have to find something else to play with.

The assayer's report on the tailing samples showed them to be very rich. Father and Mr. Latham paid an engineer to go down and make a professional report. His findings were so encouraging that Father, Brad, and Mr. Latham organized a little company, and they started to put up a mill to rework the tailings. However, before they really got under way they sold out to one of the big mining companies. They made a very nice thing out of it, a very nice thing, indeed.

"Now *please,*" Mother begged Father, "pay your debts and get straightened around."

Father said, yes, that was the thing to do.

But then he heard about the "Poso Verde," that wonderful cattle ranch that was going for a song. You know Father. He bought the cattle ranch.

I forgot to tell you about James and his river full of gold. The engineer of course reported that the stream showed color, nothing more. James was so sure he was wrong he was going to send another engineer down to make a second report. So they had to tell him what Miguel had done.

James canceled the engineer's trip, but he didn't really believe he'd been salted. He thought it was some dirty trick of Father and Brad to cheat him out of his gold.

CHAPTER 16

Man Hunt

WHEN the war came Mother and Eva May did their bit by stalking Mr. Allman.

Eva May was our cook, a cute little Negress who read detective stories. She even read them while she worked. Many a time I've seen her sitting at the kitchen table beating up a cake or shelling peas, while at the same time her eyes devoured the pages of a book propped up before her.

"So long as she does her work, I don't care how much she reads," said Mother.

Mr. Allman was the tenant in the garage house. He was a tall, sandy-haired man of about forty, quite nondescript-looking except for a scar across his cheek. From the first minute she saw him Eva May had a "feeling" about him.

She happened to be the only one at home when he arrived, directed to us by a real-estate agency, and she showed him the garage house.

"I'll take it," said Mr. Allman.

Eva May said he'd have to wait until Mother got home.

"But it's for rent, isn't it?"

"Yes, it's fo' rent, but you'll have to talk to Mrs. Drachman."

"There's nothing to talk about. The house is for rent. I want to rent it. So I shall move in."

And despite Eva May's protests he unpacked his car and took possession.

"What could I do?" Eva May asked Mother. "He say he's movin' in, and he moves. With boxes and boxes of something that rattles. I tell you I don' like that man. What's in those boxes, do you think?"

"I don't know, but I'll soon find out." And Mother went over to meet her new tenant.

When she came back she handed Eva May a small bright object. "A present for you, Eva May."

Eva May looked at it suspiciously. "What is it?"

"A can opener, that's what's in those boxes—can openers. He sells them from house to house."

"Don' look like a can opener to me."

"It is, though. Let's have some corn for lunch and we'll open up a can right now. See how it works. It's easy."

"Funny thing for a man to be selling," sniffed Eva May. "I like our own kind of can opener better."

"He seems all right, Eva May," Mother said. "I don't think he'll stay long, though. When he can't sell any more can openers, he'll move on."

We saw very little of Mr. Allman. He left early in the morning and came back late at night. Two or three times Mother sent Eva May over with a dish of something from our table, and it seemed strange to Eva May that when she knocked he did not open the door immediately but always asked who it was.

"Why for he lock his door anyway?" she demanded. "Nobody 'round here locks doors. And then he always say, 'Who's there?' before he opens it. Don' you think that's funny?"

"Now, Eva May, he's got a right to lock his door if he wants to."

"I got a feelin' about that man," Eva May insisted.

Mother might have had a feeling about him too, except that at this time her feelings were all concentrated on Father. Father had signed up for overseas service with the Red Cross, and it looked as if they were going to take him.

"But you're too old," wailed Mother; "you're forty-seven."

"Old!" snorted Father. "I'm in my prime. Your father was older than I when he went with the Confederates. A man has his duty to his country."

"You've no right to abandon your family like this."

"I'm not abandoning my family. There'll be something coming in from the laundry and the rents and you know you can always make a good living with your boarders."

"But I haven't any boarders now."

"Because you're expecting your brother and sister. That's the only reason."

"But suppose you get killed!"

"Then I've died for my country," said Father nobly, "and you'll have my life insurance."

But the Red Cross didn't take Father after all. Whether he was too old, too fat, or that they just didn't need him, I don't know. He was terribly disappointed, but of course Mother was pleased as could be.

"Don't feel badly," she comforted. "There'll be ways for you to help right here in Tucson."

Eva May thought she had a job for him the very next morning.

"Oh, Mr. Drachman," she cried to him excitedly at breakfast. "We got a German out there in that little house! You gotta do something!"

"What are you talking about?" growled Father, who was in no mood for dramatics.

"I mean Mr. Allman's a German. This morning when I come up the alley he's out there cranking his car. And the crank fly back and hit him in the arm and I hear what he say."

"What did he say?"

"It ain't what he say, it's what he talk in. It was *German!*"

"How do you know it was German?" asked Father.

"I work for a German lady once. This lady's husband, he swear a lot in German. I know how it sounds."

"Mr. Allman's supposed to be an American," said Mother. "Why would he swear in German?"

"That's jes' it," nodded Eva May, "when his arm hurt, he fergit and talk in German."

"Now look here," cautioned Father, "I might swear in Spanish."

"There *is* something funny about that man," Mother put in. "How can he have that big car and such nice clothes just from selling can openers?"

"A hustler will make a good living with a gadget like that," Father said. "Besides maybe he's got income from something else. How can you tell?"

"You know what," announced Eva May, "I think he's a spy! He go around to our forts and he say, 'Want to buy my can opener?' and that's the way he get inside and *learn* things."

"There are no forts around here, Eva May," soothed Father. "And if there were I don't think he'd get in with a can opener."

Eva May suddenly snapped her fingers. "That scar! He get that in a duel. In Germany they fight duels."

"Eva May, you read too many of those detective stories. How do you know it wasn't Swedish, Norwegian, Polish, or Russian he was swearing in?"

"It was German," Eva May insisted stubbornly.

"Well, suppose it was. Lots of good American citizens speak German." And Father went on downtown.

Mother of course had an extra key to the garage house and after a little while she said, "You can do things in wartime that you wouldn't do in peace."

"Yes, ma'am," agreed Eva May.

"We're going to go out there and look in that house."

They found nothing but a few clothes, some boxes of can openers and a large brown Manila envelope with about a hundred maps of Texas, New Mexico, and Arizona, and northern Mexico.

To both of them the finding of the maps was conclusive. Didn't spies always have maps?

Father was furious when Mother told him what she'd done. "You can be arrested, you know, for breaking into people's houses. Why shouldn't he have maps? He's traveling around the country, isn't he?"

"But why should he have maps of Mexico?"

"I have Mexican maps, haven't I?"

"But you've got your ranch down there."

"Maybe he's going to sell can openers to the Mexicans. Now don't you go into his house again."

"I think we ought to tell the police."

"What have you got to tell them—that a traveling salesman has some maps, and your servant heard him swear in what she *thinks* was German?"

It didn't sound like very much, and Mother decided to drop the matter.

But Eva May's active mind was figuring something out.

"Mrs. Drachman, there's one way fo' sure to know if he talk German."

"How?"

"If I say to him in German, quick and loud, 'Mr. Allman, you got a big black spider on yo' neck!' and then he slap his neck, then that show he know German."

"That's right," said Mother, "but can you say that in German?"

"Iffen I have the words. Can't Miss Rosemary find them for me at the university?"

So they enlisted my help. I went to the German professor and he wrote out the words in German and below them their phonetic pronunciation.

Eva May began practicing them, and all day long you'd hear her saying, "Achtung, Herr Allman, Sie haben eine schwarze grosse Spinne auf Ihrer Schulter."

Now the thing was to catch Mr. Allman in an unguarded moment. But we never saw him. He was gone before Eva May came to work and didn't get back until late at night.

"I'll ask him over for Sunday dinner," said Mother, and she wrote a little note and slipped it under his door.

"We won't tell Father and the boys about this," Mother said to me. "We'll just keep it to ourselves."

Father seemed a little surprised at Mr. Allman's presence on Sunday, but as he did with any guest, he put himself out to be nice to him.

Mother began to carve the chicken. Eva May was standing directly behind her.

Suddenly Eva May flung out her hand, pointing directly at Mr. Allman. "Achtung, Herr Allman," she cried excitedly, "Sie haben eine schwarze grosse Spinne auf Ihrer Schulter!"

Mr. Allman's hand started to go toward his neck. I'll swear it did! But then he checked it and said, "Is she talking to me? What is she saying?"

Father and Phillip and Oliver looked bewildered, and Mother and I tried to look the same.

"What's the matter with you, Eva May?" asked Mother severely. "What were you trying to say?"

Eva May shook her head from side to side. "I dunno. I think I'm crazy. I think I see a big black spider on Mr. Allman's neck."

"What language were you talking in?" asked Father pointedly.

"German. I used to know some German," answered Eva May meekly, but her eyes clicked with mine triumphantly as she went out to bring in the vegetables.

There was a little silence at the table which Mother broke with, "I think Eva May really is crazy sometimes."

"Maybe there are other crazy people in this house," commented Father drily.

Mr. Allman didn't stay long after dinner. He said he had to wash his car. As soon as he left Eva May came in.

"Did you see him?" she gloated. "He start to reach for his neck, and then he remember and stop himself."

"What *is* all this?" demanded Father.

The plot was revealed to him, and he snorted disgustedly, "Honestly, you two ought to join the secret service!"

Father wouldn't admit that Mr. Allman had started to slap his neck. "I saw him jump, but who wouldn't jump with Eva May yelling at him like that."

The next night Eva May came into the kitchen from taking out some garbage, and her eyes were popping. "Mrs. Drachman, I got another clue."

"Now what?"

"You remember how he clean his car yes'day afternoon?"

"Yes."

"He jes' drove up his car, and you know what . . . his car's all thick with dust."

"Well . . . ?"

"He don' get that dust 'round Tucson, jes' stopping at houses selling can openers. That man's *been* somewheres."

"Eva May," said Mother decisively, "tomorrow morning we're going to get in our car and follow him."

"Yes, ma'am!" And then after a moment, "But I can't drive, and you can't, either."

"I'll drive, Mother," I offered. "I've only got one class tomorrow morning and I haven't had a cut all semester."

"But won't he recognize us?" asked Mother. "And recognize the car?"

Said Eva May, "We gotta git ourselves another car

and dress ourselves up so he won't know us." Her face broke into a smile. "We'll use Jackson's car. I tell Jackson he got to walk to work tomorrow."

(Jackson was Eva May's husband, and his car was a dilapidated old Model T Ford.)

"And," continued Eva May, "les' pretend we're old Mexican women. We'll tie shawls over our heads and wear old clothes."

"But how are we going to do it, Mother?" I asked. "He usually goes about the time we're having breakfast. Unless you want to tell Father. . . ."

Mother decidedly did not want to tell Father, and for a while we were stumped.

"I know," said Mother, "we'll put the alarm clock an hour ahead. We'll have breakfast at seven instead of eight."

"That's a good idea," praised Eva May, "but you better fix his watch, too, in case he look at that."

"I'll set that ahead also," promised Mother.

The next morning Father kept looking at his watch and saying, "I keep feeling it's early. It certainly is dark outside."

"Doesn't seem dark to me," said Mother.

"Nor me either," I put in.

But Phillip and Oliver agreed with Father. They, too, thought it was dark.

"Where's my egg?" demanded Father. "What's the matter with Eva May this morning?"

Of course what Eva May was trying to do was get breakfast and at the same time keep an eye on the garage house, to see when Mr. Allman got up.

"Everything's okay," she said meaningly to Mother when she brought in the egg for Father.

"This egg isn't," grumbled Father; "you've hard-boiled it."

It seemed as if Father lingered over his breakfast forever that morning, but finally he left and the boys got off for high school.

"Man, man," cried Eva May, "I thought they'd never go. Now, we've got to hurry. He's jes' raised his shade."

We put on old coats that Mother had dug out of a trunk. We tied scarves around our heads. Mother had on a pair of dark glasses. We went out the front door and made a detour around the block to where Jackson had parked his old Model T. We got in it and waited, keeping our eyes on the alley where Mr. Allman would drive out. I started the motor to be ready.

Eva May giggled. "Mr. Drachman sure goin' to be mad when he get downtown and find out what time it is."

"And the boys," said Mother, "an hour early at high school."

"It's jes' lak you say. In wartime you gotta do certain things. You know," she went on excitedly, "if we ketch this spy, mebbe the gov'mint will give us a whole bunch of money. You'll split with me, won't you?" she demanded of Mother.

Mother promised. "If we get any money we'll split."

"There he goes!" cried Eva May.

With a loud snort and a bucking leap from the old Ford we were after him, following him up Third Street and then down Sixth Avenue. He was going like the wind, and it was hard for us to keep up with him. We passed through town and got into the residence section of south Sixth Avenue.

"Wonder when he's going to stop and start selling his can openers," said Mother.

"Don' look lak he gonna stop at all."

He kept on, with our Ford after him, until we were in the sparsely settled section across the railroad track.

Commented Mother, "He's not going to find many customers out here."

"That man ain't after customers," replied Eva May.

On and on we went. Traffic got less. Soon we were the

only two cars on the road. We were headed straight south.

"You know," said Mother, "I think he's going to Nogales."

"Sure he is. No other place for him to go."

Allman's car was getting farther and farther away from us.

"We can't keep up with him," I said, "not in this car."

"We might as well go home," Mother advised, "and when we do we're going through his things again. I don't care what your Father says."

We went back, and Mother got the key and we went into the little house again. This time we found nothing. No clothes, no boxes of can openers, no maps. Nothing.

"Why, he's left for good," cried Mother.

"Flew the coop!" gasped Eva May. "Bet he owes you rent money, too."

Mother thought for a moment. "No, he doesn't. His rent is paid for another week. It's very peculiar."

"Not peculiar," said Eva May. "We scared him with my German talk." She looked around. "He sure left everything clean. I won't hardly have to touch this place."

"Germans are clean people," agreed Mother. "That's one thing you can say of them. Well, I'm going to tell the police about this."

Just then we heard an "oo-hoo" outside. It was Mrs. Gibson, a friend of Mother's.

"I rang and rang the doorbell, and nobody answered so I came around to the back." She looked at us curiously, for we must have looked very queer, the three of us togged up in old coats and scarves. "What I came about is my uncle and aunt. They just got in this morning and I want to find them a little house. This wouldn't be vacant by any chance?"

"It certainly is," said Mother. "I'd love to have your aunt and uncle. It'll be ready in an hour."

When Mrs. Gibson left Mother went in and telephoned Father. What she told him impressed him enough so that he said he'd bring the United States marshal up to talk with her.

Mr. Hake was a hard-bitten ex-cowman, and he listened attentively while Mother, Eva May, and I told our stories. He gave a big guffaw when Mother came to the part about setting ahead the clock and Father's watch, but Father didn't think it was funny at all.

To Mother the most suspicious fact was that Mr. Allman had left without telling her good-by. "My people have always told me good-by," she insisted.

"Well," drawled Mr. Hake, "it's no crime if a tenant leaves without saying good-by, not when he doesn't owe you any money."

Said Father, "These women have got it all cooked up he's a German spy."

"He might be. He might not be. I'll phone my boys in Nogales and tell them to look out for him."

"If they's a reward for ketching him," began Eva May, "then I think . . ."

"We'll talk about that later, Eva May," Mother broke in.

"Anyway," Mr. Hake told Mother, "I'll look into it." And he complimented Mother and Eva May on their initiative. "These days we all got to have our eyes open."

"I think so, too," agreed Mother, giving Father a look.

"Well," said Mother, after Mr. Hake and Father had gone, "it's now up to the United States to do something about that man. Thank goodness we've seen the last of him."

We were in the midst of dinner that night when in burst Eva May wildly excited. She had to swallow two or three times before she could talk.

"He's back," she got out.

"Who's back?" asked Mother.

"What's the matter, Eva May," demanded Father; "have you seen another spy?"

"It's the same one. He's out there. He jes' drove up."

"Mr. Allman?" gasped Mother.

"Yes. He's out there. He's taking things out of his car."

Mother looked aghast while Father said, "Great jumping grasshoppers!"

"What'll I do?" cried Mother.

"You'd better get out there and do a lot of tall talking," advised Father.

"He's comin' in now," hissed Eva May from her vantage point at the door. She shrank back as he passed her to come in.

"There are some people in my house," he said to Mother.

"Yes," Mother got out. "Yes . . . yes, there are. I . . . I thought you'd gone away. You'd taken all your clothes."

Mr. Allman's eyes narrowed as she said this.

"I had to go into your house," Mother stumbled on.

"I had to see about something." A happy explanation struck her. "I'm going to have a carpenter up here to do some repairs. I wanted to see if there was anything to do in your house. When I saw all your things gone, I thought you'd gone, too. After all, isn't your rent up today?"

"Today? No, it's not until next week. The fifteenth."

"How stupid of me. Of course it's the fifteenth. Why did I think it was today?"

"I went down to Nogales today," Mr. Allman explained. "There was the possibility that I might stay down there. If I did I didn't want to have to come back for my clothes. I would have written you a letter."

There was something oddly defensive about his manner, as if he were apologizing to Mother.

"I'll tell those people they'll have to give you your house."

"No, don't do that. I am going on to Phoenix tomorrow. I will go to a hotel."

"That's certainly fine of you," said Father, opening his mouth for the first time. And to Mother, "Give him a check for the rent you owe him."

"I was just going to," said Mother, and she went to the sideboard drawer where she kept her checkbook and pen and ink.

Mother finished writing the check and handed it to Mr. Allman with the words, "I'm awfully sorry that this happened."

"It's all right. It doesn't make any difference. I'll say good-by now." He nodded to us all and then turned and went through the door so fast that Eva May, who was behind it listening, got bumped in the face.

"Well!" cried Father. "Well! You're a lucky woman to get out of that so easily. He might have put you in jail."

"Why on earth didn't he say something to me about staying in Nogales? Then this wouldn't have happened."

"Some people don't like to tell all their business and I guess he's one of them."

Muttered Eva May, "I still got my feeling about that man. Jes' 'cause he come back here don' mean he's not a spy."

It must have been a month later that Mother opened the paper, and there was a picture of Mr. Allman under the caption "German Agent Nabbed in El Paso." It was not the same name but, as Eva May said, "What difference do the name make? It's him, all right. Look at that scar."

Father said the scar might be a shadow, and he wasn't convinced.

As far as Mother and Eva May were concerned, it was the same man, and they both bemoaned the fact that the capture hadn't been made in Tucson.

"We'd have made ourselves some money," mourned Eva May, "or leastways got a medal."

CHAPTER 17

Here Come the Dudes

I CAN'T put my finger on the exact time that Tucson stopped being a sleepy little western town trying to be like California and became smart and swank and simply overrun with millionaires, ladies of title and fashion, celebrities of one kind or another.

It came so suddenly. We'd scarcely got our paving down and the new bus lines and changed from cesspools over to sewers, and here we were being written up in *Vogue* as a place to go when one was tired of the Riviera.

Where Tucson had had the most mediocre accommodations for tourists, now there were El Conquistador, the Pioneer, the Arizona Inn, all the Ranchos This and Ranchos That where the rich East could go western in a big way.

In private schools, newly built on the desert, heirs of Guggenheims, Westinghouses, Vanderbilts, Whitneys, and the like, acquired an education and a sun tan, and strolled about our streets in cowboy clothes and ten-gallon hats.

Where Harold Bell Wright had had the only desert home, now the foothills were covered with those sprawling adobe ranch houses—haciendas, they called them—with their gatehouses as big as the one we lived in. Such

fantastic stories about the people who lived in them! The woman who had her swimming pool dug three times, just couldn't make up her mind where she wanted it. Some other woman who'd sent to Chicago for her hairdresser to come out and give her a permanent. The So and So's, ordering a thousand dollars' worth of caviar, or was it champagne, for one party.

And the clothes that now came to the laundry! We used to go down and marvel at them. There was a woman who sent in her nightgowns to be dry cleaned. One pleated chiffon number that used to come in regularly took two men 3 hours to repleat it. Russ used to charge $5 for the job.

"Five dollars for cleaning a nightgown!" gasped Mother.

The laundry now went in for blocking Stetsons, cleaning leather jackets, fading blue jeans. The dudes would buy the levis and bring them in with the demand that they be made soft and faded right away.

"You know," said Mother, "we ought to buy up a lot of overalls and hang them in the sun all summer and then sell them at a profit in the winter."

"There's something in that," said Father. But we never did.

There was a great drive on for atmosphere. The rodeo became the event of the year. A curio shop was on every corner, or a Mexican restaurant. Even the streets were to be renamed. Congress Street was to get back its original name, El Calle del Indio Triste.

"Street of the Sad Indian!" snorted Father. "What's the matter with Congress Street?" Then somebody had the idea other streets should be named for saints. Drachman Street was to become St. Nicodemus Street.

Father was terribly upset. "It's a disgrace!" he cried. "What did St. Nicodemus ever do for Tucson?"

But the movement died down, and the streets were not renamed. Congress is still Congress Street and so is Drachman.

Some tourists went down on Meyer Street and lived

in the old adobe houses there, and it was all very quaint. Now, too, the smart thing was to have a cactus garden, and instead of digging up the greasewood and other desert flora, you went out and brought in more.

"Don't put any cactus in our garden," ordered Father. "I don't want to get full of thorns."

Father was pretty scornful of all this atmosphere until he became atmosphere himself. It started with an invitation from a group called The All States Club. They asked Father to tell them about old Tucson at one of their meetings. Father was supposed to talk for about 15 minutes. They kept him talking for 2 hours.

After that he spoke at other places—at the University Assembly, at an Elks' Convention, at church socials. He was now one of the Old Pioneers and took to wearing a big Stetson hat. He got hold of some old pictures of the early days in Tucson, and a photographer threw them on a screen while he talked about them. There were always some other Old Pioneers in the hall, and they would shout out to Father, "No, you're wrong. That's not old Pete Morse; that's old Jake Abbot." And they and Father would argue back and forth to the great delight of the audience.

Father thought he should write up the story of his life and did write some of it. It was pretty stilted. Father got self-conscious when he took his pen in hand. His stories were to be told, not written.

I was the writer in the family. By arrangement with the tenant of the garage house, I used it during the day as my study, and was busy writing love stories, with no success whatever.

The boys, of course, were still in college.

With the coming of the dudes it became hard to get servants, especially in the winter. So now we had Della again, with Ocky of course hovering in the background.

Eva May now worked for the Patmores, a fabulously wealthy family who had a mansion in the foothills.

She used to come by to see us on her day off. Usually she had half a turkey or large end of ham roast under her arm.

"Eva May," scolded Mother, "don't tell me you've become a toter."

"No, ma'am, I ain't a toter. I jes' takes what would go in the garbage."

It seemed that on the Patmore table no meat ever came back the second time. No leftovers for them. Eva May was the only servant who lived off the place, so she got the leavings.

"But what do you do with them?" asked Mother.

"I sell them around to my neighbors. I'm making me some extra money."

"I'll buy that ham from you," offered Mother. "I can see it's just like the ones they made in Virginia."

But Father was furious when she told him. "I'm not eating any rich people's leavings," he stormed.

Eva May got other loot from the Patmores—silk stockings with the tiniest of snags in them, a $175 Hickson suit with just one cigarette hole in it, bottles of expensive perfume that Mrs. Patmore was tired of.

"It's wicked for people to waste money like that," said Mother.

"They waste a lot of it at the laundry, too," Father told her. "Russ says their bill is about $200 a month.

They never wear anything twice without having it cleaned."

Then one day Eva May came in all excited. "Mrs. Drachman, I've fixed it so you can make a whole pile o' money."

"Is it honest?" asked Mother.

"It's honest, all right, and it's easy."

"Tell me."

"Well, you room and board old lady Moon—she's Mrs. Patmore's mother—and the old lady's maid and chauffeur."

"Go 'long, Eva May, people like that won't want to stay in my house. They'll stay at the Inn or the Conquistador."

"She's been at the Conquistador, las' year. The Patmores, they don' want her there no mo'."

"Why don't they?"

"Because . . . the old lady drinks."

"Drinks?"

"Yes, ma'am. She likes her bottle, and she has the bellboys git it for her. That's why the Patmores, they don' want her in a hotel. They want her in some private home. They don' care what they pay. You can charge them a whole lot of money."

"Now, Eva May, I couldn't have a drunkard in my house."

"But in your house she won't git no liquor."

"And think of the example for my children."

"Now, Mrs. Drachman, you raised your chillun right. They won't start drinking jes' 'cause they see an old lady drink."

"I don't think my husband would let me."

Eva May laughed. "When I work for you, you don' ask will my husband let me do something. You jes' do what you want."

"Why don't the Patmores have her with them?" demanded Mother. "They have that big house and all those guest cottages."

Eva May shrugged her shoulders. "I dunno, but they don' want her; they want her far away. Well, I tol' Mr. Patmore about you. He says he's comin' to see you. If he do . . ." Eva May now got to her point. "If he do, and you take the old lady, will you give me a commission like they do in the real-estate office?"

"If I take her," promised Mother, "you'll have a commission."

Mother didn't put much credit in Eva May's story because she couldn't believe any Patmore connection would be satisfied with our accommodations. So she was quite surprised two or three days later when Mr. and Mrs. Patmore came to see her. Mrs. Patmore was an extremely beautiful creature with a soft manner and big cow eyes, who let her husband do all the talking.

Mr. Patmore was small and dynamic and decisive. He took one look at the living room, another at Mother and said, "Fine! I can see you're just the person to handle this situation. There will have to be another bed in the room, of course. The maid has to sleep beside her. Since my mother-in-law broke her hip she can't turn over by herself. Oh, yes, she wears a steel brace during the day, so see that all your rugs are anchored securely. Now about the chauffeur, Eva May said there was a little house in the rear that he could have."

"But that's rented," protested Mother.

"Ask the tenants to move, please. I'll pay 3 months' rent for them somewhere else. Now Eva May said you had no liquor on the place. That's important. You have no liquor?" he demanded of Mother directly.

"No liquor, but . . .

"That's terribly important. My mother-in-law has an unfortunate weakness when it comes to liquor. Somehow in a hotel she always manages to get hold of it. And then it is most embarrassing . . . most embarrassing. Forgive me, my dear," he said to his wife, "but you know it is true."

Mrs. Patmore nodded sadly. "She yodels."

"Yodels!" cried Mother.

"You might as well know the whole truth," Mr. Patmore continued. "My mother-in-law was formerly in vaudeville . . . as a yodeler. I believe she called herself the national yodeling champion. Did you ever hear her —Milly Moon?"

Mother shook her head.

"When she is not herself, she yodels." He shook his head. "I would pay for her to stay anywhere in the world, but once a year she wishes to come out to see us."

"But naturally," said Mother, "she wants to see her daughter and grandchildren."

"Naturally, naturally. But it makes it very difficult for all of us. Now may I have your price for the three of them, for about 3 months, I think?"

Mother hadn't even decided to take them and started to say as much when Mr. Patmore broke in, "I realize the conditions are unusual and difficult, and you should be remunerated accordingly. I am prepared to offer you . . ." And he mentioned a sum that made Mother gasp.

As she said afterward, "It was all that money. I couldn't think straight."

"Come, come," said Mr. Patmore, as Mother sat there staring at him, "will that be enough?"

Gulped Mother, "Quite enough, but I . . ."

"Fine! Then it's all arranged. Oh . . . one other item. She likes to make her own cold cream. Why, I don't know, but she always has. She uses lard and lanolin. It seems to make quite a mess. Last year she went out and made it in the hotel kitchen. The chef was going to leave. So once a month could she make cold cream in your kitchen?"

"She can make the cold cream, all right . . ."

Mr. Patmore rose to his feet. "If you'll have the tenants out of the little house by Saturday. The chauffeur is driving out. Mother and the maid will arrive by train on Monday. The chauffeur and the maid are married. Vince is their name, Mr. and Mrs. Vince. We are most lucky to get them. English servants, best in the world. They worked for Lord and Lady Leffing. Like tea in the afternoon, though. No difficulty about a cup of tea for them, is there?"

"Tea is easy, but . . ."

"Fine! Fine! All this meets with your approval, my dear?" he questioned his wife.

Mrs. Patmore smiled sweetly and said it did.

"Then I'll write a check for the first month." He drew out his book, made a few quick squiggles and handed the check to Mother. "How much is the rent on the little house in the rear?"

"Thirty-five dollars," answered Mother, staring unbelievingly at the piece of paper in her hand.

Mr. Patmore made some more squiggles. "Here is the 3 months' rent for the tenants. I think that is all, then. Can you think of anything else, my dear?"

Mrs. Patmore couldn't think of anything else.

They bade us good-by and were gone in their big limousine before we'd come out of our daze.

"What have we got into?" Mother said at last.

"I don't know, Mother, but I'm afraid it's something."

Mother stared at the check. "To think of people wasting their money like this."

"They might as well waste it on us as on anybody else."

"What will your father say?"

"He'll have a fit, and then he'll want to borrow the money."

Mother laughed. "Well, let's go tell Della."

We went into the kitchen.

"Della," Mother said, "I've raised your wages. We've taken on a yodeler."

As so often happened when Mother had a surprise for Father, he also had one for her. That night he got his surprise in first.

"I'm going to make a trip to Louisiana. There are some wonderful oil wells down there."

"Oil wells!" cried Mother. "That was one thing you hadn't gone into. Well, it's a good thing I've got a boarder who's paying me a lot of money."

"Who have you got?"

"Mr. Patmore's mother-in-law."

Father thought she was joking. "Why not Rockefeller's mother-in-law?"

"It's the truth. Mrs. Moon—that's Mrs. Patmore's mother—*and* her maid, *and* her chauffeur are going to stay here!"

But when she told him the whole story he burst out with, "What do you think you're running, a Keeley cure place? Suppose she has delirium tremens, sees pink elephants!" But he couldn't help being impressed by the Patmore connection and the size of the Patmore check.

"What are you going to do with your money? Want to buy some of this oil stock?"

"I do *not!*"

"No need to take my head off. I was just asking. You'll be sorry when those wells come in."

Vince, the chauffeur, arrived on Saturday, driving up in a big limousine. He was a harassed-looking little cockney who seemed most anxious to explain to us just why he was working for Mrs. Moon.

"Things are very hard in England now, ma'am, very hard. In England we couldn't get what Mr. Patmore pays us, not by half. Half! Not by one quarter. We came over with Lord and Lady Leffing. But after he died Lady L. knew she couldn't keep us, not with the death duties and all. So when Mr. Patmore offered us this position, and at such a salary, ma'am, what could we do but take it."

"Of course," said Mother hurriedly, feeling she shouldn't be talking this way to a future boarder's servant.

"I must say the old lady's difficult, ma'am. And when

she gets hold of liquor . . ." He shook his head. "It's 'orrible, that's what it is."

"Well, she won't get any liquor here."

"I hope not, ma'am, but she's tricky, very tricky. Have you seen her, ma'am?"

"No, I never have."

"She's . . . she's . . . Well, ma'am, you'll see her."

She was arriving Monday afternoon. I'd closed up my typewriter and was in the parlor with Mother. Della was hovering about. Even Ocky was sitting on the coping outside.

"Here they are, Mother!"

Two big limousines had driven up. Vince and his wife—a little wisp of a thing—got out of one car and began taking out the bags. From the other the Patmore chauffeur helped down Mrs. Patmore and . . . Mrs. Moon.

We'd speculated on what she'd be like. We thought we were prepared, but we weren't. No one could have imagined her. She was a perfectly preposterous-looking creature!

She was half Sarah Bernhardt, half Apple Annie, a short top-heavy woman, starting with an enormous wig, black and frowzy and much too large for her, then an enormous bosom bedecked with strings of beads and brooches, and then suddenly tapering down like a seal to unbelievably tiny feet. Powder and rouge lay on her face like a mask. Painted eyebrows, mascaraed lashes, painted lips, and gleaming false teeth completed the picture.

As she came up the porch, her steel brace clumping

noisily, we could see that her face was contorted with fury. She had expected to go to the hotel. Her mouth no doubt was all fixed for the drink some bribed bellboy would provide for her. But instead she was coming to us.

"So you run this private asylum, do you?" she shouted at Mother when Mrs. Patmore tried to introduce her.

"Please, Mother," Mrs. Patmore begged. "Come see what a nice room you have."

"Nice room!" she snorted. "It's a jail, that's what I'd call it. Who are you?" she demanded of Della, who was in there pretending to straighten the bed. "One of the keepers, I suppose."

Della just stared at her, not believing her eyes.

"Can't you talk? Oh, well, one more won't matter. I already have two. Those!" With a contemptuous gesture she indicated the Vinces, who were now carrying in the bags. Mrs. Vince looked ready to drop.

"If there's anything you want," offered Mother coldly, in her best landlady manner.

Mrs. Moon turned on her. "Want! What I want is not to be in this hole. But what good does that do me? When you're old and you haven't any money you're pushed around. You do what other people want."

Said Mrs. Patmore patiently, "You're coming out to our place for dinner, Mother. The children want to see you. So we'll go now and Mrs. Vince will have everything unpacked for you."

To Mother she said, "We'll send her back about eight o'clock."

The old woman laughed a raucous laugh. "Eight o'clock! They can't stand me any longer." She thumped out beside her daughter, looking like a crippled bird of prey.

Little Mrs. Vince collapsed into a chair.

"Buck up now, Maudie," urged her husband. "Can't flop now."

"Ever since New York," she moaned, "cooped up in a stateroom with *her!*"

"What you need, Maudie, is a nice cup of tea."

"We'll get it for you," said Mother.

As Mother measured out the tea, she said to me, "I've made a terrible mistake. But I haven't cashed his check. I'm going to give it back to him and tell him she can't stay here."

"But you can't do that," protested Father, when she told him at dinner. "You've made a bargain with Patmore. You can't break it for no reason."

"For no reason! If you could see her!"

"You say she wears a wig, she's painted. You can't turn her out because of that."

"She asked me if I kept an asylum. She said our house was a jail, a hole."

"Oh," soothed Father, "she was probably worn out from her trip. Now don't do anything for a few days anyway."

After dinner Father had to go downtown for an appointment at the office, and Phillip and Oliver went up to the S.A.E. house for some fraternity business.

A little after eight Vince brought in Mrs. Moon.

"Did you have a nice dinner?" asked Mother politely.

"Nice dinner! No food's good without a drink. Will you give me one?"

"I'm sorry. We have no liquor in the house."

With a disappointed grunt Mrs. Moon swished into her room.

We heard her thumping about, berating Mrs. Vince in a loud voice. Then there was a sharp cry and the words, "Damn, clumsy fool!" Evidently the brace was being taken off. Then after a little while Mrs. Vince opened the door and said to us,

"Begging your pardon, but would you like to come and see Mrs. Moon's hair?"

"Hair?" asked Mother. "Did you say hair?"

"Hair, ma'am. She's very proud of her hair. She'd like you to see it."

Wonderingly, we went in. There before the mirror of the vanity sat Mrs. Moon covered in her hair. What we had thought was a wig was her very own hair. I've never seen so much hair. As she sat there it dragged on the floor.

"Did you ever see anything like this?" demanded Mrs. Moon. We admitted we never had.

"And you never will," she gloated. "I'm the only one in the world with hair like this. And because she's too lazy to brush it, this stupid fool wants me to cut it off."

"No, ma'am, but because I think it gives you those headaches."

"Hair like this is worth a few headaches." She ran her hands through it. Then to us, "Sit down. Sit down. You can watch it being brushed."

Neither of us thinking of any way to get out of it, meekly we sat down.

With long, gentle strokes Mrs. Vince began brushing

while the old lady started counting. "One, two, three, four . . ."

At the end of a hundred strokes Mrs. Moon turned away from the glass and said to us, "You may go now. Tomorrow night come in again."

Meekly we bade her good night and went out.

"Mother," I said, "you don't suppose we've got to watch her hair brushed every night!"

"I haven't cashed that check yet."

"Of course," I admitted, "it's an easy way to earn money, just watching her hair being brushed."

"And Eva May expects a commission," added Mother.

"And you've raised Della's wages."

"Poor old thing! It must be awful to be old and not have your children love you."

For a minute we felt sorry for her, and then we heard her scream, "You ——!" It was a word that had always meant soap in our mouths when we'd used it as children.

"You see," said Mother. "We can't have that in the house."

"No," I agreed.

We went to bed, and after I'd been there awhile I heard the light snap on in the dining room and someone rummaging around in there. I thought it was Mother and paid no attention to it. Then the rummaging stopped, and the light was turned off. I must have been asleep for a half hour or so when I heard the most unearthly noises coming from Mrs. Moon's room. It wasn't screaming or calling or singing. It was . . . yes, that's what it was . . . it was yodeling!

Mother came rushing in from the porch. "What can it be?"

"She's yodeling, Mother."

"But she mustn't do that. She'll wake all the neighbors."

We got into our robes and knocked at the living room door. White-faced Mrs. Vince opened it. Mrs. Moon was sitting up in bed, her head thrown back, letting out those unearthly yodels.

Mrs. Vince had an empty brandy bottle in her hand.

"But, ma'am, where did she get it? I was in the bathroom having my bath, and when I came out she was drinking the last of it."

Mother took the bottle. "My heavens! My heavens!"

"Your fruitcake brandy," I cried.

"But it was in the sideboard, away in the back. I've had it 5 years. Uncle Brad brought it to me from Nogales."

"Oh, ma'am, you said you had no liquor on the place!"

"I'd forgotten about this. I use it only once a year."

"I heard her, Mother. I thought it was you."

"But how did she know it was in there?" demanded Mother.

"A sideboard's a likely place to look, ma'am. How much was in the bottle?"

"It was about half full."

Mrs. Vince shook her head. "We're in for trouble, I'm afraid."

Mrs. Moon stopped yodeling. "I'm going to get up. Vince! Vince! Put on my brace."

"Please, ma'am, stay in bed."

"My brace, you ——! I've already been up once without it. Do you want me to fall and break my hip again?"

Hastily Mrs. Vince hitched on the brace, wrapped a robe around her. She thumped over to Mother.

"You never saw me on the stage, did you?"

"No, I didn't."

"You missed a lot then. I was *good!*" She lurched toward me. "And didn't you see me?"

"No," I said, shrinking away from her. It was my first

experience with anyone who was roaring drunk, and I was terrified.

"You didn't see my act where the orchestra leader gives me his drum and I kick a hole in it?"

"I didn't see you."

"Why, here's the drum," she cried, her eye lighting on a tin wastebasket by the bureau. Quick as a flash she drew back her foot and gave it a tremendous kick. It sailed through the door and into the entrance hall.

With a raucous cry she clumped after it, her two long braids of hair flying out behind her. "Get it next time!"

"Don't do that," ordered Mother. "You'll break something."

"Oh, ma'am, let her have it or she'll do something worse."

Round and round the room she went kicking the wastebasket, which went banging into the furniture. "What's the matter with this — drum?"

"Won't you yodel for us?" cried Mrs. Vince, trying to distract her. "The ladies would like to hear you yodel. Come, stand here by the piano and do it for them."

Like a sleepwalker she came over to the piano. Clutching at it for support she began to yodel again.

"You know, ma'am, when she's like this, the best thing to do is to give her more liquor and put her out."

"But there isn't another drop on the place."

"Can't we get some?"

"I don't know where." (It was prohibition then and alcohol was not to be purchased, as now, at the corner drugstore.)

Mrs. Moon's face was a reddish-purple color. Her eyes were bulging.

"Oh, ma'am, I don't know what to do. She looks 'orrible. I'll call my husband; you watch her."

"I'll call him," I offered quickly, "and *you* watch her."

"And phone your Father to come home, too," said Mother.

Mr. Vince said he'd dress and come right over. A few minutes later he came in the back way at the same time that Father was coming in the front.

"What in God's name?" gasped Father as he stared at the apparition by the piano.

At the same moment Phillip and Oliver came in from their fraternity meeting, and they, too, stared in horror.

Mrs. Moon beckoned grandly to them. "Come in. Come in. Plenty of seats down front. Sit down so people can see. SIT DOWN!" she roared at them.

As if hypnotized, they sat down, as did the rest of us.

"Now, as a special encore, I will do the echo song for you."

The room shook with the volume of her voice, and then she did the echo. For all she was an old woman and drunk as a lord, you could tell that once she had been very, very good.

She finished and stood there waiting. "Clap, you ——!"

We clapped.

Bowing grandly, she backed off an imaginary stage and sank on the davenport muttering to herself.

"Where did she get it?" cried Father.

"My fruitcake brandy. She found it after we went to bed."

"We must get some more and put her out, sir," said Mrs. Vince.

"But I don't know a bootlegger. I haven't the slightest idea where to get liquor."

My two brothers, looking sheepish, said maybe they knew where they could get some.

"See here," said Father, getting his wits together, "we're not giving her any bootleg poison. Call Patmore and have him bring a doctor. She looks pretty bad to me."

"Oh, sir, do we have to tell Mr. Patmore? He'll be very angry. . . ."

"I don't care if he's angry or not. This is his responsibility."

The chauffeur went to call him. Mrs. Moon now stood up and began to sing us bits from *Pinafore*.

Vince came back. "He's coming right away. He hadn't gone to bed."

"Did you tell him to bring a doctor?"

"I did, sir."

Patmore must have burned up the roads, for it seemed as if it were only a few minutes before he and the doctor were there.

When he came in Mrs. Moon had started kicking the wastebasket again.

"I thought you didn't have any liquor in your house," Mr. Patmore flung at Mother. Then to the doctor, "All right, all right. I'll get her into bed. I've done this before."

He took a bottle out of his pocket and waved it before Mrs. Moon's bulging eyes. "Come on, Mother. Get back into bed and I'll fix you a nightcap." Holding the bottle just out of her reach he backed into her room. She followed him. The doctor went in, too, and Mrs. Vince.

As the door shut, the chauffeur let out a big sigh. "She's bad, ain't she?"

"What will they do to her?" asked Father.

"Oh, she'll have another drink, only the doctor will put something in it to knock her out quick. She'll sleep till tomorrow afternoon. Then we'll have to watch her more careful-like."

"We're not watching her here," stated Father firmly, "because she isn't going to be here. I'll tell Patmore he'll have to take her away tomorrow."

But he didn't have to tell him, for when Mr. Patmore came out he started right in talking. "I know, I know. It was a mistake to bring her here. She needs to be in a sanitarium, and tomorrow that's where she's going. Now I contracted for her to stay 3 months and I'm perfectly willing . . ."

"Heavens, no!" cried Mother, managing to break in. "I haven't even cashed the check you gave me, and I'm going to give it back to you."

But Mr. Patmore wouldn't hear of that. "We've caused you a lot of trouble. We've made you move the tenants out of the little house. I insist you keep the check."

And they argued back and forth with Mother trying to give it to him and Mr. Patmore refusing.

Finally Mr. Patmore won, and Mother kept the check.

When he and the doctor had departed she said to us, "That's the most money for the least work I've ever done."

"I wouldn't trade all his money for what he's got in there," said Father, nodding toward the living room.

"Nor I," agreed Mother.

CHAPTER 18

Mother Retires—Almost

PHILLIP was the first one of us to get married, and to a boarder, at that. Only they were practically engaged before she became a boarder.

Betty Whittledge was an apple-cheeked girl from Kentucky with an irresistible Southern accent. Her father, an Army doctor, was at a station in Texas, and Betty had come to Tucson for her last year at the university. She was a Pi Phi and lived at the house. Phillip had an immediate and enormous crush on her, and at Christmas vacation, because the Fort was quarantined with some contagious disease, Betty didn't go to her parents but came to visit us.

She shared my room and luxuriated in having a whole bed to herself and a whole bureau and half a closet. The Pi Phi house was terribly crowded just then, and poor Betty was in a room with five other girls and on the sleeping porch had to sleep in the top part of a very narrow double-decker bed.

"Ah tell you," she drawled, "Ah don't dare turn ovah for feah Ah'll fall out."

When it came time for her to go she said, "Ah certainly do hate to leave you-all."

"Why do you?" asked Mother. "Why don't you stay on here with us?"

So Betty wrote to her parents, got permission from the Dean of Women to live off the campus, and moved in with us. Mother charged her $35 a month.

Betty put on Phillip's S.A.E. pin, and they said they were engaged. We didn't take them seriously. Phillip after all had just turned twenty and had another year in school.

Betty graduated and next fall came back to teach school. She stayed with us again. Phillip managed to keep up his grades and do his courting, too. He already had a job waiting for him in a printing company. In June he and Betty were married.

Mother gave back to Betty all the board money she'd paid her. "I've been saving this up for you. You can use it for furniture or anything else you like."

Father gave them an equal amount for their honeymoon. "Blow it in, kids."

They were supposed to be away at the coast for two weeks, but they came back in one.

Said Betty, "Ah got to thinking how much moah furniture we could have if we had less honeymoon."

They were going to have a house three blocks from us. Continued Betty, "Ah got anothah bedroom set. In case we want to rent our front bedroom."

She was a girl after Mother's own heart.

Oliver was the next to go. Alice West, a little redhead from Phoenix, had intrigued his heart. She was a Junior at the university. Oliver would have been a Junior, too, if he hadn't flunked out. Not because he wasn't smart—I really think Oliver has more brains than any of us—but because he wouldn't study. Oliver had a job in a wholesale grocery company and was saving his money for the time when Alice would get through school. But they couldn't wait. When school was out that year they eloped to Los Angeles.

"Now why did those crazy kids do that?" asked Mother.

"Well," philosophized Father, "at least we like the girl."

But Alice's family were very much upset about it. They had sacrificed a lot to send her to college, and now they thought she would have to stop.

Mother rose to the occasion. "Of course she isn't going to stop school. Betty stayed with us and she can, too. She can go on and get her degree."

Father said, "I gave Phillip and Betty a honeymoon, so I'll give you what I gave them."

Oliver was all for going back to the coast for a few more days of holiday. "I think I can fix it at the office."

"We'll do no such thing," insisted the redhead severely, who, for all she looked like a cute little flapper, was very practical. "We'll save that money for our house."

Again Mother had a daughter-in-law she could approve of.

I still lingered on the family tree. Two or three lads I'd marked out for my own had left me in the lurch.

"They aren't the ones for you," Mother tried to comfort me. "I never did think any of them were meant for you. When the right one comes along you'll know it."

I didn't believe her and resigned myself to being an old maid.

Yet Cupid in the person of fat old Mr. Ferry was already in the garage house. Mr. Ferry, a once extremely successful playwright, now lived on the income from a small trust fund and on memories of past glories.

"I've got a friend coming out to visit me," he told me one day. "He's a writer, too, writes westerns, so he thinks he ought to see something of the West. John Winchcombe-Taylor is his name. He's an Englishman, fought in the last war. You'll like him."

I wasn't enthusiastic. I visualized him fat and middle-aged like Mr. Ferry, probably with a limp from some old wound.

I was utterly unprepared for the slim, blond man—he looked twenty-five, although actually he was ten years older—Mr. Ferry introduced me to a week later. I was unprepared, too, for the sudden blinding realization: "But here he is; this is the one!"

Being English and conservative, it took John a little longer to grasp the situation. In fact it was 3 weeks to the day before he got around to proposing.

Mother gave a tea to announce the engagement. We decided on Mexican refreshments, to have a drink made of coffee, cocoa, and whipped cream, and to serve with this some delicious little Mexican cakes called *pastillas*.

Unfortunately the two old Mexican women who were making the *pastillas* for us misunderstood our order and, instead of sending us the sixteen dozen as we'd asked for, sent us *sixty* dozen. We were swamped with little cakes. Of course we couldn't make the Salazar sisters take them back, even though it was their mistake.

"Never mind," said Mother, "we'll sell them to our friends."

I'm sure she didn't intend to sell them at the tea, but when guests began to "oh" and "ah" about how good they were and ask where they could get some, Mother reasoned she might as well start her sales immediately.

She brought out some paper bags, and, in between greeting guests and receiving congratulations, she counted out pastries and made change.

I noticed my friends going out with paper bags in their hands and caught Betty's eye.

She and Alice wandered over to where I stood at the door. "Mothah's selling the refreshments," Betty giggled in my ear.

All three of us laughed. It struck us as funny. It was so like Mother—and really quite sensible. After all, the guests wanted the cakes, Mother wanted to sell them. Why not make the transaction right then and there?

But my English fiancé when I told him about it, was *not* amused. Selling food to guests! It struck him as in the worst of taste, and I suppose it was. He was appalled.

Poor John! He has never quite got used to the family; nor, I must admit, has the family got used to him.

But as Mother always says, "Well, my dear, if he suits you, that's all that matters."

To John his home was his castle, not a place to be shared with others. When lean times came as they do to any writer, we lived on less by ourselves; we didn't take in roomers and boarders.

Mother couldn't understand this.

"But you've got that extra bedroom. At least you could rent that, even if you didn't give board."

I talked to John again.

"You can have a roomer if you like," he said evenly, "but not me, too. So choose."

"It's a hard choice, honey, but I'll take you."

Mother couldn't quite forgive him for this attitude.

"Your Father and I took in boarders. Phil and Betty rented their room. Alice and Oliver would have probably done it, too, if they hadn't had Jim and Anne so soon. Does he think he's any better than we are?"

"Of course not, Mother, but he has different ideas. Besides, his business is different. He's home all day. Father and the boys go out to work."

"Well," said Mother, "it's none of my business. I guess I'll let you run your house the way you want to, and I'll run mine."

But when from time to time she had to turn people away because she didn't have room, it irked her dreadfully. "Such a nice couple came to me. It would have been so convenient if they had roomed at your house and taken their meals with me."

Remarked John, "What extraordinary energy your mother has! It's not enough to have her own house full of people. She wants to make an annex out of ours."

Mother's being so busy with boarders at least solved one problem for us children. We didn't have to worry about our aged parents left lonely and forlorn in the old homestead. For the old homestead was jam-packed with boarders. Father and Mother were so busy with all the people on the place it was hard to get a date with them.

Yes, they wanted to see us, but they were going down to Nogales with some of the boarders or taking them to the rodeo, or they had a bridge tournament on or a picnic out in the country.

And then the end of the world came. Father died. Hale and hearty one day, giving his "Old Tucson" talk at the Rotary Club, and lying so still and quiet the next.

"But I was going to go first," Mother kept saying in tragic bewilderment.

It was October. No boarders had arrived yet although several were coming.

All of us—Mother and we children—decided that Mother should rent the big house, so full of memories and necessitating so much work to keep up, and go into the little garage house. How stupid we were. As if any adjustment weren't easier to make in one's accustomed surroundings, as if work weren't the only medicine for sorrow.

But we could see that with what Father had left her and with his insurance to pay off the debts, she was going to be on that street he'd talked about all his life—Easy Street. So why should she take in boarders? And without boarders why should she stay in the big house?

Mrs. Long rented it for a guest house and Mother began the sad task of sorting out the accumulations of a lifetime. She couldn't bear to throw anything away, and down into the cellar or up into the attic went beloved but useless objects as well as such trash as old bottles, old tennis shoes with the soles out, handleless cups, broken picture frames, the half a dictionary we children had sat on as babies.

Mrs. Long gave the house such a cleaning as it had never had before. Rightfully she demanded that new shades be put in, that leaky faucets be fixed, that countless small repairs be made. As for the litter in the cellar and attic, she called me about that.

"I don't want to talk to your mother; she seems to get so upset about that old trash. But really I need the space."

"We'll call a junkman," I told her, "and we'll have him take it away without Mother knowing it."

But she caught us in the act and almost had hysterics out there in the alley. Her treasures going to the junkman! She snatched half of them back despite my protests of "Mother, darling, you haven't room!" The junkman kept saying, "Take it, lady, take it. I don't know what you want with it, but take it."

The half a dictionary Mother shoved under her bed, old muffin tins crowded the already bursting cupboards. The rest of it was somehow stowed away. The little house bulged at the seams.

Mother felt she didn't want to be alone and got a companion, a young girl who was working her way through the university. Lottie slept on the day bed in the room that was used as the parlor and did what work there was to be done before she went to school and after she came back. For Mother there was nothing to do. She could sit and hold her hands. She began to have sick spells, to spend half her time in bed. We saw with panic she was becoming feeble, *old*.

Mrs. Long had the big house full of people. She wore a white uniform and served the guests their food on trays in their rooms. Rigidly she adhered to instructions concerning diet.

But people didn't seem happy with Mrs. Long. They would stay for a few weeks and then leave.

Mother tried to help her. "You ought to serve your people in the dining room; you ought to try to entertain them a little."

"But if I let them eat in the dining room, they'd want to sit around and talk to me and I haven't time for that. It's an old house on a dusty corner," she told Mother accusingly. "I have to be everlastingly at it."

So the guests continued to get excellently cooked meals in the solitude of their own rooms, and Mrs. Long was, as she said, everlastingly at the house—washing windows, waxing floors, ironing curtains, getting dust off picture moldings.

But it takes more than diet, more than a shining spotless house. Mrs. Long couldn't keep her rooms rented. She got behind in her rent. One month, two months, three months.

"I don't want to put her out," Mother said, "but it doesn't seem to be the right place for her, does it?"

A family conference again. Mother saying resignedly, "Well, if I have to take it back, I have to take it back."

"Just for the summer, Mother. Next winter you can rent it again."

So Mother moved back. I was out of town for a week. When I returned I found Mother in the midst of carpenters and plumbers. She looked guilty, but otherwise her old self.

"Mother! What *are* you doing?"

"Well, I'm turning the parlor into a bedroom, and making a bathroom out of that closet, and glassing in the front porch so that can be the parlor. And I'm dividing up the back porch and making part of that a bedroom and putting a bathroom out there, too. In that way I can take eight or ten people."

"Ye gods, Mother!"

"After all, if I stay here, I'll have to have a cook, and if we're cooking for the two of us, we might as well be cooking for more."

"Of course, Mother," I said weakly, watching her walk across the floor to advise with the carpenter. Her old quick step. Why, Mother was young again!

"I'm going to build a patio wall at the back," she went on, "and an outdoor fireplace—it will be nice for steak fries. And you know the attic is all floored over the top. I could put two rooms and a bath up there. Not this year, but maybe next. I know it'll cost a lot, but I'm not getting much interest on that money down at the bank, and there's one thing about bathrooms, they never fold up on you."